PRAISE FOR ELIZA REID

THE FIRST LADY NEXT DOOR

"Eliza Reid is brilliant, passionate, and accomplished—yet funny as heck and so down-to-earth. Read *The First Lady Next Door*, and you will feel you have made a truly remarkable new best friend."

—Jeannette Walls, #1 *New York Times* bestselling author of *The Glass Castle*

"With her lovely debut memoir, former First Lady Eliza Reid shows women (and anyone paying attention) how to set their own course and defy expectations. She does so with a disarming humor, deep self-reflection, and a core set of values that never waver, even when her life takes dramatic turns."

—Stacey Abrams, #1 *New York Times* bestselling author, politician, and voting rights activist

"What do you do when your ordinary life suddenly includes royal carriages, state visits, photo sessions, and invitations to the White House? I raced through this delightful, thought-provoking memoir in which Eliza Reid explains how she made the most of an unexpected opportunity by finding and using her voice as Iceland's first lady."

—Gretchen Rubin, #1 *New York Times* bestselling author

"An intimate, engaging memoir that details Reid's life as Iceland's first lady, this book is also a potent argument for female identity and being true to yourself even when you're on constant display. This is a warmhearted, smart read that is a real delight."

—Susan Orlean, *New York Times* bestselling author

SECRETS OF THE SPRAKKAR: ICELAND'S EXTRAORDINARY WOMEN AND HOW THEY ARE CHANGING THE WORLD

"Riveting."

—*New York Times*

"*Secrets of the Sprakkar* is a fascinating window into what a more gender-equal world could look like and why it's worth striving for. Iceland is doing a lot to level the playing field: paid parental leave, affordable childcare, and broad support for gender equality as a core value. Reid takes us on an exploration not only around this fascinating island but also through the triumphs and stumbles of a country as it journeys toward gender equality."

—Hillary Rodham Clinton

"With warmth, wit, and insight, First Lady Eliza Reid explores the reasons why Iceland is one of the best places on earth for women, as well as the challenges still ahead in achieving full gender equity. *Secrets of the Sprakkar* is an illuminating, inspiring, and absorbing book about how a more equitable society could elevate us all."

—Cheryl Strayed, #1 *New York Times* bestselling author of *Wild*

"What a world of possibilities Eliza Reid unveils in this warm and wonderful book! It made me want to pack my bags and move to Iceland."

—Ruth Reichl, *New York Times* bestselling author of *Save Me the Plums*

"A warm and intimate exploration of what one small country can teach the world about gender equality. Eliza Reid charts her personal journey from a Canadian farm to Iceland's Presidential Residence, and along the way proves to be the best possible guide to the historical, geographical, and cultural factors that helped women thrive and built a vibrant modern society."

—Geraldine Brooks, Pulitzer Prize–winning author

"The fact that the Icelandic language includes the word 'sprakkar'—an ancient term that translates to mean 'extraordinary women'—in its lexicon tells you a great deal about the country of Iceland. And in her marvelous memoir, Eliza Reid tells us a great deal more: not only about her life in Iceland but also about gender equality in action and the sense of purpose that all of us seek. This is a charming and necessary book."

—Meg Wolitzer, *New York Times* bestselling author

"Everyone who visits Iceland quickly learns that the little country contains some of the world's most extraordinary women, their lives rooted in a social and political culture that nurtures equality between men and women without ignoring the pleasures and complexities of family life. It's a pleasure to see that culture marked out for us through the sometimes wry but always beautifully personal and perceptive lens of the remarkable Eliza Reid."

—Adam Gopnik, *New Yorker* staff writer

"Charting her own love of the nation and her journey to becoming its first lady, alongside histories of other formidable women, Eliza Reid's *Secrets of the Sprakkar* sheds light on Iceland's unique approach to gender equity—an emblematic look at what's possible in the fight for women's rights worldwide. A fascinating, hopeful, and inspiring read."

—Esi Edugyan, bestselling author of *Washington Black*

"Reading *Secrets of the Sprakkar* is like sitting down with your favorite, smartest, warmest girlfriend and hearing all about the extraordinary women, history, and culture of her tiny adopted country. Reid celebrates Iceland and its attitudes toward women while also discussing where it has some room for improvement. By the time I finished this book, I felt I had traveled to Iceland and gotten to know its beauty and quirks and, most importantly, its sprakkar."

—Ann Hood

DEATH ON THE ISLAND

"Gripping."

—*Washington Post*

"I loved this book. Eliza Reid is so assured in her plot, her characters that it's hard to believe this is her first novel. *Death on the Island* is compulsive and propulsive reading. Not only wonderfully evocative of a little-known area of Iceland, it is also surprising, with twists even a seasoned crime reader won't see coming. A brilliant debut that promises more to come."

—Louise Penny, #1 *New York Times* bestselling author

"An intriguing mystery, an exotic setting, and a Christie vibe—what's not to love?"

—Shari Lapena, international bestselling author of *What Have You Done?*

"Now, here's something new: *The Good Wife* meets Agatha Christie beneath the northern lights of Iceland. In *Death on the Island*, Eliza Reid—who served as that country's first lady for eight historic years—evokes its extraordinary atmosphere, its cultural rituals, even the quirks of its language; better still, her protagonist—the intrepid yet vulnerable wife of a diplomat—is tactful but fierce, a heroine to thrill fans of *Scandal* and *Madam Secretary*. And the mystery, cunningly structured as a series of tick-tock countdowns, pays homage to locked-room classics while blazing a path that's defiantly modern. This is a fresh, transporting, emotionally involving suspense debut, that rare crime novel you'll want to discuss with friends. Maybe even beneath the northern lights."

—A. J. Finn, #1 *New York Times* bestselling author
of *The Woman in the Window* and *End of Story*

"*Death on the Island* is a wonderful and compelling debut, welcoming a new and unique voice to the Icelandic crime fiction genre."

—Yrsa Sigurðardóttir, international bestselling author

"With its twisty golden-age plot and a fascinating Nordic noir setting, this novel is perfect for lovers of each."

—Ann Cleeves, *New York Times* bestselling author

ALSO BY ELIZA REID

Secrets of the Sprakkar: Iceland's Extraordinary Women and How They Are Changing the World

Death on the Island

THE FIRST LADY NEXT DOOR

THE FIRST LADY NEXT DOOR

A Memoir of Iceland, Identity, and Unexpected Adventure

ELIZA REID

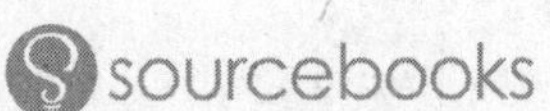
sourcebooks

Cover design by Brittany Vibbert/Sourcebooks
Cover photograph by Baldur Kristjáns
Internal design by Tara Jaggers/Sourcebooks

This book is a memoir. It reflects the author's present recollections of experiences over a period of time. Some names and characteristics have been changed, some events have been compressed, and some dialogue has been re-created.

Published by Sourcebooks
1935 Brookdale RD, Naperville, IL 60563-2773
(630) 961-3900
sourcebooks.com

Cataloging-in-Publication Data is on file with the Library of Congress.

Printed and bound in the United States of America.
MA 10 9 8 7 6 5 4 3 2 1

To the people of Iceland, who are a continued inspiration

To spouses of world leaders, current and past,
from whom I learned so much

And to Guðni, whose bravery led me to this wonderful adventure

En þori ég ,vil ég, get ég?
Já ég þori, get og vil.

[But dare I, will I, can I?
Yes, I dare, I can, I will.]

—Chorus of the song "Áfram stelpur" ("Go Girls"), anthem of the 1975 Women's Day Off in Iceland

"Each of us needs to imagine something that can take us beyond where we are now, in a direction that we want to go, and be part of making that happen. To be a deliberate part of change."

—Chris Hadfield, *An Astronaut's Guide to Life on Earth*

CONTENTS

1

Over the Hill

My husband, Guðni Th. Jóhannesson, announces his candidacy for President of Iceland, May 5, 2016. Pictured here with me and his five children.

About six weeks before I turned forty, my husband, Guðni, snapped a photo of me laughing with my three young sons and toddler daughter piling on top of me. Pandemonium was my daily reality, and it made me sentimental and practical in equal measure. After all, it's a reminder that all chicks leave their nests, and one day, I would miss the constant chirping.

The image captured me as I'd like to be known: Mother. Planner. Wife. Immigrant. (Not included here but helpful to highlight from the outset so you understand where my priorities lie: I'm also the maker of Iceland's best—and likely only—Nanaimo bars, that uniquely Canadian treat.)

That picture isn't curated or photoshopped, and it's one of my favorites. Its charming imperfections—four wide-eyed young pups jumping and tickling, the mirth on my unmade-up face highlighting my double chin, split ends only visible if you zoom *way* in—showed I was living a full life, one with love and laughter. I may not have had a stylist in my contacts, but nor did I have a single gray hair.

So forty was looming; that was okay. In the Olden Days, when my parents had turned forty, there were jokes about being over the hill and changing suppertime to 5 p.m. By 2016, however, things were a bit more complicated. Sure, I had laid the groundwork for my life's legacy, now that I had a nice career and lots of kids. But I expected there to be more adventures, more fun. I wasn't over the hill! I was merely a sleep-deprived, working parent with young children and a hectic but happy life.

Far from about to tip over it, I felt so distant from the hill that I even allowed myself an ambitious dream for celebrating the big four-oh. As much as I'd loved previous birthdays getting together with friends, I hoped for something more once-in-a-lifetime, the memories of which I'd feed off for the next decade and beyond. Guðni and I were in the thick of parenting young children, so I was imagining more of a romantic escape *à deux*. Not a potluck party in our little house in Reykjavík—but Paris.

Just the name conjured visions of a carefree, urbane existence I was already beginning to forget from my preparenthood days. In Canada, Paris is often seen as far away, rarefied, and chic. In Iceland, it's less so. It's a flight away, sure, but so is every foreign destination, and hardy Icelanders often see international travel as a means of finding cheaper clothes and stronger cough medicine. Plus, Guðni had never been before.

Admittedly, we had four children aged eight and under together and no nearby relatives who could watch them. Since moving to Iceland in 2003 (after spending five years in the UK where we had met), Guðni and I had been lucky enough to travel occasionally for work or to visit family in Canada, but once we became full-time parents (his daughter from his first marriage spent every second weekend with us), we hadn't so much as gone to a late movie together. I would not allow this stark reality to be an impediment in my forty-year fantasy celebration, however.

Could we afford it? We had just moved from our 1,200-square-foot house to a larger fixer-upper farther away from Reykjavík city center, with an expanded mortgage to match. On the other hand, Guðni was inching closer to the ultimate promotion at the University of Iceland, full tenure as a professor of history, and I had cobbled together numerous freelance writing projects that brought in regular income. Anyway, as Guðni optimistically reminded me: "We're rich in the bank of love."

But on dark winter evenings after the kids went to bed, as I folded laundry and scraped snot off the sofa, the idea of Paris was all too irresistible. I would close my eyes for a moment and picture my tall husband and I strolling hand in hand down a tree-lined *rue*, a striped-shirted accordionist playing Edith Piaf classics next to the Seine. It would be so romantic, so *je ne sais quoi*. The perfect way to celebrate forty.

Guðni was less enthusiastic and more realistic about my middle-aged fancy. His pragmatism complemented my occasionally quixotic enthusiasm. He never burst my bubble, just let the air out gently until my feet once again touched the ground.

"Will you take me to Paris when I turn forty?" I had suggested eagerly about a week after his fortieth birthday; his was a full eight years before mine, and for that reason, my desired festivity was likely not yet on his radar. Guðni had celebrated his own big day exactly as he wanted: a low-key dinner just with me, his then fourteen-year-old daughter, Rut, and our baby son, Duncan.

"Sure, sounds good," my hubby had replied casually, something noncommittal in his tone that I chose to ignore. It was his smile that convinced me he would be heading off to research hotels right after we spoke. He'd have eight years to plan it to perfection.

After that first suggestion, I gave him a little reminder nudge on a roughly annual basis, and every time, the response was that same happy but enigmatic smile, the one that I chose to interpret as "I've got it all under control." If Guðni had it all under control, I was free to imagine how the birthday trip would pan out. It was going to be great! Snot-free weekend, here we come!

As my fortieth grew nearer, my inner organizer started to kick in, even though I knew Guðni was surely on top of things. I wondered who he had convinced to look after the kids (aged two, four, six, and eight) while we escaped to Paris. I wondered how we could afford such a trip, even if staying in a cheap hotel for only a couple of nights. I wondered whether he had made a reservation at a Michelin-starred restaurant or whether we would stumble into an intimate bistro and get drunk on French wine.

My birthday is in the first week of May. At the end of March, I couldn't see any dates blocked off on the four-month laminated University of Toronto calendar we used to track our family activities. No one had mentioned plans to take the kids for a few days. Could it be that my darling hadn't yet bought the tickets and booked the hotel?

Cynicism began to creep into my thoughts. This was going to be lose-lose, I thought. Either I would swallow my disappointment, lie, and tell Guðni that it was all a near decade-long joke, or I would throw my hands in the air and organize it all myself with the disgruntled resignation of women through the ages who have had to bear the burden of the mental load.

I had to admit to myself that Guðni hadn't initiated discussion of the birthday trip in years (probably ever, actually), but he had recently been talking about a potential summer vacation by booking a week at a discounted union-rate summerhouse in the Icelandic countryside. Did dewy mornings and itchy midge bites excite him more than the capital of romance?

That snotty sofa and the endless laundry seemed to mushroom as I began to accept that my pipe dream had been just that: airy escapism from a perfectly happy but rather hectic existence. I didn't want to be the passive-aggressive wife who announced a week before my birthday, "Right, when do we leave for Paris?" It was better simply to reserve the tiny union summerhouse for whichever July week we'd be assigned and be happy with a few days in the countryside doing puzzles and playing Memory with the kids. There would be more bluster than *belle époque*, sure, but it would be cozy and affordable, and it wouldn't cost me any marital discord.

As it turned out, less than a month before my big day, Guðni fell upon an excuse to stay in town that eliminated any hope of a minibreak or even a week in a summerhouse that July. Yet the outcome of that utterly unexpected development turned out to be even sweeter than all the profiteroles in Paris, an adventure greater than even the City of Light could inspire.

On my special day, as I officially journeyed over the hill, with me and all five of his children by his side, Guðni announced that he was running for president of Iceland. It was an astonishing development that we could never have predicted. (And certainly wasn't on the four-month University of Toronto calendar.) In fact, it was the first time Guðni had ever sought elected office or ever considered the possibility of doing so. The election was scheduled for the following month, in June.

The next day, I found my first gray hair.

What images do you conjure when you see the term "first lady"? I expect you picture a well-groomed woman of at least middle age, hair perfect, a bright smile ready on her face. She's wearing pearls and an elegant outfit showcasing local designers. What do you imagine this first lady doing? To be sure, she is supporting her husband, a strong and decisive leader, a head of state. She does this by clapping enthusiastically when he delivers speeches, nodding sagely at insightful remarks he makes, and holding his hand as they arrive at star-studded events.

But what does she do when she's on her own? She usually has her own causes, does she not? These causes are often connected to the soft power of the feminine sphere: literacy among young people, public health awareness, support of the arts and culture. Whatever the first lady does, it is almost always complementary to her husband's goals. She is the muse to his genius, the gentle touch to his firm leadership. She is a perfect hostess, the comforter in chief, the smooth side to her husband's rough edges.

It is, to quote the headline of a *New York Times* op-ed I wrote in 2019, an "incredibly weird job," especially in a nation known colloquially as the best country in the world for women. Was I about to be an anachronism?

The fact is, with a very few exceptions, being a first lady is not a job at all. Volunteer in chief is a more apt title. Even then, not many spouses of heads of state have defined roles or responsibilities. And many first ladies, or at least many of those I met and the type that I chose to be, do not fit into the mold I just described.

Even before my husband won the election in late June, it seemed as if my most common descriptor was "Guðni's wife." Once he signed his oath of office on August 1, I became the *forsetafrú*, or literally "president's lady." (There is no Icelandic term for "first lady," but I chose to use it in English because it is familiar to people.)

From the day Guðni announced his candidacy, though, I felt the need to maintain and even promote my own identity. Suddenly I was spending significant time contemplating how to do that. Where would Eliza go while the *forsetafrú* garnered column inches? I didn't know exactly how I would tackle what was clearly an exciting and unexpected opportunity, but I was determined that Eliza would not disappear.

Early in the campaign, a stylist called me at home in preparation for the election flier we would need to print, which would feature a photo of our whole family.

"Can you describe your personal style?" he asked me as I wedged my phone to my shoulder, changed a dirty diaper, and used my last available resource—arched eyebrows and a stern look—to signal to my toddler that the television was on too loud.

"Well, I haven't bought a new pair of shoes in five years, and my maternity pants still fit," I answered in a distracted tone. I invited the stylist to come by and meet me; maybe he could glean a signature look from my worn jeans and '80s hair clips.

Five minutes after the stylist appeared at the door, six-year-old Donnie bellowed down the hall: "Mom, come quickly. There is blood everywhere!" I raced to him and discovered his younger brother, Sæþór, nearly hyperventilating, a big gash under his lip from a softball bat swung by a playmate. I cleaned him up, and several hours later, we had a single happy family photo to use for the campaign brochure. Bonus: The makeup artist gave me her blusher compact, the first one I had owned since high school, with a sympathetic look that said I needed it more than she did.

Somehow, over the chaotic weeks from my fortieth birthday on May 5 to the election on June 25 and then the inauguration on August 1 and just beyond, I realized I would need to hit the ground running if I was to make the most of this chance. There were no training wheels, no prep class. I had limited time to squeeze all the juice from this fruit. I wanted to leave a legacy, be able to look back on this all-too-brief moment and know that I had done everything I could, the way I wanted to do it. But what way was that?

I'm a rule follower. I'm the person who declares the sweater that cost twenty dollars over import limits when crossing the border. I read the instruction manuals cover to cover for every appliance, from toasters to dishwashers.

So while I was thrilled (and excited and nervous) about the once-in-a-lifetime opportunity to serve my adopted country, I was also intimidated. What if I broke a rule? What if I brought dishonor to Iceland? To my husband? To the dignity of a respected office? Was I allowed to talk about whatever I wanted, whenever I wanted? What was I supposed to wear when we met kings and queens? Could I express opinions on social media? Order a tequila shot in a bar on a Friday night?

I didn't know the answers, and I didn't know whom to ask. (I couldn't ask my husband. He was as in the dark as I, and the transition he was facing was exponentially more significant than mine. Also, he never read the manuals.)

Try as I might, it was a challenge to find much information on head of state spouses from other countries. Again, perhaps it's a sign of how little attention we give to people who serve in these roles (unless, of course, they mess things up). But over the years, I have had the tremendous privilege of meeting many of my counterparts, several of whom have become friends. I learned about sacrifice, stoicism, enthusiasm from them, and I learned about my own preconceptions of this weird job.

Identities are imposed upon us at various stages in our lives. As children, we form ourselves into the molds our parents establish, perhaps according to gendered expectations or birth order. As adolescents, we strive to be the cool kid or the attractive athlete or the edgy outsider. As adults, our job titles often define who we are and where we fit into society, sometimes adding wife or mother to our professional identity. Later in life, when we're over the hill, we're written off in terms of the contributions we can make but face expectations of what people in our positions and roles ought to do. We put each other in boxes, setting invisible boundaries that we are told—sometimes overtly but often more discreetly—we cannot cross. If we ask why, we're told it's because it has always been that way.

Uncomfortable though it was to realize that as first lady, I was steering a ship without a compass, using an appliance without reading the directions, I knew from the outset that I needed to be the one who would decide how I would be defined. I needed to be my biggest champion, and I needed to make my own rules to follow.

In the weeks between Guðni's election and the inauguration, my friends—all of them still as astounded by my life's unexpected turn of events as I was—often asked me what I was going to do in the role. I said I did not want to squander the opportunity, that I wanted to use the platform while I had it, but that there was no handbook on how to be the spouse of a head of state, so I wasn't sure where to start.

"That will be your legacy!" they told me. "You'll write a handbook for those who succeed you."

The idea didn't appeal to me. There shouldn't be a handbook on how to serve in this role, because it isn't a formal position, and I believe it should not come with rules or expectations. Besides, that's an awfully specific situation for a handbook. It would be like writing a travel guide to the moon.

But slowly, an idea began to take root. Only a handful of people in the world will ever experience being married to a head of state, but everyone at some point in life lands where they never expected to, a place where they struggle to seize an opportunity (or even chase it in the first place) while staying true to themselves. Serving as first lady taught me how to use my voice, how to navigate change in life, how to make the most of unexpected opportunity. To do so effectively required self-confidence, creativity, humor, the support of friends and family, and the ability to fake it when any of those were in short supply.

As first lady, I learned to use my position to draw attention to matters important to me, from wearing secondhand clothing to ensuring locals heard my accented Icelandic in speeches. I mostly managed to ignore the irony of using my platform to advocate for gender equality when I only had the platform because of something my husband had achieved.

This book is for everyone who has ever found themselves in a situation they never anticipated, whether you are married to a head of state or not. It's a book for everyone who wants to believe in fairy tales but lacks the requisite fashion sense. It will inspire you to harness the discomfort of a rule-free environment to push your own limits. Along the way, you'll encounter a prescient Central Asian family, the underappreciated game of touch football, and even, when you're least expecting it, Paris.

All of it is based on my firm belief that every single one of us can be a force for positive change in the world if we lean into the risks and make the most of the chances we are given.

This book also begins against the grain—with the very first rule I broke.

2

Following the Rules

Summer vacation at the cottage
doing what I loved best—reading.

Bert: Ernie, how do I look?

Ernie: With your eyes, Bert.

—*Sesame Street*

The first time I broke the rules, I didn't know I was doing it. While that act of vandalism didn't give me a taste for spray paint and baseball bats, it did remind me to trust my own instincts.

When I was three years old, my father moved my mother, younger brother, and me to England for one year while he began his PhD in English literature. Dad flew over to London a few weeks before the rest of us and found a small cottage, aptly named the Dairy Cottage, to rent in the Oxfordshire countryside near the town of Wallingford. He secured the small two-bedroom home and then found a used Morris Minor car to ferry us all around.

My memories of that time would likely be nonexistent were it not for the stories my parents told us years later of our English adventures. Like the time the electricity went out in the middle of bathtime, and in the sudden darkness, my mother managed to rinse off shampoo, towel dry two toddlers, and find the necessary coins to feed the meter and get the system turned on again. Or the morning our landlord's favorite horse, Smiler, dramatically expired of a heart attack on the pasture directly in front of the house.

We returned to Canada in the summer of 1980 in time for my father to go back to his job as a high school English teacher while he worked on his thesis in the evenings.

In order to finance their time abroad, my parents had rented out our semidetached home in Kanata, a newly developing suburb of Ottawa. It turns out the people Mom and Dad chose were not ideal renters: they paid late—or not at all. They stubbed their cigarettes out in the carpet. They ran a taxi business from the living room. In the end, we had to stay for several weeks with my maternal grandparents as my father brushed up on the law and took the renters to small claims court. Eventually, he was awarded enough damages to make the house livable again.

My parents did the fixing up themselves—my father after a full day of teaching, my mother after an arguably fuller day looking after two preschoolers. And then one evening, they invited my brother and me to witness the fruits of their labors: My mother had just repainted my bedroom in a calming pastel green. It looked lovely, and I was excited to make the space my own. After showing me this renovation, she left me alone in the room while she went downstairs to talk to my grandparents.

I remember standing in this empty room, *my* room, and gazing around its naked walls, thinking about how much work my mother must have done to get it ready for me. Why not help her out with the decoration? I have no idea how I procured it, but I found a black indelible marker, walked to the largest wall by the window, and drew a big house with one door, two windows, and a chimney releasing a swirl of smoke. Next to the front door, I drew a stick-figure version of myself, posing by some perky flowers. I drew a sun shining in the sky and some fluffy clouds next to it. Then I drew a path from that smiling girl by the door around all four walls of the bedroom in a circle back to the picture of my house. For the final touch, I closed the door to my bedroom and added a floor-to-ceiling abstract scribble of whorls and lines.

Standing back, I surveyed my work. It looked pretty good. Was everything there that should be? I thought so. Sun, check. House, check. Happy girl and flowers, check. All corners of the room touched by the art? Check. Strange then that something niggled at me, some tiny voice in my head whispering that all was not quite right.

I shut the bedroom door and raced downstairs to my mother.

"Mommy, come upstairs!" I cried. "I have a surprise for you!" I was so excited to see her reaction. She was certain to be almost as thrilled as I.

As soon as I flung open my bedroom door and saw the expression on my mother's face, I realized what it was that had been tugging at my conscience. Our household rule: *Never draw on walls.* As legend has it, I burst immediately into tears. Was Dad going to turn his newly acquired prosecutorial skills on me now? Would I go to jail? Breaking the rules did not feel very good, but not meeting expectations, those unwritten standards my family set for me, felt even worse. I was, of course, forgiven, although my mother needed to apply several coats of paint to cover my art.

My mother loved to tell that story, but she had a variety of tales in her repertoire, one for every occasion, and we all (a second brother came along when I was five) had our favorites. Long before *Friends*, we requested "the one where you wore your dress backwards" or "the one where you brought the wrong sandwich to school." It was only as an adult that I recognized my mother's tremendous skill in spinning yarns—complete with captivating characters and narrative arc—from even the most mundane moments.

There was often a moral or a message in her stories. At the very minimum, a chance to make light of ourselves, to learn not to take ourselves too seriously, to accept our imperfections. But by making us the heroes—or sometimes antiheroes—of our own adventures, my mother taught my brothers and me that we had a place in the world, that our actions mattered, that we belonged. Storytelling was a tool kit for managing life, an instruction manual for the expectations and rules of my family.

There were a lot of stories, especially on weekends, when my parents, brothers, and I gathered around the dinner table. Sunday night dinner was sacrosanct. My father dressed in better clothes. There was usually a roast involved. When it was beef, my father always carved the outside slice, my favorite, and gave it to me. When it was lamb, my father emitted a discreet bleat at some point during the meal. He was the king of dad jokes before it was a hashtag.

When my brothers and I were in a particularly quarrelsome phase, my mother had the idea to hold "I appreciate" nights at Sunday dinner. One of us was the designated subject of the praise, and the others would have to go around the table and say one nice thing about us. Inevitably, this tool to promote positivity descended into barbed insults instead: "I appreciate Ewan because he only farted at me five times today" (except we were not allowed to say *fart* at the dinner table).

While Mom focused on cooperation and consensus building,

Dad firmly but kindly taught us the rules. *All joints on the table must be carved. A fork is not a shovel.* We often complained about his rigidity concerning table manners, but Dad always said, "You never know when you'll be invited to Buckingham Palace."

For the first decade of my life—with the exception of the year in England—we lived in the semidetached home in Kanata. Kindergarten began when I was five. I was excited about making new friends and walking all by myself down the road to John Young Elementary, but I was nervous too. What if something went wrong? What if I was late for school on the very first day of my formal education? Would that blasé attitude follow me for my entire academic career? I suggested to my perennially tardy mother that we do a dry run of the walk to school. That way, I could calculate how long it would take to get there (five minutes on foot) and work backwards to figure out when I would need to wake up every day.

One never knew when contingencies could come in handy. So I created my own preparedness doctrine, which was to have a plan for even the most unlikely eventualities. After I had aged out of preschool television programs such as *Polka Dot Door*, *Mr. Dressup*, *Today's Special*, and *Sesame Street*, I watched a popular Canadian game show called *Just Like Mom*. Mother and child were tested on their knowledge of each other. The gimmick of the show was a section where the kids had a limited amount of time to bake something, say, chocolate chip cookies, using a selection of ingredients presumably provided by a local sponsor. The mom who correctly guessed her own child's creation won the most points. The winning team was awarded a trip to Canada's Wonderland, a theme park near the fabled big city of Toronto. I wanted that trip, so I made a plan (conveniently skipping the steps that involved us actually qualifying to appear on the show). My mother and I would agree in advance on a secret ingredient, something that would be anomalous in a dessert—ketchup, say, or English mustard—and then she would be able to figure out which concoction was mine, thereby winning us the coveted vacation. (Spoiler: not only was I never a guest on the show, but I have still never visited Canada's Wonderland.)

I had other plans too. I loved to read, so I organized all my books alphabetically by author and placed a discreet label with my name and a book number inside each cover. The numbering system allowed me to create various ranking lists of the books and to build a lending library, the only clients of which were my brothers. By age ten, I was forcing them to borrow books from me—neither had any interest in reading—and then following up with "book due soon" notices slipped under their bedroom doors. The notices I wrote by hand on paper selected from my vast stationery collection.

I saved and organized other things too. In summers, when we drove north to Sault Ste. Marie to visit my Grandma and Grandpa Reid, I collected fallen crab apples from their garden at one cent apiece and saved the money to buy an array of porcelain cups fit to host a tea party for Princess Di herself. Just in case. I also acquired salt and pepper shakers and *sometimes* allowed my mother to use them on the Sunday night dinner table. After my mother's mostly failed efforts to teach me (never my brothers) how to iron, I would humor her by practicing on my collection of handkerchiefs.

My prized possessions, however, were my postcards. If I visited a new place and had some pocket money, I bought a postcard. Every time someone went away, I was sent a postcard. Not only were they letter keepsakes and pretty images, but they provided virtually endless opportunities to categorize: By location! By sender! By sending date! By size!

Childhood really was *so much fun*. I had a wonderful group of girlfriends from school. (No boys. Gross.) We baked cookies and played dress-up and listened to records. When my friends couldn't play, I ironed my handkerchief collection or straightened my salt and pepper shaker collection or read books.

Another one of my hobbies was playing bridge at my maternal grandparents' place in the city. Grandma Brown taught me how to play, and I loved it, assiduously reading the sample bridge hands printed in the newspaper. I traveled with a porcelain bridge score card, my favorite gift from a clearly astute relative the previous Christmas. Seeing how bereft I was at being unable to play when my grandparents were busy, my mother suggested that I post an ad on the school notice board to start a bridge club among other grade 5 students. No one signed up. Not to worry, Mom said. They would be begging to join once they learned how to play the game. Maybe I could offer lessons!

One of my other interests was politics. In 1984, when I was eight years old and in grade 3, there was a federal election in Canada. The result—a large Progressive Conservative majority that would usher in Brian Mulroney as prime minister—was not really in question. Despite the predictable outcome, I followed all the relevant news closely. I didn't understand why children weren't allowed to vote. After all, I knew the names of all the major candidates for my riding constituency, and when the New Democratic Party candidate came knocking at our door to share a campaign flier, I blushed as if I'd met a rock star. On election night, I begged my parents to let me stay up past my bedtime to watch the results as they came in. Given Canada's six time zones, they came in late. Shrugging, my parents went to sleep and let me feed my inner political junkie. It would be good practice for when I became prime minister, they said. Although I didn't know any girls interested in that job, I didn't think that meant I was excluded from the club. And even though I'd been taught how to iron and clean the bathroom while my brothers took out the garbage and mowed the lawn, I had also been taught that I should never let my gender limit my career choices. Nor was I led to believe it should steer me along a certain path. I had two unmarried, childless aunts who had busy and happy lives. Their example, and those recounted to me of my very independently minded grandmothers and great-grandmothers, taught me that marriage and children were not a prerequisite for a fulfilling adulthood.

Anyway, I didn't really want to be a politician when I grew up (I wanted to be a flight attendant, because then I could travel), but I reasoned it could be a potential backup career, so in my unofficial contingency plan, I nurtured the skills a politician might need, namely a competitive nature, the gift for public speaking, and an affection for the spotlight. I signed up for drama lessons at the Ottawa Little Theatre. During our weekly classes, two men in dark suits stood silently outside the door of the rehearsal room, guarding us all. It was only during the final performance for parents that I realized I'd been taking classes with the son of the prime minister. For many years, learning trust falls with Ben Mulroney was my go-to brush with fame story.

Starting in grade 4, students in my school were trained in public speaking. We had to choose a topic, research it, write a three- to five-minute speech in English or in French, memorize it, and deliver the speech to our class.

One key to a good speech was to pick a topic that was not too obscure but not so personal that the teacher suspected you hadn't cracked the *Encyclopedia Britannica* (e.g., how I spent my summer vacation). That first year, I increased my odds of winning by writing and delivering my speech in French, a feat only a handful of my classmates attempted. Unfortunately, my subject was Halley's Comet, which was passing through the earth's atmosphere for the first time in seventy-five years, and nearly everyone else chose it too. Despite the unoriginality of the topic, *la comète de Halley* managed to secure me a class win.

Before you start to think that life was all public speaking, bridge playing, and groundbreaking postcard organization, there were also plenty of areas where I did not excel. Like sports. I had broken my arm three times before I was eight and was petrified of injuring myself again. The kid picked last for the team in gym class? That was me, every time. I completely understood why. I never went skiing when the class took a trip to Mont Cascades, and on skating days, I only ever managed one shaky circle around the rink per hour, my hand gripping the boards the whole time.

None of that bothered me, though. I had loving parents, siblings who could only harass me to a limited extent because they were younger, very fun friends, and fascinating hobbies. The fact that I would never play pro sports did not cause me a moment's worry. (Spoiler: Never say never. Stay tuned.)

Then, all of a sudden, the world around me changed.

When I was ten years old, at the tail end of 1986, we moved to a 150-year-old house that was worn at the edges but chosen for its generous spirit. It sat on four acres of land, and my parents had dreams of a chicken coop, a duck pond, and a small barn for sheep, a perfect "hobby" from their other work. Our new home was several miles past the city limits and well into what city slickers often called "the sticks," the boring bit on the way to the cottage. One example of the isolation to which we had moved: Our home telephone was still on a party line. One long ring followed by one short one meant the incoming call was for someone in our house; other rings didn't usually sound on our phone but were meant for whichever other family or families shared the line. It was not unusual to pick up the receiver to find another conversation already taking place. Then you had to wait your turn.

Even if this place had proper heating, unlike the English Dairy Cottage, I thought it was a tragedy to move to a new house where phone calls to friends incurred long distance charges, where there was no access to public transportation and, woe is me, no cable television. It seemed to me that the phone never rang, or at least never for me.

In my new neighborhood, I was a fish out of water, unused

to kids who woke early to help milk the cows and spoke with a distinctive Ottawa Valley accent. I was bused several miles back to Kanata so I could continue at a different school that offered French immersion. Even if the countryside was alien to me, I was looking forward to the new school and was ready to launch the bridge club and trade postcards. But to those new suburban kids, I was the country bumpkin. The one who had boring bangs, didn't shave her legs, and didn't know the names of any members of New Kids on the Block.

The kids in this unfamiliar place didn't care about my public speaking prowess or my interest in organizing. That crisp white bridge club sign-up sheet on the school's notice board stayed empty, and my postcards remained neatly filed away in their shoeboxes in my closet.

I felt like I was the only girl in the class who did not tuck the front of an Ocean Pacific or Vuarnet brand T-shirt (with bra straps showing underneath) into a pair of black bicycle shorts with a neon stripe down the side. I didn't know how to curl my bangs and spray them to showcase a stiffly coiffed starburst on my forehead. During our daily fifteen minutes of "USSR" (that's Uninterrupted Super Silent Reading), I poured over Agatha Christie novels or *The Lord of the Rings* while my new classmates read the latest Sweet Valley High or The Baby-Sitters Club.

I can't remember exactly how much I was teased or in what way. My mother had always told me that people teased me because they liked me, but this didn't feel like that. This felt more like I was the only person in the class who didn't get the joke, which was me.

That first year in the new school, when the annual speech writing event rolled around, I was too scared to deliver my remarks in front of the class. I was convinced I would be laughed out of the room. The fear of the shame was so great that I had to brave the next scariest thing: telling my parents why I couldn't do it. They were compassionate and understanding, sensing immediately that I wasn't looking for a lazy way out of doing homework but was genuinely frightened about the repercussions. They spoke to the teacher, and I was allowed to deliver the speech alone to her during recess one day.

My world was suddenly less friendly. Problems were nuanced. Divergence from the norm was mocked, rebelliousness—within well-defined boundaries of *mainstream* rebelliousness—encouraged. The stories I had been soaking up all my life, which created the scaffolding for what family and safety meant to me, didn't seem to be relevant in this edgy new world. I had always thought good girls finished first, but for a time, it felt like following the rules, the only thing I knew how to do, the only thing I felt *comfortable* doing, wasn't going to get me anywhere (certainly not on *Just Like Mom* or a national bridge championship). And despite the loving cocoon of a supportive family, out there, I would have to carve my own path—and possibly break a few rules.

3

Ontario's Fastest Typist

My dorm room in third year at Trinity College, University of Toronto, fall 1996. The futon was the first grown-up piece of furniture I bought, and it's still at my parents' house in a guest room.

"Slow comes the hour, its passing speed how great."

—Adage printed on the clock in Strachan Hall,
Trinity College, University of Toronto

Change takes time. After that first year in a new school, I made a handful of friends and joined the school band, playing the clarinet. I still didn't know how to style my bangs properly, and my name was never whispered together with a boy's, but I was no longer anxious about what each school day might have in store.

At the graduation ceremony on the last day of grade 8, when I was fourteen, I won the John Beatty Award for Citizenship, given to the student who was, in a nutshell, the kindest and most engaged. My parents told me that this, the prize for kindness, was the most important award of the evening. I'd won ribbons for achievement in specific subjects before, but this was the first accolade I had received that was school-wide. Ah, the sweet taste of acknowledgment! Public appreciation motivated me, as did the ice cream cone my mom bought me at Balderson's (which insiders knew provided larger-than-average scoops) that evening as a special treat.

High school beckoned, and I was relieved I wouldn't be studying with most of the kids who had been causing me grief; I would attend a regional catchment school for people who had been designated "gifted." My mother had always told me not to let labels like that go to my head, that everyone was gifted in some way, but at least in this new school, I'd be in smaller classes and fast track in math. Things were looking up!

First of all, there were many different clubs to join: I was in the band, the vocal jazz choir, the drama society, the yearbook committee, peer mediation, and student council. After my first year, I volunteered my summer weekends at the local hospital.

If middle school had forced me to develop my inner strength, I thought perhaps high school would help me to grow more physically adept—or at least to try. After briefly flirting with the idea of trying out for the rugby team, I joined the curling team, where the risk of breaking my arm a fourth time was small. Sweeping a broom along a flat slab of ice was more my speed than contact sports. Even better, our team finished second in the entire Ottawa area that season…out of two teams.

In fact, the accolades began to pile up. On the heels of the curling near victory in grade 9, I discovered that I had won a prize as Ontario's fastest typist. Well, to be more specific, I was the recipient of the Ontario Business Educators' Association's award for Novice French Typing, which went to the student with the fastest typing score of anyone in the province who took typing in French that year. It was my first (and only) province-wide accolade, therefore kind of a big deal, even though my mother wouldn't drive me all the way to Pickering, a suburb of Toronto, to receive my prize in person because it would cost too much in gas money. "Ontario's Fastest Typist" featured heavily on my CV for at least a decade after that.

Buffering my résumé with such praise encouraged me, because I still craved a plan for my future, some sort of guidebook to lead me to my yet undefined adult success. I was growing up after all.

I wore lipstick to school. In my bedroom, I replaced my chart of the kings and queens of England with a large, laminated complete guitar chord poster. I made my own mixtapes.

I didn't have much time to play bridge with Grandma and Grandpa anymore, but I was an award-winning nice person and a silver-medal curler, and I could type about sixty words per minute *en français*. It wasn't long before I had paid for my driving lessons and got a part-time job selling shoes at the local shopping center.

In 1993, there was another federal election in Canada. I was seventeen and not old enough to vote yet, but my interest in politics had only grown since the day I stayed up past my bedtime to watch the '84 election results come in. I was taking a class in politics in high school, and our independent study assignment was to volunteer for a campaign. After all, we were in the nation's capital, and federal election season was heralded like an early arrival of Christmas. I chose the candidate I thought most likely to cruise to victory rather than the one I supported, because I thought the experience of serving on a winning team would be more fun.

It was the last time I would allow pragmatism to rule over principle when it came to my political views. The local office wasn't really interested in having extra people help, especially, it felt to me, young kids who couldn't yet vote. I had no access to internal polling—heck, I had no access to the coffee maker—but the campaign vibe struck me as chaotic rather than collected. On election night, that party was decimated, winning only two seats from a 295-seat Parliament.

My new rule: Follow your values, not the allure of glory.

That guiding light led me through high school, even if I didn't articulate it that way. I demonstrated my values through my clubs, volunteering, and work. I had plenty of friends too, even if I was firmly in the band/nerd clique.

Ultimately, I was still a rule follower, a reader of manuals. While others were dropping LSD on the school bus or getting grounded for arriving home drunk past curfew, I was the designated driver who had never put a cigarette to my lips. Just being in the presence of people who bought Labatt Blue using a fake ID felt rebellious to me.

Socializing for me in those years meant movie nights, occasional dinners out at the local Swiss Chalet or Subway, and a great many informal hangouts in the family rooms of friends' houses, talking earnestly about the meaning of life and how we would change the world, even though our world wasn't really all that big yet. I had spent that single year in England and had been to a few American states, but my knowledge of geopolitics didn't extend much beyond an awareness of the recent fall of the Iron Curtain and memorizing world capitals, though I was curious enough to know that there was an awful lot I didn't know.

While the meaning of life didn't include dreams of marriage and kids, it did include dissecting *crises du coeur*. I often felt as if all my friends had more interesting love lives than me, that I would never be one of the girls with a string of handsome, popular, and interesting boyfriends. I didn't envy those girls exactly, but I did try to feel comfortable about not being a serial girlfriend, despite magazines, films, and television indicating it was the key to happiness. I dated one guy for over a year, a geological age in adolescent terms. After that ended, I had contentedly come to terms with the possibility that I might not have another romantic relationship for a long time, though I had several male friends. After all, why should I aspire to be a secondary character in someone else's story? Was my ambition really to be known as so-and-so's girlfriend? What could one possibly accomplish in the supporting part?

In the autumn of 1994, when I was eighteen years old, we packed up our beige Mazda MPV, and my parents drove me the five hours along the 401 highway to where I had accepted an offer to attend Trinity College at the University of Toronto. That first night, I asked if my mom would stay in the residence room with me, even if it meant we'd need to squish into the single bed I was allocated. She generously obliged. After that, I was alone in the big city, alone in my single dorm room with its college-issued desk, bookshelf, and dressing table. Where would I hang up my guitar chord poster? Would I splurge and rent my own phone line for my room or just use the shared one that stood in a little cubby at the end of the hall?

Those big decisions could wait. Alone and on my second night in the dorm, though it was well after midnight, I thought it would be a great idea to knock on the doors of nearby rooms and see if anyone else had moved in. After a few vain attempts, I tried the room immediately next to mine. A moment later, a very bleary-eyed blond woman peeked around the door. She introduced herself as Ildikó. I had woken her from a deep sleep—it was the middle of the night after all—but she seemed to forgive me. Thus would begin a long friendship that often involved me banging on the wall that divided our rooms in the middle of the night and only stopping when she drearily trudged over to mine to patiently listen to what unimportant nugget of conversation I wished to bestow.

I soon discovered that Trinity was the eccentric sibling of the U of T colleges. When I accepted my place to study there, I was completely unaware of its reputation as the breeding ground for the great and good of Canadian society, churning out more than its fair share of politicians, Rhodes scholars, and luminaries of cultural, political, and business life. But I learned soon enough. We wore gowns to eat in the dining hall and said a Latin grace before sit-down meals, the large clock of Strachan Hall looming over us and reminding us of the William Cowper line *slow comes the hour, its passing speed how great*. Other colleges made fun of Trin students for being snobbish, old-fashioned, and out of touch. But I drank the Kool-Aid early on. I thought we were, to quote the Latin (of course) name of the school paper, the salt of the earth.

I dove head-on into all of it but primarily the student societies and the drinking. In the most egregious violation of my scrupulous adherence to laws, I began consuming alcohol, even though at eighteen, I was a year younger than the legal drinking age. No one seemed to be bothered by such technicalities, especially at campus parties, where a plastic cup of keg beer cost one dollar. I soon learned that if you volunteered to serve that beer for an hour, you could drink for free the rest of the evening. That hit the sweet spot of my tight student budget. There were plenty of other shenanigans going on, but I steered clear of all that, although on occasion, when emboldened by the Labatt Wildcat lager flowing through my system, I would offer to hold a friend's cigarette when they went to the bathroom, thus ensuring I looked rebellious enough to smoke without actually having to inhale. My fingers stank after those moments, but I was pretty sure it was worth it.

Trinity had its social hierarchies, naturally. Unlike high school, where the kids from the gifted program didn't sit anywhere near the top of the pyramid, at Trinity, the entire cohort was composed of those geeky kids, so I needed to find a new subniche. I was certainly not one of the athletic ones, not with the privileged private-school kids, and definitely not a big-city girl. I was the small-town friendly—bordering on naive—social butterfly who never wanted to leave a party early in case she missed something important.

Now that I was in the big school in the big city, I wanted to do big things, to squeeze the most juice I could from the experience. One of Trinity's proud and ancient societies, the Trinity College Literary Institute, or the Lit for short, was one of the country's oldest debating clubs. The Lit held weekly debates on Thursday evenings, during which teams of two would argue a previously publicized resolution. It might sound dry, but the debates were generally very funny, and crucially, there was free beer for everyone who showed up.

As someone who religiously attended these events, even though it meant I missed the Thursday must-see TV lineup of *Friends* and

ER, I was delighted when I was asked in the winter of my first year to be one of the debaters. I accepted; I figured it was my duty after drinking so much free booze over the term. The debate I agreed to was different: It was the only one of the year in which the resolution was not determined in advance but announced at the beginning of the evening itself. Speakers had about half an hour to prepare their remarks, while everyone else poured themselves another pint.

As mentioned, the key to these debates was wit. You had to be funny, blending inside jokes about the school, an awareness of current affairs, and overall logical reasoning. I was the sole first-year student taking part in this debate, and I was intimidated. The people running the Lit were third and fourth years and almost always men, though I didn't pay any attention to the gender imbalance at the time. I was nervous because I didn't have the crutch of advance preparation and practice. Still, I had always been a strong public speaker: I'd done some improv in high school and never minded performing, except for that one time in grade 6. I had a good general knowledge of current affairs, could easily entertain friends with funny stories, and knew bridge and curling terminology inside out. I had all the ingredients I would need to be a big success at my Lit debut.

Well, I bombed.

I wasn't funny. I didn't have a cogent argument. I stammered and stuttered. I blushed and showed my nerves. And even though I could tell almost immediately that I was a flop, I had to keep at it for five agonizing minutes.

No one laughed outright at me. No one came up to me and

teased me afterwards. I couldn't feel people whispering and pointing behind my back. And in fact, no former Lit member I spoke to when writing this book could remember a single detail about my speech. But the moment is seared into my mind. I wanted the ground to swallow me whole.

Yet the sun still rose the next morning.

If the sun was up, I could be too. I may have been a disaster, but I couldn't think of a future occasion when I would be asked to deliver a witty speech with little to no advance preparation. I would never have to face that particular humiliation again. It was time to try a different challenge. I dusted myself off after the rhetorical pummeling and pivoted to the prospect of a near-physical one. In my third year, I joined our college's women's intramural touch football team, the legendary Smashers. Even though this was a noncontact league of women in rugby shirts who ran around a campus field for matches that began at 7 a.m., most team members were athletic. Players needed to be able to run fast, run fast backwards, pass a football, catch while running, and be familiar with something called a buttonhook. I could do none of these things.

What I could do was yell. So I enthusiastically volunteered for the position that no one else on the team wanted: steamboat counter. For the uninitiated, the steamboat counter is the person who faces the quarterback as a play begins, arms raised, steely glare in the eyes, oozing intimidation. After all, it's touch football, so you can't race forward and tackle your opponent. The quarterback only has five seconds in which to pass the ball, so it is the steamboat counter's significant responsibility to count these five seconds loudly and clearly enough for her teammates to hear as they run and to holler *ball* as soon as the pass is made. The name comes from the fair pace at which the seconds need to be counted. It wouldn't be sportsmanlike to race through *onetwothreefourfive*, unleash my wrath, and kill the play. Rhythmically yelling *one steamboat, two steamboat, three steamboat* provided a universally accepted pacing. (Although, perhaps somewhere in the southern United States I had a similar counterpart who was dubbed the Mississippi counter).

For the first time in my life, I dominated in a sport. Well, to be fair, I dominated in this particular niche role in a sport. No one could match the stage-voice caliber of my steamboat counting, my frantic arms flailing in front of an often-bewildered opposing quarterback, the fervent way in which I called *ball* the moment the pigskin soared into the air.

Once, I even completed a sack when I intimidated the QB so much that she forgot to make the pass. My fellow Smashers were so ecstatic at this single, inconsequential failed play that they poured onto the field to celebrate with me. We nearly got a delay of game penalty.

That season, the Smashers were undefeated and won the University of Toronto's intramural championship. In celebration, we finished off a case of cheap champagne by 9 a.m.

Were there classes amidst all the adventure? Of course, somewhere. I had decided to complete a specialist degree in international relations, which was a combination of history, political science, and economics. But social events and extracurriculars were front and center in my life. I rarely left a party until it shut down, just in case

I missed some big drama that everyone would be talking about the next day (I believe the kids call this FOMO now). I sang in the chapel choir and was copresident of the dramatic society.

In my final year, I made my first—and to date only—foray into elected office when I ran for and won the position of head of college. At that time, one woman and one man were elected each year to lead the student body for Trinity. The heads of college steered committees that controlled the budgets for student societies, schmoozed with donors to the college, headed up one of the university's only student-led discipline committees, was the primary liaison between students and college administration, and generally acted as a leadership example for the student body. Heads of college also lived in nicer dorm rooms. My room in the final year had a futon that mostly served as a sofa, a small beer fridge, and the residence's only fax machine.

Head of college was a busy role. I chaired a panel that kicked someone out of residence for stealing from a student club. I spoke to women who had been sexually harassed in the residence and those accused of such violations. I sat next to a homophobic, racist man at a dinner for major donors and, in my immaturity, didn't know how to react. As a twenty-one-year-old, I probably handled much of it differently than someone with more life experience would have, but I did my best and trusted in my integrity. I liked the responsibility. I liked speaking to students, to alumni, to donors. I liked being a well-known face on campus, someone people spoke to in the halls.

It was also my final year of school, and I needed a plan. A

degree in international relations was ideal for a move into diplomacy. A career traveling the world, managing bilateral crises, promoting my country's interests, and hobnobbing with global leaders sounded pretty interesting to me. The deal-breaker was that all foreign service careers began in unsexy Ottawa, and in my mind, that represented a step back. I wasn't quite ready for the real world, so I considered graduate school. Ideally, I would get a chance to live abroad, and the world-famous schools in the UK were top of my wish list. By March of my final year, I was still waiting to hear from my top choice, Oxford University. There were no guarantees that I would get in. My grades were good but not outstanding, although I had strong reference letters and extracurricular activities.

One weekend in March, I returned to Ottawa for a quick break. I went to the movie *Good Will Hunting* (partially filmed at the University of Toronto) with a high school friend, and we stopped at a nearby bar afterwards for a drink. The place was dark and felt a little creepy, but the beer was cheap. My parents had insisted I bring their latest tech toy with me: a cell phone. They said I should have it with me in case the car broke down on the way home. My friend Chris and I were chatting about how strange it was to have this mobile device with us that, barring the exorbitant costs, you could just pick up to call anyone at any time! So in some inexplicable fit of bravado, I dialed my number over in Toronto, and my roommate Ildikó answered.

She wasn't interested in the technology I had used to reach her. "There's a letter here for you. From Oxford," she said breathlessly.

"How big is the envelope?" I asked. Acceptance letters usually arrived in large, thick envelopes because they contained brochures on financial assistance and residence. A "thank you, but competition was tough this year" rejection took only half an A4 sheet. I waited for her response.

"It's thin," she said as my heart sank. "But it has the word 'URGENT' stamped on the front."

Chris was giving me a curious look to see what was going on. "Open it!" I pressed Ildikó as she agreed and said she would run to get it. The seconds ticked by. I wondered how much this call was costing and thought I would need to cut my parents a check soon.

"It's an acceptance! You got in!" she virtually screamed over the phone.

I turned to Chris. "I just got into Oxford!" I exclaimed joyfully, then realized instantly that holding a cell phone in my hand and yelling about getting into one of the world's most elite institutions was not necessarily going to endear me to all the other patrons quietly enjoying a pint around us.

In that moment, though, I didn't really care.

I had a new plan, a next chapter, and some cell phone–incurred debt. I was an ordinary girl off to have extraordinary adventures. It was exciting and daunting, but I reminded myself that I had added new gear to my tool kit for life: an appreciation for the importance of kindness, honed chops in student politics, and a willingness to try new things.

There would be questions, of course. How would I pay for it? When would I go? What would I do when the one-year program was finished? I figured I'd maybe stay another year or two and work in England and then return to Canada to build the rest of my life.

For now, though, in that dingy bar in the small town where I'd grown up, to paraphrase from the biggest film moment of that era, I felt like the queen of the world.

4

Across the Pond

After final exams at Oxford University, wearing the "subfusc" uniform that is mandatory for exams, spring 1999.

"When spring comes, you will get good fortune... Just like rice grows, you will be able to reach the highest position."

—No. 13 "Best Fortune," purchased in Tokyo, June 2003

Stroke it! Faster! Harder!" Her voice was firm but pitched with an urgency that bordered on the frantic. Ever the rule follower, I did my best to obey, although I don't think I was naturally so skilled at hard, fast stroking as some others. I was committed to improvement, though.

I had several opportunities a week to try. Practices for the St. Antony's first (and only) women's eights rowing crew were three times a week at the brisk hour of 6 a.m. on the picturesque River Isis, approximately a twenty-five-minute walk from my room in college. I rowed in the position of bow, but even from the other end of the boat, I had no problem hearing the strict commands of our cox, an ebullient doctoral student of Weimar Germany, who steered and led the crew.

Despite no improvement in my physical prowess, I never seemed to avoid venturing into the sporting world. After the curling team and the undefeated Smashers, my latest attempt at athletics lay in joining the rowing crew when I was a graduate student at Oxford in the winter of 1998–99 at the age of twenty-two. St. Antony's was composed entirely of graduate students, more than half of them from outside the UK, so our team was a motley gang, with members hailing from not only Canada but also Germany, Hungary, Greece, and Australia. Our mates over on the men's team were equally as diverse, including from the United States, Mexico, Colombia...and Iceland (a country I knew nothing about but that sounded cold and distant).

But that was the nature of my new environment. Technically, I was living in England, shopping at Sainsbury's, reminding myself to say *trousers* instead of *pants*, and looking right and then left when I crossed the street. But in the cocoon of my tiny Oxford graduate school, I was resident in a miniature United Nations.

If I felt my world had expanded by moving to Canada's biggest city, then it had virtually exploded once I got across the pond. I had thought speaking French gave me a leg up on life, but most of my new friends were fluent in at least three of the world's most common languages and often threw in something like Aramaic or Estonian for good measure. Lunch discussions at the Hilda Besse dining hall often revolved around taking bets on how long a new coalition in the Dutch Parliament would last or whether the economic recovery package the IMF had offered Thailand would successfully stabilize the baht.

Although Oxford (and Cambridge) had been the inspiration for the gown, high tables, and other ancient traditions that Trinity in Toronto had so espoused, I was glad to have a break from it and attend one of the newest and most informal colleges at Oxford. St. Antony's was established in 1950 and, with its emphasis on regional studies and international relations topics, was often known as the "spy college" during the Cold War. I thought that was pretty cool. Spies were almost like diplomats—and they were let in on more scandalous secrets—but crucially, they didn't have to live in Ottawa, a town I still associated with childhood and not adult ambition. Maybe I had a new career prospect.

After a year as the head of the student body at Trinity, I was ready to take a break from politics and clubs. I went to just as many parties at Oxford, though. The on-campus "late bar"—so known because it was open later than the traditional 11 p.m. of British pubs—was a favorite hangout. It was there that I learned about Dutch coalition negotiations, where to find the cheapest kebabs, and how to apply for further funding.

Each week, I met with my supervisor and prepared short essays. I didn't need to attend classes because I was a graduate student, but I did need to read a lot to prepare for each assignment. The university's world-famous Bodleian Library may have the legal right (established in the early seventeenth century) to request a copy of every book published in the UK, but it was not easy to reach them for research purposes: you had to visit in person (a fifteen-minute walk away), order the book(s) you needed, and return again several hours later once said books had been gathered from deep within the storage bowels of the library. After that, it was only possible to read the books within the walls of the Bodleian itself.

Canadians were a dime a dozen at St. Antony's. We always seemed to know people in common, which made everyone else think the country was even smaller than it was (and possibly that we were breeding spies for export).

Many nations were only represented by a single student, though. One day, a good-looking man with curly hair, who was dressed in a black leather jacket, sat next to me in the dining hall at lunch. We were all getting to know each other, and it wasn't unusual to sit next to strangers.

He offered his hand to me and said, in an accent I couldn't

place, "My name is Guðni [he pronounced it Good-nih]. I am from Iceland."

"Ah, you're the Icelander!" I exclaimed. I proceeded to ask him all the questions I would later discover everyone asks when they meet someone from this country: "Is it cold there?" ("Not as much as you'd think.") "How many people live in Iceland?" ("Well, there's me, Mom, my brothers..." In truth, it was not quite three hundred thousand at the time.)

Guðni seemed surprised that I had never heard of the Blue Lagoon and didn't know that superstar Björk was one of his countryfolk, but he held his disappointment in check. We talked a bit more over lunch and saw each other occasionally on campus after that. I found him interesting, kind, and very funny in a bone-dry way. He knew far more than I about Dutch coalition negotiations and even more about the "cod wars," fishing disputes between Iceland and the United Kingdom over territorial waters and also the topic of his doctoral dissertation. If Guðni could make the law of the sea accessible and interesting, then I knew he was a good storyteller. Unlike so many at the college who were clearly rising stars in a galaxy of future world leaders and business luminaries, Guðni had the drive to be the best in his niche field but had no ambition of otherwise having his name recorded in the history books.

A few weeks later, I met him late at night at a student party and was shocked to discover that he was a full eight years older than I was ("*thirrrrty*," he said to me, rolling the *r* as if he were speaking in Icelandic) and divorced with a young daughter back in Iceland.

This really was a cosmopolitan place if I was chatting with a father who had been previously married!

At yet another party, the rowing crews that we had both joined held a fundraiser, a sort of dating raffle. A row of Styrofoam cups stood along a table, and each was marked with the name of a (usually male) member of the rowing team. Anyone who wanted to support the team or perhaps get a chance to enjoy a kebab with a fit rower could buy five paper tickets for one pound, mark those with our names, and put them in cups of our choice. At the end of the evening, the cup owners were to draw one name and take that person out for dinner.

This was my moment! I liked Guðni and wanted to get to know him better but didn't feel like I could ask him out. I had no idea how he felt about me (he was always friendly to chat with, but I thought maybe all Icelanders were), but I hadn't had any indications that he was going to ask me out either, unless dictated by the rules of a raffle.

I bought ten tickets and put about eight of them in Guðni's cup. I reckoned that this greatly increased the odds of him drawing my name. Beyond that, I couldn't possibly be committing myself to much more than dinner and small talk about the tenacity of the Icelandic Coast Guard, could I?

Twenty-four hours later, I enjoyed a delicious three-course Italian dinner at Guðni's expense. Soon enough, Guðni and I were a couple, but we didn't want to think too much about the future. I would be finishing my degree in June, and although I wanted to stay in England and work, at least for a couple of years, I didn't yet have a job secured. Meanwhile, Guðni was in the first year of his doctorate, but his funding sources had ended, and he would not be able to afford to return to the UK and complete the degree unless he had a scholarship.

Fortunately, by the end of the spring term the following June, things became a bit clearer. I had been hired by a large multinational company as part of a graduate recruitment scheme—a program for recent graduates that gave new employees an opportunity to work in numerous divisions of an organization before choosing the best departmental fit. I wasn't going to be a spy, but I was going to get share options. Before the job was set to begin in the autumn of 1999, I undertook my first solo trip: six weeks on an Interrail pass visiting various European cities, including Copenhagen, Warsaw, and Vienna. Although I'd been a bit nervous before I left, I discovered that I loved traveling on my own. There was so much to see and do, many interesting people to meet (both locals and other tourists), many postcards to add to my collection, and much blissful planning to undertake—from pretrip visa applications and ticket booking to reviewing train schedules and hostel vacancies. The excursion ended with a return to Canada for a month…via my first visit to Iceland.

The weather was outstanding on those first few days in what I didn't know then would one day be my permanent home. The sun shone brilliantly, and the wind was virtually nonexistent, as if Nature was pulling out all the stops to woo a potential future citizen. Guðni and I spent our time in a summerhouse on the Snæfellsnes peninsula, not even stopping in the capital. He had secured new funding, now at the University of London, and he'd be returning to the UK as well. For us, finally, it was full steam ahead.

Six months later, we moved in together. (Icelanders move fast to shack up thanks to a lack of moral hang-ups and a traditional dearth of affordable housing. It took me a while longer to come around to the idea.) I was twenty-four and he was thirty-two. We rented a small furnished flat in the Hampshire town where I was working. My job in marketing wasn't very satisfying. I was a fish out of water in terms of the unspoken British class hierarchies (no one knew where to place me because of my Canadian accent) and because I was a young woman in a relatively male-dominated environment (I was told I wouldn't be sent on business trips to certain countries because of my gender and was often asked to serve tea at meetings). My ignorance of all the corporate jargon also didn't help. I didn't know what synergies were, how to leverage low-hanging fruit, or whether paradigm shifts were a good thing, and I didn't really care. My graduate trainee final report said of me that "We discussed, and she accepted, where her 'North American' openness was beneficial and where she could be misread... She has learned a great deal and is a bright graduate who needs to be 'overloaded' to get the best out of her... Eliza relates to and is accepted by most people. She is a person of integrity and wants to give."

Frankly, I wasn't cut out for the corporate world. But I did get to travel, and I had made several friends.

In any case, as Guðni finished up his doctorate, we had a decision to make. He would be returning to Iceland to be close to his daughter, Rut, as she grew up. Would I join him? Iceland was the only option for us if we wanted to be together. And we did.

I handed in my notice and began planning another solo trip. I figured that since I was moving to a new country where I didn't speak the language or have a job lined up, I might as well arrive broke too. This was true, but I was also itching to plan an even bigger, longer trip than my interrailing of four years earlier. I had always wanted to visit more far-flung regions of the world, expand my horizons, and test my resilience, independence, and confidence in a fun way. I wanted to do this alone so I didn't have to adapt my plans to anyone else or justify my bizarre foibles, such as never eating eggs at breakfast or insisting on keeping my printed photos in chronological order.

Where would I go? How would I get around? Where and how would I get visas? Cash traveler's checks? Find accommodation? Buy postcards? In my free time, I pored over travel magazines and searched the internet for fun things to do. I carved out a nearly one-hundred-day itinerary that began in Moscow, went through Central Asia, up to Siberia, and then to Mongolia and on to Japan, Singapore, and through Southeast Asia. (My first plan, which included a month in China, was scuppered when the SARS pandemic closed borders.)

But before the trip began, there was one thing left to do. I knew I wasn't moving all the way to Iceland to test the waters or see how it would go. I was making a commitment to both a person and a country. As a rule follower and somewhat of a traditionalist, I wanted that to be codified and officially recognized in some way.

On one of our last weekends in England, Guðni and I traveled to Cornwall in the southwest of the country where he conducted an interview with a retired admiral for his doctoral thesis. I smuggled a bottle of champagne into my backpack. Just before we headed into town for supper, I told Guðni I wanted to ask him something.

"We're moving to Iceland soon," I began, stating the obvious. "And I'm going on this big trip. So I wanted to know if you would marry me?"

Actually, I can't really remember what I said, and even if I did, some things get to stay between a couple. The point is that I proposed to him, I did it without a long, cheesy speech, and he said yes. We had never discussed getting married before.

It hadn't occurred to me to wait for him to pop the question. I have never understood why, in heterosexual relationships, a marriage proposal was the prerogative of the male. I wasn't about to leave jewelry catalogs lying on the coffee table or casually drop my ring size into dinner conversation (had I even known there was such a thing as a ring size). I had a voice and something to say. Why not do that?

When I flew off to Moscow a few weeks later, I wasn't wearing an engagement ring. Since Guðni hadn't even done the proposing, how would it be fair to ask him to buy me a ring? I also didn't want to wear anything of value that might attract thieves. But who needs rings? Guðni wanted to marry me too, and our dazzling commitment (and the rest of our checking account) went into loading our combined worldly possessions into a shipping container bound for Iceland.

I had no ring, but I did have a mosquito net, six pairs of underwear, two ninety-minute mixtapes, one of those fancy new digital cameras with a 16-MB memory card, and a detailed itinerary called "Eliza's Big Trip."

Of course, I wanted to be as organized as possible but also leave (scheduled) room for moments of spontaneity. My first long journey would be the train from Moscow to Tashkent, capital of Uzbekistan. I had booked the ticket for the seventy-two-hour journey in advance, and it departed from the city's Kazansky station at around 11:30 p.m. On my only day in the Russian capital, I used my morning to take the metro from my hotel, the mammoth Hotel Rossiya, to the train station and the specific platform of my departure so that when I returned later under cover of night, I would have a good idea of how long the journey would take me and move around with more self-assurance, which I thought made me less of a target for theft or harassment.

It was a beginning typical of my personality, more party planner than party animal. After all, what's more fun than spontaneously planning exactly where the day's journey will end? And after I stepped into my train compartment and greeted the young Tatar couple with whom I would share the three-day journey, I knew I would have time to figure out my next steps. (I would also have time to read Guðni's entire doctoral dissertation on the Anglo-Icelandic Cod Wars. My first assignment upon reaching Tashkent was to find an internet café and email him all my suggested edits. That's long-distance love for you.)

About a week later, I arrived in the Uzbek city Samarkand,

a stop on the ancient Silk Road that was a primary trading route between China and the Mediterranean during the Middle Ages. I had created my whole itinerary based around a brochure photo I had seen of that city's Registan Square, a splendid trio of imposing azure and beige madrassas built in the fifteenth century. Now, instead of classrooms for religious pupils, it was home to various souvenir stalls. I stepped into one of them, with colorful handsewn tablecloths hanging outside the doorway, and met a woman whose name I later learned was Mohabbat. I wanted to negotiate the price of ten faded Soviet-era postcards to add to my collection. She spoke no English, and I spoke no Tajik or Russian, but I was determined to communicate with her. With the aid of my tiny phrase book and with some initial small talk, I learned that she was inviting me to dinner at her home.

My intuition told me that I would enjoy some excellent hospitality if I agreed to Mohabbat's request. That evening, a bumpy taxi ride deposited me in a suburban neighborhood of Samarkand, where multistory apartments framed a dusty courtyard. Mohabbat, her husband, Rofi, and their four boys—Rahim, Amin, Azim, and Aziz—lived in a four-room flat on the second floor.

Rahim spoke the English of a tour guide, so he acted as interpreter for the evening. "Please, you are welcome," he said and gestured to a low table surrounded by cushions and laden with Uzbek specialties.

In porcelain bowls were nuts, apricots, raisins, strawberries, tomato-cucumber salad, and cabbage with dill. Chilled Baltica beer and giant nigella-flecked naan breads were clustered in the corners.

Once Rofi had cleansed his hands and uttered a prayer of thanks, Mohabbat presented the star of the show, a massive pottery bowl of steaming plov, a glistening Central Asian version of rice pilaf. As the guest, I was presented with the dish's choicest cubes of mutton fat.

Then we opened the vodka.

As a precautionary measure, I meekly requested *malinki, pazhalsta*, a mangled Russian version of "small, please," but Rahim grinned and filled the teacup almost to the brim.

Rofi and I took turns composing toasts while Mohabbat flashed me a gold-toothed smile of encouragement and the boys listened in silence. First to my health, then to their longevity. The teacup was filled to support my upcoming nuptials and, on the fourth round, to my fertility.

"To your many unborn sons," proclaimed Rofi, his eloquent-sounding Tajik translated by Rahim. I drained my teacup of vodka in one go.

The vodka bottle empty, I slept on the floor of the same room where we had eaten. I awoke early with a fuzzy head, the laughing children and barking dogs outside a prelude to the day. Before I climbed into the cramped minibus that would shuttle me back to the tourist trail, Mohabbat scribbled her address down in Cyrillic on a scrap of paper. We promised to write.

It wasn't just the locals who were kind to me. In Siberia, I met a Swiss couple named Martin and Susannah who were taking an extended honeymoon, spending several months in the region. We decided to visit the shores of the world's deepest lake, Baikal, together. Legend has it that if you dip your hand in the lake, you'll live one year longer. If it's a foot, you'll get five more years. And if you swim in this body of water where summer temps are only around 8°C, then the bonus is a full quarter century. Neither Susannah nor I had bathing suits, but we reasoned that skinny-dipping might earn us an additional decade on top of that.

Gently making our way down a slope to a rocky beach, we asked Susannah's new husband to be our official photographer and capture the proof of our dips. We quickly raced into the chilly water and ducked down to our necks, yelling "Take the picture! Take the picture!" so we could run out again as soon as possible. I only learned later that we had jumped up so quickly Martin hadn't captured a good brag-worthy photo of a dip in Lake Baikal but rather an image of two pale, topless women leaping out of the gray water, a sort of Siberian, no-frills *Birth of Venus*. Ah well. Seeing as I had already secured many sons with my teacup of vodka in Samarkand, the extra longevity would come in handy.

Despite my joke that Martin was the rare man who saw another woman naked on his honeymoon, we all got along well. I even spent a few days camping with my Swiss friends in Mongolia's Gobi Desert. After that, I flew to Tokyo. I had no accommodation booked and was arriving so late that I had decided just to spend the night at a café and try to find a hostel room in the morning. On the train into town, however, a young woman my age began chatting with me, and she ended up inviting me to stay at her residence that night.

"I'm not really allowed guests," she confided. "But I'll sneak you in." Once again, I trusted my instincts. Chizuru was a generous host. She and I also promised to stay in touch, even though I wasn't sure when, if ever, I would be back in Japan.

Two months into my trip, on one of my regular but infrequent stops at an internet café, this time in Hanoi, Vietnam, I opened an email from my father stating that my paternal grandmother had been diagnosed with terminal cancer. When I had seen her last, earlier that spring in Canada, she was her usual energetic self, driving around in her used Volkswagen, swimming laps in the apartment building swimming pool. But now, as I sat in a humid café on the other side of the planet, I learned that doctors did not expect her to live more than a few weeks.

In the bottom of my backpack, I carried my old Nokia cell phone from the UK, the one that charged astronomical fees to make a call. I called my family and managed to say a few words with Grandma. I was her only granddaughter, and I tried to figure out how I would cut my trip short and afford a last-minute ticket to Canada to see her. But she wouldn't hear of it. She didn't want me to stop a once-in-a-lifetime journey to race home and watch her die. It was better to have the memories of her healthy and well.

I obeyed her, although I felt a mixture of relief that I didn't have to curtail the trip and guilt that I had heeded her wishes so quickly. But she was right; two weeks later, from another internet café, this time in Phnom Penh, Cambodia, I learned that my Grandma Reid, retired nurse, baker extraordinaire, and unofficial budgie whisperer, had died the day before. She had just turned eighty-four.

That evening, accepting hugs from some new backpacking

friends and sipping cheap lager, I felt both very far away from everything that was familiar and grateful for the compassion of others. A couple of weeks later, it was over. In almost one hundred days, I had visited eleven countries and seven time zones, and I never once felt afraid. Nor had I ever felt lonely, but I wrote in my diary several times how excited I was to be getting married and grateful for a partner who was so supportive of my independent nature. I had developed the fortitude to be more laid-back when problems or surprises led to unanticipated developments. And I had had glimpses into how similar people are yet also how incredibly privileged I was through the random luck of my place of birth. My trust in humanity was bolstered, and I reminded myself to act with the same generosity, patience, hospitality, and kindness to strangers that I had encountered on my travels.

A prediction I had bought at a temple on my brief stop in Tokyo promised that when spring came, I would get "good fortune." Between proposing to my boyfriend, raising vodka-fueled toasts with strangers in Uzbekistan, and skinny-dipping in a mystical lake, I figured I had stuffed the raffle box of life with many tokens marked Eliza. I loved to plan for all eventualities, but part of the reason that gave me security was that it freed up more bandwidth to tackle life's unpredictable surprises when they struck.

That same Japanese fortune also assured me I "will be able to reach the highest position." On August 18, 2003, wearing the same fifty-liter backpack I had carried since early May, I left Bangkok, Thailand, on a flight to London. A couple of days later, I flew to Reykjavík and a brand-new start at the edge of the Arctic Circle.

5

Keep Your Seat Belt Fastened While Seated

With Guðni at the Jökulsárlón Glacial Lagoon, late 1999 and long before Iceland's tourist boom.

"It may be dark and cold right now—but I know I'm home."

—From my first Daily Life column for *Iceland Review* online after I returned from seven weeks in West Africa, November 2006

Fyrirgefðu, ég talar bara pínulítið íslensku. Excuse me, I speaks only small Icelandic. This grammatically challenged phrase was one of my go-to conversation starters during my first months and, frankly, probably years in Iceland. Anyone who has visited this country knows that English is widely spoken. Locals long ago discerned that if they ever wanted to make something of themselves beyond the subarctic island, they would have to learn more than the ancient language of the sagas. So English is taught in schools from an early age, and films and television programs are subtitled rather than dubbed (with the exception of those for preschoolers).

For native English speakers, our mother tongue can, counter-intuitively, pose a challenge to learning Icelandic. If everyone you interact with is more skilled in your own lingua franca, why switch, especially for any subjects more in depth than ordering a restaurant meal or making small talk about the weather. I was determined I would make a go of it, though. After all, I wasn't moving to this island for a test run. I had made a commitment to be here while my partner's daughter was growing up, not to see whether I could cope with the winter darkness and smelly hot water.

And while there was no denying that I had immigrated to Iceland for love, I wanted to stay for me. I wanted, craved, my own group of friends, my own financial independence, my own hobbies.

While I was grateful for it, a happy relationship was but one component of a well-rounded life.

I committed early on to learning Icelandic as effectively as I could, as quickly as I could. This was, after all, the key to helping me contribute best to society. I had met a few "old-school" immigrants who were nearly flawless in the language, but many others still struggled with more than simple conversation. Even the first lady at the time, the immensely popular Israeli-born Dorrit Moussaieff, was far from fluent. I realized that I could function without knowing the word for monkfish (it's *skötuselur*), but I didn't think Iceland would get under my skin in the same way if I didn't master its language.

I had had some advance practice. Ever since Guðni and I had become a couple, I had been trying to learn the basic rules around the three genders, four cases, and incomprehensible "middle voice" of Icelandic grammar. I knew that *hv* together was pronounced like a *k*, that there were about twenty-four different ways to decline *headache* (depending on the word's number, gender, and grammatical role in the sentence), and that you never, ever, needed to say *please*.

I had a few stock phrases too, including guidelines on wearing seat belts during flights, thanks to hours spent staring at the tray table in front of me while flying up to Iceland for visits. And I wore that proverbial harness tightly in those first months. If I was flying through the turbulence of living in a new country, I needed the security of knowing the language and of finding a predictable office job.

Whenever I began any interaction in Icelandic, the person to whom I was talking almost immediately switched to English. A simple reminder of the fact that I was learning made them think twice before changing. (The other rule I picked up quickly was to order at least five items of everything, thus avoiding the question of which gender and declension to use for numbers one through four.) Before I took on the formal grammar, which overwhelmed me, I was discovering how to make my own rules for learning Icelandic.

Acquiring proficiency was but one of my objectives on the single sheet of paper titled "Eliza's Big Plan" that I had written and printed out to guide me when I arrived in Iceland. The Big Plan also included tasks of varying significance, from opening a bank account to sending photos to friends I had met while traveling to buying an apartment and, most urgently, finding a job. Most importantly, the Big Plan gave me a framework of *what* I should do *when* to build a fulfilling life for myself in Iceland. Whatever "a fulfilling life" meant, it had tantalizingly few rules; I was always better at trying to let that part develop organically.

In addition to committing to learn Icelandic, I was determined to find a position that did not involve exploiting my fiancé's contacts.

"So many people in Iceland get their job because of contacts," Guðni had warned me.

I shook my head stubbornly and took that as a challenge. "Not me. I'm finding something purely on my own merits."

About a week later, fate handed me an opportunity. Guðni spotted an ad in the local newspaper for a "marketing specialist." (All right, so he helped by reading the paper.) A small start-up was looking for someone with sales and marketing experience and fluent English to join their team. I met every one of their criteria.

I called the company and asked to talk to the head of human resources.

"You can speak to me about that," said the woman who had picked up the phone.

"My name is Eliza Reid, and I am going to apply for the marketing specialist position," I explained. "I'm calling to ask the name of the person to whom I should address my application."

"You can send it to me," she answered and gave me her details.

It was only after I got the job that I discovered that I had been speaking with the CEO. There was no dedicated human resources department in the small company, but I was the only applicant who had called to ask for these details. She later told me that from that point on, the job had been mine to lose.

One thing to tick off from Eliza's Big Plan.

Around this time, we also put in an offer to buy a two-bedroom apartment in downtown Reykjavík. We would move early in the New Year. Tick item number two.

"When I'm organized, everything is much nicer," I wrote in my diary. "I'll get through this culture shock stuff."

The "culture shock stuff" was nothing too significant. I griped about the weather, that most days were "a combination of cloud, fog, and rain." I found setting up a bank account and getting a national ID number relatively straightforward but didn't like that it took companies up to half a year to update their databases, so even though I had the ID number, which is key to being able to do almost anything in Iceland, it was months before I could rent a movie at the local Blockbuster. And of course, I blanched at the cost of imports: everything from chicken breasts to gasoline. Without any irony, I raged at the lack of crème fraîche and halloumi cheese in the stores. Green and red peppers from the low-cost grocery store were often moldy, sandwich cheese only available in "bland" or "blander," and a sweet potato was as rare as gold dust. Still, Guðni reminded me that life was better now than in 1970s Iceland, when apples were an exotic fruit reserved for the Christmas season and vegetables generally came in two forms: canned or frozen. Of course, when not grumbling about moldy peppers, I had to laugh. All those grievances were borne of a well-cheesed childhood in a country of overabundance.

There were also plenty of amazing things, not the least of which was the beauty of the island. "Saw the most gorgeous sunset," I gushed in my diary. "Makes me so happy to be living here! I sat down on a bench by the sea to watch the sun slowly sink. Breathing in the clean air, smelling the sea, hearing the waves beat against the rocks. And the colors! Just highlighted against a little band of cloud…all mauves to pinks to oranges and then sunset red with one band of deeper light shining straight up. Just beautiful!"

To put it another way, I was lucky. Within a few months, I had a job in my field of experience, I was moving into a nice apartment, I had made a fun group of friends, both from my workplace and from my Icelandic class, and I had time to fawn over sunsets.

I was also planning a wedding! Well, sort of; my mother did most of it from Canada, and I was happy to delegate. Guðni and

I got married the following July at the local United church in the village near my parents' home. My two bridesmaids were Ildikó, who had remained a good friend despite the number of times I woke her up in the middle of the night at university, and Katja, former quarterback of the mighty Smashers touch football team. We had a Mountie acquaintance greet the foreign guests, my talented high school friends supplied the music, and my new husband's family told all the Canucks that the Icelandic word for "cheers" was *typpi*, which actually means penis. Guðni and I then embarked on a perfect honeymoon to Newfoundland and Labrador. (By the way, I kept my last name. After all, thanks to Iceland's mostly patronymic naming system, why become the son of my husband's father?)

Guðni and I returned from our summer wedding to the impending Icelandic autumn, my second one living in the country. It was on one of those crisp days soon afterwards, near the end of August (fall comes early in Iceland), that I was summoned to the CEO's office and told that I was being laid off. There were some excuses given, some sympathetic smiles delivered.

I was devastated.

Was it something I had done? Was I bad at the job? Had I inadvertently broken a rule? Whatever the reason, my seat belt had come off, and there was turbulence ahead. I was also worried about the financial aspect. Guðni was working on a postdoc research project, and I was the primary breadwinner for our tiny family. How would we pay for our inflation-indexed mortgage without my income?

Guðni was tolerant, patient, and encouraging, and my newfound friends were sympathetic and supportive. As the weeks and months ticked by, I picked myself up to figure out yet another Big Plan.

I put together another spreadsheet, another chart, another to-do list; I was systematic about tackling this challenge too. As I researched local companies where English was the working language, I went to the gym every morning—turns out unemployment is great for staying in shape!—joined a choir, and volunteered at a hospital shop run by the Red Cross.

It was a period of highs and lows. Every time I applied for a position or met someone new at a party, I hoped this was the connection that would get me a challenging, well-paid job. Every time I was turned down—ostensibly because my (Oxford!) degree wasn't in business or marketing or because my Icelandic wasn't good enough even for a company whose clients were exclusively in English-speaking markets—I would sink into a funk and despair about ever finding fulfilling employment. I leveraged every contact I had, including appearing on a morning radio show hosted by my Icelandic teacher, all in Icelandic, during which I made a poorly worded pitch for a job. No one called.

It was taking much longer to find work this time around. In the meantime, I'd need to keep busy. In the choir where I sang, I finally plucked up the courage to ask the group a practical question in my beginner's Icelandic: Would we be required to wear *búðingur* for the upcoming concert? We were not. *Búningur* with an *n* in the middle is the word for uniform that I was looking for. *Búðingur* with the letter *ð*, which is what I said, is the Icelandic word for pudding. Turns out the proof is not in the pudding but in how quickly you can laugh at yourself when learning a new language.

To show the depths to which I was prepared to earn some cash and stray outside my lane, I even made my pro sports debut: A friend of a friend contacted me to ask if I would be interested in dressing for a match between two basketball teams in the top Icelandic league. These teams were allowed to have one citizen from outside the European Economic Area on their squads, and there was a final date to sign up a foreigner. The rub, however, was that the team could switch out the foreign player later on. The season deadline was coming up, and this team wanted to add a player with a foreign passport registered on their roster so they could leave the option open of finding a semipro to join them for the playoffs. I was offered $100 to dress and sit on the bench.

Given my varied background in athletics, from the curling team to the Smashers to college rowing, I was thrilled about my first pro experience. I was even more excited because I came from a basketball-loving family: My father had been captain of his university team and had been a coach for decades. My brothers both played basketball. My aunt was captain of her college team, and my uncle competed in the sport at the Commonwealth Games.

But *I* went pro.

With Guðni in the stands to cheer me on, I warmed up with the team. Just before tip-off, the captain, recently returned from studying in the U.S. on a basketball scholarship, told me that if the game was going well, they would let me play. My husband begged them not to. "She's not being modest!" he pleaded. "She is really, really bad at sports." This was true.

Fortunately—or not, as you see it—the game didn't go so well for my team, and I was kept on the bench for the entire match. But the newspaper the next day had a write-up of my participation, probably one of my first appearances in the Icelandic press. It reported that I was a new team member but that I "did not feature" in the match. Guðni cut out the clipping and stuck it to our fridge door with a magnet.

Still, the rather passive adventure gave me a jolt of positivity. Maybe I was growing. Maybe I still belonged in Iceland, even if no one wanted to hire me for anything beyond legally dubious bench warming. Maybe I could really make something of myself here.

But beyond the unlikely diversion of athletics, I would need to gain some professional experience to land a lucrative nine-to-five gig. I had another idea: writing. I pitched a story to *The Reykjavík Grapevine*, the country's only English-language newspaper, about how to find work as an immigrant in Iceland. They promptly replied that they weren't interested in that but did ask me to compose a feature on, in a master non sequitur, the Eurovision song contest.

An unexpected chain reaction began. That piece was well received and led to more assignments. Someone from an English magazine, *Iceland Review*, hired me to write advertorials and then feature articles. Companies that saw my work hired me to proofread or write marketing texts for them. Within a few months, I was cobbling together a full-time job on my own terms, one that built on my love of storytelling to connect with others. I realized that my career didn't need to be about the rat race and time sheets. Maybe I could be my own boss.

As I found my professional groove once more, in a place I had never dreamed of looking—my own home office—about two years after I had been laid off, I started to think big again. If I was building a career in journalism and travel writing, maybe I could make that international. I embarked on more of my beloved planning, this time for a seven-week solo trip around several nations in West Africa. I spoke to a leading newspaper in Iceland and got a commission to publish a five-part series on my visit after I promised my itinerary would include a stop at an orphanage supported by Icelanders in Togo's capital, Lomé.

Once again, I took great pleasure in the planning of my trip, from researching the best antimalarial medicine to selecting songs to transfer onto my new portable MP3 player. I spoke to friends and acquaintances who had visited the region, though I had no contacts who were actually from the seven countries I would visit. I researched the best route to Timbuktu and the top towns to see in Burkina Faso. I knew I'd wear a physical seat belt every time there was an opportunity, but I was as prepared as I could be for the inevitable instances when I would have nothing to cling to. Meanwhile, Guðni, who still warmly encouraged all my adventures, even if he had no interest in joining me, began work on a new project that fascinated him—a book on surveillance of left-leaning activists in Iceland during the Cold War, in particular government-sanctioned wiretapping, based in part on documents he had accidentally uncovered in Britain's National Archives. *Enemies of the State* would become a critically acclaimed bestseller.

As Guðni camped out in the archives, after a journey that had begun more than eighteen hours earlier, I descended the steps of my airplane into the oppressive humidity of the night in the Senegalese capital, Dakar. At the bottom of the steps, a van was waiting to shuttle everyone to the terminal. Next to the van was a young man wearing a long white kaftan. He was holding a sign for "Mme Reid." My new kaftan-wearing companion was Arona, a friend of a friend from my days working in England. Arona and his wife, Mariama, hosted me in their central Dakar apartment while I explored the city. They were well connected enough that they could get airside access to receive guests and the use of a VIP room to wait for baggage and passport control. Who knew that airports had VIP rooms? That on occasion a fortunate passenger could bypass the entire arrival chaos? It was an unexpected treat at the outset of a no-frills vacation and one I reckoned I would never experience again.

Several sightseeing-filled days later, I was ready to move on to the next country. In my guidebook, the train between Dakar and Bamako was billed as one of Africa's last great train journeys, and my plan was to enjoy it, perhaps invoking some nostalgia from my days in Siberia and Central Asia. The Malian train took about three days to complete the 760-mile journey.

I was on my way to the station for the scheduled departure time of 1 p.m. when I discovered that the express had been delayed, not an unusual development.

A few minutes before the new scheduled departure time, the faded green-and-yellow cars of the express inched into the station. Hundreds of passengers crowded on. Many were traders, mostly in the free-for-all seating of second class, with their sacks of onions and rice and fabrics. First class had assigned seats and the same torn cushions and dirt as second class.

I had opted to splurge on my ticket and had purchased a couchette, which entitled me to one bed in a cabin of four. Each bed was composed of a piece of hole-filled foam, about three inches thick, and an extremely dirty cover sheet (everyone had brought their own linens).

We boarded the train at about 7:30 p.m., by which time the sun had set. There were no lights on the train until it started moving, so we passengers were in complete darkness, with only malaria-carrying mosquitoes and cockroaches for company. (My compartment mate kindly pointed out all the creepy-crawlies to me with her flashlight.) As we waited to depart, the heat continued to rise, the air was stifling, and I was a sweaty mess. I couldn't help but think of my husband, who had told me that that evening, he had been invited to a dinner at the presidential residence for the first time, thanks to the visit of a renowned historian. I bet there were no bugs greeting him there, I thought.

At 11:30 p.m., after four hours on board the stifling dark train and several very pleasant conversations with the other incredibly tolerant passengers, I took a stroll along the platform to casually inquire about the delay. I was told by friendly officials (who first wanted to know where my husband was) that the train would leave once all the traders' bags were loaded, and I was assured this would happen before midnight. Inside the main terminal building, I could see there were literally hundreds of sacks left to load and a group of men standing around them not doing much of anything.

So against my better nature, I became a quitter, returning to the train, bidding farewell to my brief travel companions, and staying one more night at Arona and Mariama's before flying to Mali the next morning. Even though the scheduling amendment flew in the face of my plan, I felt really good about my decision. I didn't have to prove my travel mettle to anyone, plus, courtesy of Royal Air Maroc, I got to study *keep your seat belt fastened while seated* in Arabic.

In Mali, I visited the legendary Timbuktu. I took the twenty-first century version of the ancient camel trains there—a 4x4, windscreen beautifully intact and air in all the tires. After two weeks in Mali, it was on to Burkina Faso and then Benin. It was a 684-mile journey from Burkina Faso's capital, Ouagadougou, to Benin's de facto capital, Cotonou, on the coast, about a twenty-hour bus ride. In my quest to avoid having to take public transportation at night due to safety concerns, I came up with a cunning plan: take the bus as far as Natitingou, a city in the north of Benin, and then continue early the next morning to Cotonou.

So I called and reserved my ticket for Natitingou. Then I arrived at the station and purchased the reserved ticket for Natitingou. I showed my ticket for Natitingou at the door of the bus and again to the conductor when the journey started.

Two and a half hours into the trip, the chauffeur announced he was going to... Togo. So much for the plan to avoid driving late at night. I never did find out where the confusion lay, but I was now in it for the long haul—and a new country.

Hours later, after a supper break of tinned sardines squished on a baguette, we stopped briefly where a big discussion ensued with some youths at the side of the road. Turns out they were "our mercenaries," and the chauffeur was negotiating their fee to accompany us on the bus in order to protect us from possible bandits at roadblocks. That's when I noticed the machine guns slung over their shoulders. In the end, a suitable price wasn't reached, and the youths stayed on the road. I wasn't sure if that was good or not, but there was no time to dwell on the threat of armed robbery; I was worried about the driver. He must have been exhausted. He had been driving since 7 a.m., and everyone else on the bus was sound asleep (except me—rigidly looking out the window, as if willing him to stay awake).

We arrived safe and sound in Lomé at 1 a.m., where I faced a throng of taxi drivers focused on the lone foreign face to get off the bus. I agreed on a price with one and followed him to what turned out to be an unmarked taxi. Just outside the gates of the bus station, he pulled over, and his "friend" jumped in with him—for "security" I was told. Then they told me my hotel was nine miles away in a village outside the city.

I had to think on my feet. All the rule books would have told me to ditch this ride and get another, but that would have meant disembarking somewhere in central Lomé in the middle of the night with nowhere to go. Meanwhile, my intuition felt that they were legit people and the "security" of the extra person in the car was to protect the driver against rogue clients. I quickly concocted a fabrication, explaining that I knew the owner of the hotel and he was waiting up for me to arrive. A police officer who stopped us at a checkpoint soon afterwards confirmed the distance of the hotel. That made me feel better. And when I finally arrived at 2 a.m., the taxi drivers wanted to wake up the owner to confirm that I had been deposited safely!

Although a big takeaway rule of life from my trip was that it was impossible to plan anything around West African transportation, it turns out that my visit to Dakar airport's VIP room was not the only glamorous moment of the journey.

I arrived early in Ouidah, Benin, after a blessedly uneventful shared taxi from Togo. I was the only guest at the Hotel Oasis in the center of the city. After settling in, I collected a few things and left the room to find some lunch.

A friendly group of people loitering around a restaurant at the hotel gestured for me to enter—"*Ici, madame!*" I looked in; it was crowded for some function. But then even the police officer guarding the entrance invited me in.

And that is how I inadvertently crashed the gala lunch commemorating the coronation of the supreme chief of the vodoun religion, the Daagbo Hounon Tomadjlèhoukpon Hounwamènou.

There I sat for a delicious three-course meal and chatted about this new supreme leader. One of the guests at the table, an engineer named Rodrigue, asked me if I wanted to visit the daagbo the next day.

At the leader's compound the next evening, there was lots

of singing and dancing. The man himself was seated in a largish receiving room with plenty of well-wishers surrounding him as well as an (empty) bottle of whiskey.

Rodrigue introduced me as "an adventurer" (which, as someone who was too scared to ride a bicycle, I found ironic) who was writing about her trip.

Soon the daagbo invited me to come and have a chat with him in a smaller reception room.

He asked me what I thought of Benin. I replied I was fortunate to have had the chance to meet him on this auspicious occasion. "Yes, you are," he replied. Then he asked for my email address so I could have a little correspondence with the "king."

It was my first brush with royalty.

Soon afterwards, it was time to return home and write my five-part newspaper series. As I recalled my travels, I thought of all the people I'd met—from the supreme leader of a major religion to strangers selling their wares on a Malian street who invited me to break the Ramadan fast with them. The trip had reinforced my optimism in humanity after a couple of difficult years in Iceland. It was just what I needed.

I had now been living in Iceland for just over three years, and in that time, I'd been hired, been fired, switched careers, bought a small house (we moved after eighteen months in the apartment), warmed the bench of a top division basketball team, offered to wear pudding to a choir concert, took hundreds of hours of Icelandic lessons, and knew how to make nearly any kind of water potable with iodine.

I was stitching together diverse experiences without assiduously following a step-by-step setup manual but learning to trust that each little square of adventure would patch together into some sort of security quilt of experience.

I didn't realize it at the time, but suntanned and back in my new home in Iceland, I was preparing for the great unbuckling: parenthood.

6

In a Family Way

Guðni and I had four children in just under six years, and this is typical of the few group photos we have. Our two-year-old has clearly just realized he is no longer the baby of the family!

"We could sit together in the evenings, me studying and you sewing and crocheting."

—Gunnar Thoroddsen to Vala Ásgeirsdóttir, October 1940

In 2005, the year before I took my trip to West Africa, Guðni and I had moved to a century-old timber house in the western part of Reykjavík. It was painted a sunny yellow and had a red aluminum roof and a small, enclosed backyard. The whole thing was about 1,100 square feet; the two of us shared a tiny home office, each with our own desk facing opposite walls. If we turned around to face each other, we almost bumped knees.

We called it the Sit Room, after the hub for vital decision-making on our favorite TV show, *The West Wing*. I composed my trip travel pieces from the Sit Room. Meanwhile, Guðni was writing his sixth book, a biography of a former prime minister, Gunnar Thoroddsen, who'd had a long, happy marriage with his wife, Vala. Guðni jokingly taped a note on the door of our Sit Room that Gunnar had written to Vala in 1940, predicting a happy future together, each contented in their own gender-predetermined roles. (Guðni knew how to tease me about sexism.)

Now that I had returned from a successful trip, it was time for what we hoped would be the next chapter in our journey as a family: having children. My doctor had told me I needed to wait a month after finishing my antimalarial medicine before trying to get pregnant, but in any case, he added it would probably "take quite a while."

I got pregnant that first month. I was thirty years old and would be thirty-one when the baby was due.

Being knocked up was a manual reader's mecca. There were books and websites that covered the guidance of virtually every step of baby gestating. A weekly "how your fetus compares to a fruit" guide! Recipes to suit every mood swing, food craving, and pregnancy trimester! Glossaries for symptoms, bodily changes, and vanishingly rare but enticingly nerve-racking possible complications. I devoured it all (and a lot of dill pickles and ice cream).

It felt good to be pregnant. Sure, I got a sore back and had difficulty sleeping by the end, but I didn't have bad morning sickness or really any other of the more irritating side effects of pregnancy. I wasn't glowing exactly; I had gained more than forty-four pounds by the end and removed my wedding ring around the seven-month mark after my finger got too swollen. But it all boded well.

My mother had offered to come from Canada and help once the baby arrived. Until she mentioned the idea, it had genuinely never occurred to me that she might want to come and that I might need her around. After all, I had left home when I was eighteen and not lived close to my parents since then. But she certainly wouldn't be a hassle, so I said that it would be fine for her to fly over.

"Fine" is perhaps the biggest understatement I have ever made. My mother was a godsend. She had booked her tickets to arrive a few days after my due date, thinking she could best help after I had returned from the hospital. My midwife was convinced the baby would arrive a couple of weeks early, so to get to Iceland at due date plus three days would be right when things were getting busy for Guðni and I as new parents.

However, despite all my rule books, I hadn't paid enough attention to the premise of babies operating on their own schedules. Duncan was not merely overdue. He was induced two weeks past my due date and required so much induction medicine that the midwife needed a doctor's approval before administering it.

When I was growing up, every time I watched television with my mother and someone went into labor, she would roll her eyes, turn to me, and say dismissively, "It's not that bad." My mother is an optimist—remember, this is the woman who convinced me a bridge club would be the perfect addition to my middle school. I like to think I'm an optimist too. So, I reasoned, if my positive mother thought labor and delivery was straightforward, so would I.

I was wrong.

I could blame the fact that my labor was induced when my body wasn't ready. I could blame the anesthesiologist for positioning the catheter in such a way that the epidural had no effect whatsoever on me. I could blame a system of shift midwives that left me with a caregiver I had never before laid eyes on looking after me—popping in and out of the room, really—only ten minutes before the birth.

Really, I think it was that I wasn't prepared for the fact that giving birth just hurts like the dickens.

Shortly after midnight, fifteen days past my due date, Duncan was born with the help of a method delicately called vacuum extraction. He was blue, but he cried immediately, his skin pinking up as he sucked oxygen into his little lungs, and I figured this was just how newborn babies looked. In any case, this meant my pain was over. Almost. I had to have surgery after the birth and ended up returning home with him when he was a few days old.

By the time all this happened, my mom, who had arrived ten days before, was scheduled to leave the next day with my dad, who had arrived the day after Duncan was born. Just when I finally realized how helpful it was to have Mom around—cooking, cleaning, swaddling the baby, and generally being wonderful—she was returning to her home thousands of miles away. What was I going to do?

I didn't know how we could afford it, but I offered to buy her a ticket to return six weeks later. Mom readily agreed.

Mom was a shining example of an amazing parent, a woman who nurtured and supported all her kids. For her, labor was a moment of connection with a child, one of life's beautiful passages.

I didn't yet have that feeling. Even though Duncan was healthy, I kept reliving the unpleasant parts of his birth. I was physically and mentally exhausted. I loved my son, but the love did not overwhelm the feeling of "is this it?" and the guilt that accompanied that sentiment. I was supposed to be ecstatic, a natural nurturer like my mother. I wasn't supposed to be trudging around with a scarf tied around my breasts because they ached so much from nursing. I wasn't supposed to be scared about falling asleep at night because I'd have nightmares of labors gone wrong. Was I already a failure as a mother, only a few days into the gig? I couldn't help but compare myself to my own mother, and as a parent, I didn't come close.

Mom hadn't had any problems with her shift to parenthood. Why wasn't it that way for me?

I didn't tell Mom any of this. Her positivity was simply her personality, not some passive-aggressive calculation to increase my guilt. She would have felt awful if she thought her attitude had added to my unease.

After what felt like a stopover-length visit, it was time for my parents to leave. At least I knew my mother would be returning soon. I told myself I could tackle this until then.

I gave my mom a kiss and hug and got a bit teary, unusual for me. (Those postpartum hormones!) Then I gave my dad a hug too.

Dad is a proud male member of the baby boom generation. He doesn't talk about his feelings often, except for how much he loves being married to my mother.

Dad gave me a squeeze and leaned in.

"You're doing great," he whispered in my ear. "Your mother was a wreck."

It's the best thing he has ever said to me. Mom wasn't trying to paint a false picture; she had just forgotten all the negative stuff! In that instant, I felt normal again, as if I had been given permission to feel like myself, like a regular new mom but one who could still be a good mom. Maybe even in time, I would forget the bad stuff too.

I wasn't a perfect parent, but of course no one is, and after that, I learned to accept my imperfections. Duncan had parents and extended family who loved him, and that was the important thing. I was also so grateful to have had some parenting experience from the weekends when my stepdaughter, Rut, would stay with us. That had happened only after we moved to Iceland when she was nine years old, so to paraphrase an Icelandic idiom about being unaware of something, I "came from the mountains" as far as parenting infants and babies was concerned.

I had more manuals to read too: week-by-week guidance on everything from rolling over milestones to solid food schedules to bowel movements. So much poop. Never in my life did I expect as an adult to carry on so many conversations about feces. But parenthood can surprise you.

I was also an immigrant parent, whatever that meant. I was already learning that there would be different traditions in this realm, just as there were in other areas. Most of them were positive. It was socially acceptable to breastfeed anywhere. When Duncan needed a nap, I'd bundle him up and leave him outside in his pram, whether that was on our back porch, near a friend's house or balcony, or outside a café if I were meeting a friend.

Was Duncan also a Canadian? I'd filed the paperwork for him to be. I spoke to him in English, while Guðni and everyone else around him spoke Icelandic. He had an Ottawa Senators onesie. As he got older, of course it would be up to him. As my firstborn, he was also the object and beneficiary of my planning and organizing skills. I took hundreds of photos, recorded every new twitch and sound.

When Duncan was four months old, I returned to work. This meant commuting to the Sit Room with the door closed. I also worked at *Iceland Review* two days a week and contributed to an online trend the publishers wanted us to try: blogging. My colleagues and I were each responsible for one of five Daily Life columns that needed to go live by 11 a.m. each day. The insight into the daily life promised by the blog's title varied greatly depending on our moods, the news of the day, and the amount of caffeine we had ingested. Meanwhile, Guðni took his paternity leave.

At around the same time, on an otherwise ordinary Tuesday, a letter arrived in a plain white envelope that looked like it contained an annual pay slip for the upcoming tax season. The contents of the letter totaled just one sentence in Icelandic: "It is hereby announced, in accordance with Paragraph 1, Article 7 of Law 100 (1952) and with Article 5 of Law 81 (2007), that you have been granted Icelandic citizenship." An enclosed certificate repeated the proclamation and was personalized with my name and ID number. It was signed by the minister of justice and a lawyer.

With that, I was an Icelander. To an outside observer, I didn't look any different. I still owned more fleece tops than high heels and still wore my sky-blue ski jacket to dinner parties. I rarely used the subjunctive case when speaking Icelandic, and I almost always declined the word *cow* incorrectly. But that formally worded announcement of my success stirred something in me, some feeling of acceptance by my adopted home, that I hadn't expected by just filling out a few forms and paying an ISK 10,000 administration fee.

Just before Duncan turned one year old, Iceland's economy imploded. Its three major banks collapsed, and inflation spiraled out of control, leading tens of thousands of people to lose their jobs and savings. The nation was featured in major international newspapers. Regular protests grew into what became known as the Pots and Pans Revolution, named after the household implements angry citizens brought with them to make noise outside Parliament. Eventually, the government collapsed as lawmakers too bore the brunt of the public's ire for their failure to implement rules that limited unsustainable rapid growth. Like all mortgages in Iceland, ours was indexed to inflation, meaning that as daily costs soared, so too did the principal of our loan and the monthly payments. Guðni lost his job as a lecturer at the private Reykjavík University, and I was laid off from *Iceland Review*.

Once again, the future looked uncertain, but now we gazed upon it in a sleep-deprived haze. I had several freelance assignments that paid the bills, but what about Guðni? Was there even such a thing as "freelance historian"? It didn't sound like a career that promised security. Like so many other Icelanders at this time, we looked at opportunities in neighboring countries, though we really wanted to stay in Iceland. If push came to shove, we might be able to find better paying (if less fulfilling) full-time jobs with companies in their marketing or PR departments, but neither of us wanted that. It was the uncertainty rather than the financial reality that caused me the most stress.

Then I got pregnant again.

Despite my first birthing experience, I was excited. Now that I knew a little bit more about what pregnancy entailed, I had more confidence. I had the maternity clothes, the pregnancy cookbooks. I was worried my labor would be induced again, but now I could better control my breathing and knew to ask about alternative pain relief options.

Donnie was born a mere nine days past his due date, without the need for inducement. The epidural was blissfully effective. My mother arrived a few days before and stayed longer this time. Everything was peachy.

Once again, I took several months of maternity leave before Guðni took his paternity leave. Duncan had started preschool around the time Donnie was born, and he continued even though we were home with baby; preschools in Iceland are heavily subsidized, and parents aren't encouraged to keep older sibs at home even if one of them is taking parental leave.

I got back to work on freelance projects, and there were enough of them that we could make ends meet. It was professionally challenging, but I had enough free time to freeze homemade baby food and organize weekly mom-and-baby meetings with a new group of friends. When Donnie was about a year old, I even got to go on a business trip, to Albania of all places, to attend a conference for a charity I was working with. That separation was the end of breastfeeding him, so I was excited to go out with colleagues for drinks in the evenings and relax a bit on my own schedule.

A couple of weeks after I returned to Iceland, I discovered I had been pregnant the whole time.

Was this part of an Eliza's "Big Baby-Making Plan?" Or was it preordained? The sage prediction delivered during a late-night dinner in a suburban Samarkand apartment was coming true. Truth be told, I was a planner of details, not the big picture. I had never had a specific number of children in mind; I didn't even know if I wanted to have children! All that would have depended on having a partner with whom I wanted to raise them and on whether biological fortune would shine upon us.

In Icelandic society, there is a lot of support for new parents, with plenty of parental leave and subsidized childcare. That made me feel I had more control over the size of the family Guðni and I wanted. We didn't have a final tally in mind, but we were definitely getting our money's worth from our reusable diaper investment. Besides, by the third time around, I felt even more confident. I was getting great at this parenting and pregnancy stuff! I loved wearing casual maternity pants every day! Who needed sushi anyway?

I still had bouts of irrational fears. Sæþór was in a breech position until very late in the pregnancy, and that sometimes kept me up at night. Did that mean I had a uterine cyst? Was there an undiscovered congenital defect? What if I needed to call an ambulance when I went into labor and our tiny street was too narrow for the vehicle to drive up and collect me?

But Sæþór arrived without difficulties, with one of those fantastic, effective epidurals. Calm and serene, he was an old soul—I saw it from the moment he was placed on my chest. My baby boy, with an unusual emotional intelligence, had a broad, open face that made him look like he had done this whole living thing before.

The day after his birth, we returned home to a joyfully chaotic household. Three-year-old Duncan was eager to help his newest little brother, stroking his head and rushing over to hand him various stuffed animals that the baby probably couldn't even see yet. Donnie, who at twenty-one months wasn't much older than a baby himself, would toddle over with his own bottle and showed a kind, if more distant, interest in the new arrival.

Even though regular deep sleep became a vanishing luxury, it was all tremendous fun. So one dreary winter evening, I plotted with my friend Erica, an American expat whose husband was a diplomat posted to the embassy, why not create a rewarding professional project too? Maybe I was adhering to the adage that if you want something done, ask a busy person. But it felt right. Over drinks and lunches, walks and dinners, Erica and I brainstormed how to create an annual event that we called the Iceland Writers Retreat, to be held in Reykjavík, a UNESCO city of literature. It would be a welcoming gathering for people who loved to write, no matter how inexperienced they were. We'd invite famous authors to teach small workshops and then introduce people to wonderful Iceland through its literary heritage. We were excited and nervous, a combination of emotions that has always shown me I'm on the right track.

On the day Erica and I had a meeting scheduled with our first potential sponsor, I found Guðni in our small kitchen looking weary. The weariness was understandable; he'd been up since 6 a.m. It was a cozy scene: pitch-dark outside, Christmas lights around the window, porridge on the stove, two toddlers eagerly asking for superhero temporary tattoos bounding at his feet, and a third wee one banging the table for more food.

I picked Sæþór up, glancing at Guðni and giving an almost imperceptible nod. It took him a second to realize what that signified. He raised his eyebrows. *Really?* I nodded once more, unable to suppress a small smile.

I was pregnant again.

"Wow," he said dazedly to me a short while later once the kids were out of earshot. "Wow."

Something about having four children in fewer than six years seemed to give people permission to take the gloves off. "Was it an accident?" some would ask. "What are you thinking?" asked others. Once we found out we were having a girl, there was even more: "Will you finally stop now?" or "That was a big gamble." We simply felt incredibly fortunate.

If I dutifully recorded every twitch and every craving of my pregnancy with Duncan, Edda was the subject of woefully little documentation. I noted in my diary that I was pregnant, then in the next entry, I was about seven months along and being assigned near bed rest for high blood pressure. It was the summer, and poor Guðni was full-time with three boys who weren't even school-age yet, all of them on summer holiday. I felt fine but was told to avoid moving around or standing up too much and could only watch my three energetic puppies and their immensely patient father entertain them.

Despite the mild health concerns, things went well with Edda's birth too. I returned from the hospital the day before Duncan started elementary school and was just able to walk, slowly and cautiously, with him for the big first day. The local school only went up to grade 7, and as we made our way down the path to Grandaskóli, I remarked that there would only be one year when all four of them would be in the same school.

"What do you mean?" Duncan asked.

"Well," I said, "I know she's only a few days old now, but when Edda starts school here, Sæþór will be in grade three, Donnie in grade five, and you'll be in grade seven, the oldest grade."

Duncan firmly shook his head. "No, no, that's not right."

I wondered what he meant. The math wasn't too complicated. I gave him a quizzical look.

"The next baby won't be old enough for school yet," he explained simply. To him, ours was just a family where a new baby appeared every second autumn.

I couldn't quite bring myself to tell him the truth about that assumption. Duncan, despite his initial disappointment that he now had a sister and not another brother on the way, was just as doting as the others. Meanwhile, I had dramatically increased my coffee intake and was working hard at growing the Iceland Writers Retreat (we'd hosted Pulitzer Prize winner Geraldine Brooks in our first year and had just heard that Barbara Kingsolver would be joining us in our second go).

But within a year or so, Guðni and I began to find that space was at a premium in our lovely little house. We gradually decided that we might need to upgrade to somewhere a bit bigger, even if moving meant uprooting the kids to a new neighborhood and school.

It was bittersweet to leave our home of ten years, the place where we were raising our wonderful children. Where we hosted birthday parties, Christmas drop-ins, academic meetings, and moms and babies mornings. Where Donnie used to sip a bottle of milk in my lap so very, very early on a Saturday morning. Where the boys loved to play hide-and-seek despite the house's size, reveling in all the nooks and crannies. Where twenty-month-old Edda could wave goodbye to each of us and toddle off to play on her own in the yard outside, still close enough for me to watch her all the time. Where I made homemade jam from berries I'd picked in the garden. I'd miss the almost daily play fights on the sofa—with a worn, spare mattress pulled out from behind for protection—or the handball, soccer, basketball, and hockey matches played with two goalposts placed directly in front of windows, an antique buffet, and a very heavy soapstone carving. I'd miss watching the boys learn how to ride their bikes in front of the house. I'd even miss the much too early Sunday mornings when every child had managed to crawl into our double bed and Guðni and I looked at each other with a mixture of happiness and exhaustion.

We had made wonderful memories there, but the future beckoned yet again. Now that I had likely finished my run as a baby maker, I could turn to baby raising and writers' retreat organizing. Life was full, I was often tired, and I still dressed in a way that once led Donnie's preschool teacher to excitedly ask if I was expecting yet again! But we busy people get stuff done. Exhaustion isn't linear; my baseline had adjusted, and I reveled in the joy of our young family and the thrill of being an entrepreneur. Would the Iceland Writers Retreat be my opportunity to leave a lasting mark on the world? Would my contact with renowned authors spark an idea within me so that one day I would evolve from magazine writer to published book author? I still didn't quite know what I wanted to be when I grew up, but I felt like every new project was a building block to fulfill some future professional ambition whose specifics were tantalizingly opaque.

Forty was around the corner. I knew by now that having specific targets for the future was futile, but I was comfortable with the security of the chaos. I may not have had a fancy car or ever have taken a resort vacation, but in all the main KPIs of life (hey, maybe I had absorbed some business lingo!), I was scoring high. And now I enjoyed the fun from a new home, one where we planned on living for many years to come.

7

Panama

It took about eight hours to shoot this happy family photo that was used in campaign materials for Guðni's presidential run, spring 2016.

March 29, 2016: Your application has been received.

—Confirmation of application to rent cottage from Union of Icelandic Journalists for week of July 15, 2016

The spring I was thirty-nine, the only elected office Guðni held was that of head box unpacker, voted in by his four young children and weary wife. On the first night in what we thought would be our forever home, there was pepperoni pizza (for all) and beer (for the two of us) as we sat happily among stacks of books and piles of Lego. The kids still shared two bedrooms between the four of them, but now they had more space and there were spare rooms in the basement for when they got a bit older. Best of all, they had a big new backyard. We undertook the most urgent renovations soon after moving in—new windows downstairs and a sturdier staircase to the basement—and left the others for an unspecified future when there would be more disposable income. We caved in to pressure and bought a trampoline, one of the most popular outdoor structures for children in Iceland. I planted potatoes in the garden. The kids started at new schools: Duncan and Donnie in grades 3 and 1, Sæþór and Edda in preschool.

The house was a little farther from the center of town than our old place but still walkable. Most days, we didn't need to use our car. Everyone seemed happy and settled in our new home. As we unpacked the final carton, we both felt relief that we wouldn't have to move again for a long, long time.

Professionally, I was doing well too. The Iceland Writers Retreat was going from strength to strength. We'd been growing every year, were named one of the world's best writing retreats in *The Sydney Morning Herald*, and had great press from media and faculty alike. I worked one day a week for a large company doing copy writing in English, edited Icelandair's in-flight magazine, and occasionally acted as a local reporter when international outlets such as France 24 or NBC needed details of an Iceland-based story. It was enough to cobble together a reasonable income and gave me the freedom to control my schedule. The kids—now one, three, five, and seven years old—were mostly sleeping through the night but not yet old enough to be alone or to be truly helpful keeping the house tidy. If either Guðni or I had to go abroad for a few days, the other had to carefully juggle all the kids' calendars and our own professional commitments, not to mention personal sanity. On those occasions, I used to joke that after getting the kids their breakfast, packing them off to school, settling down to work, shopping for groceries, doing the laundry, picking up the kids, cooking supper, putting them to bed, doing the dishes, and finishing work… the ten minutes of remaining free time before I collapsed were really special.

Guðni had also found his professional stride. He was an associate professor of history at the University of Iceland. After the uncertainty in the years immediately following the economic crash of 2008, he was in a stable job that he loved. His office had a sofa! There was unlimited free coffee! (Though it was I who was more excited about the perks. Guðni doesn't speak in exclamation marks.) He taught courses on fishing disputes, presentation of historical work, and (ironically, as it turned out) counterfactual history.

He also supervised graduate students and, best of all, had allocated time to research and write his own projects.

Guðni loves to write. While mere mortals relax in the evenings with some Netflix, Guðni will read to the kids, get them to sleep, sit in front of his laptop, and write a book that has dozens of pages of notes at the end. He has online folders on numerous general topics in which he puts links to articles, quotes from books, and social media posts so he has a built-in and updated archive for whenever he begins the next project.

By early 2016, as we approached our one-year anniversary in the new house, he had already published eight books, including the biography of Gunnar Thoroddsen that he wrote from our Sit Room (which was a critical and commercial success) and an acclaimed breakdown of government formation in the 1970s and 1980s. (Only in Iceland does coalition negotiation feel less like politics and more like family drama.) Based on these books, regular appearances on current affairs programs and radio shows, and the occasional newspaper article and public lecture, he had earned a reputation among public policy wonks as a knowledgeable, witty, and neutral commentator. I got a little thrill whenever we were out and about and someone recognized him or told him they had enjoyed one of his books.

Guðni was now working on his next project, a history of the presidents of Iceland. A few approved biographies and memoirs of former presidents had been released, but this was to be the first book-length academic review of their times in office. Guðni was riding the buzz he always got from discovering new details of famous figures and building a captivating plotline around them. And if it were a success, it would help him secure enough cred within the university to be promoted to full professor, a professional pinnacle.

I'm going to disrupt the narrative at this point to give you a short but necessary primer on Icelandic civics. Iceland (as you may have guessed by now) has a president. The president replaced the Danish monarch as head of state once Iceland announced its independence from Denmark in 1944. The president is directly elected by the people every four years, with no term limits. To run for president, you need to be an Icelandic citizen (not necessarily born in the country) aged thirty-five or older and collect the signatures of between fifteen hundred and three thousand voters from around the country (controversially, that number has not changed since the foundation of the republic, despite the voting population more than tripling since then). A president does not represent a political party, although sometimes presidents have come from political ranks.

Does the president of Iceland have political power? Yes and no. Not in the day-to-day operation of the country, but a president has to sign all laws and can choose to veto a law, although this has only rarely been done. A president also helps to steer coalition negotiations following a parliamentary election, notably by using his or her power to choose which leader has earned the mandate to try and form a government.

We also have a prime minister in Iceland. In contrast to the figurehead president, the prime minister is a politician. He or she is almost always the head of a political party represented in our Parliament, the Althing. We have numerous parties in the Althing, because members are elected based on a system of proportional representation. For example, at the time of writing, there are six parties with representatives in Parliament. This means that several parties need to work together in a coalition to form a government. A person does not campaign for the position of prime minister. He or she is chosen by the members of the parties who form a majority coalition in government.

Are you still awake? If so, remember that this is the kind of nerdy detail that my husband *loves* to analyze.

At the beginning of 2016, in his annual New Year's address, Iceland's president, Ólafur Ragnar Grímsson, announced that he had decided not to run in the election that was scheduled for June 25 of that year. Ólafur Ragnar (we're all on a first-name basis in Iceland, though we generally also include middle names for formality) had served in the office for two decades, since 1996. Perhaps as a remnant of Iceland's membership in a monarchy, it was often not seen as polite to run against an incumbent president. The only competitive elections were generally when there were no incumbents in the race. So 2016 was shaping up to be an exciting year for politicos.

In a presidential campaign in Iceland, it doesn't pay to seem too keen on the position. One needs to display modesty, to appear as if the nation has called you to (grudgingly) do your duty and put your name forward. Too much enthusiasm and hubris would be crass. Perhaps this is because, broadly speaking, the people of Iceland hold a deep respect for the presidency and for the person who holds that high office. Polls regularly show high trust in the institution of the presidency, voter turnout in presidential elections hovers near 80 percent, and even though people express strong differences in a campaign, the nation has always more or less united around the winning candidate once the results are clear.

For Guðni, an exciting presidential campaign meant an opportunity to take part in more interviews—not because he relished the limelight but because he enjoyed talking about these subjects. Perhaps, he mused hopefully to me that winter, he would even be asked to appear on television on election night itself to analyze the results as they were announced.

In late March that year, I visited Chicago for the first time, leaving Guðni to manage the chaos of our young household. The winter wind was still blowing across Lake Michigan, the Chicago River still greenish in areas after its annual dyeing for St. Patrick's Day celebrations. I was in the Windy City to take part in a festival to promote tourism to Iceland. Organizers brought over an Icelandic band to perform a free concert, a visiting chef teamed up with a local restaurant to offer an Icelandic menu of fish, lamb, and dairy desserts, and I had prepared a presentation about Icelanders' love of literature and my experience running the Iceland Writers Retreat.

At a convivial dinner the evening before everything kicked off, conversation among our team inevitably turned to the upcoming presidential election. This was about three months before the big day, and while a few people had declared their intention to seek the nation's highest office, casual gossip gave no individual an obvious lead.

My dinner mates and I speculated about some possibilities. The head of that influential institute? The politician from the biggest party? Perhaps the television personality would go for it? There was nothing so entertaining as acting as unofficial pundits for our nation. In fact, with a population of only about 350,000, many of us personally knew one or two of the people whose names had been floated. Even I, who had only been living in the country for thirteen years, had come across a few of them. I hardly knew the dynamics and history well enough to accurately speculate on what would happen, though. I enjoyed following the news, but I had absolutely no clue who would be my adopted country's next head of state.

I returned home to the usual domestic anarchy. Things were so crazy that I immediately agreed to Guðni's suggestion and went online to book a week at a discount-rate cottage that July, just to have something to look forward to—on the assumption my fortieth birthday Parisian escape wouldn't materialize. That Sunday evening, Guðni told me he was looking forward to watching a much-anticipated current affairs program on what would colloquially become known as the Panama Papers scandal. In a global scoop coordinated by the International Consortium of Investigative Journalists, which included a team from RÚV, Iceland's national broadcaster, the program identified several world leaders who had funds kept in offshore tax havens, based on a leak of over eleven million documents from Panamanian law firm Mossack Fonseca. The leak identified twelve heads of state or government in papers that showed about two trillion dollars had passed through the firm. (In early 2024, twenty-seven people who had been charged with money laundering connected to the leak went on trial.) The next day, the Panama scandal made headlines across the globe.

In Iceland, the repercussions were much more local but no less seismic. That Sunday evening show featured an interview with Iceland's prime minister, Sigmundur Davíð Gunnlaugsson, which had been prerecorded a few weeks earlier. The discussion began on a banal note, the Swedish interviewer asking general questions in English on the Icelandic tax system and the prime minister's opinion on people in general keeping funds in so-called tax havens. He then began to ask questions to clarify whether the prime minister had any personal connections to offshore companies.

"As I say," answered the prime minister, "my assets have always been up on the table." Then came a question delivered on an equally bland note: "Mr. Prime Minister, what can you tell me about a company called Wintris?" The tension increased. The prime minister awkwardly explained what the organization was but said, "I'm starting to feel a bit strange about these questions because it's like you are accusing me of something."

The conversation switched to Icelandic as a local journalist jumped in to ask about more specific information. Less than two minutes later, the prime minister stood and walked out of the interview. Watching on television, it felt as if the nation collectively gasped. Only eight years after Iceland's devastating economic collapse, it appeared the nation's head of government had been hiding some serious financial misdeeds.

Monday morning dawned with sun and blessedly little wind. It was one of the first days of the year when you might not need your winter jacket. The unusually pleasant weather may have played a role in what was to come, for on such a day in Iceland, it was an unofficial rule to leave the house and absorb one's required dose of vitamin D. The crowds began to gather outside the Althing that afternoon. At one point, they may have totaled up to twenty-two thousand, more than on any single protest day of the so-called Pots and Pans Revolution of 2008–09 that brought down a government deemed complicit in the third largest corporate bankruptcy in world history. Like then, protestors demanded change. I'd love to say that I was there, at the forefront of making history in Iceland, but I wasn't. I was finishing up freelance projects, as usual, though I had one eye on the television because I had a feeling that these protests were different. I sensed a desire for change that seemed disproportionate to the scandal itself. That Monday, Guðni was asked to appear on the nation's most popular current affairs news program to comment on the crisis.

Things moved quickly from there. On Tuesday, April 5, more protests were scheduled. In the late morning, the prime minister announced on Facebook (Icelanders' social media platform of choice at the time) that he would like to call an election if he did not have enough support among his colleagues in the governing political parties. He then headed to Bessastaðir, the presidential residence, to meet with outgoing president Ólafur Ragnar Grímsson.

Have you been paying attention? I snuck something in there that you and most people in Iceland may not have noticed immediately: A prime minister cannot call a parliamentary election without the formal approval of the president.

One person who was aware of that was my husband. That day, he was called to the national broadcaster to appear alongside constitutional lawyer Ragnhildur Helgadóttir to comment on the ongoing crisis. He was on air for almost six hours, and together, he and Ragnhildur analyzed the roles and responsibilities of the president and the ensuing public disagreement between the prime minister and the president on the nitty-gritty of the constitution.

Tens of thousands tuned in to the broadcast. Confused about the critical role knowledge of procedure played in whether the PM would resign and new elections would be held, viewers watched Guðni and his colleague explain the situation using neutral, understandable language. At one point, they even acted out a four-decade-old exchange between the then PM and a journalist about calling for a snap election. Once again, I was missing out on history in the making; my Icelandic wasn't good enough to follow banter about the constitution, but I knew I could ask for an English précis over dinner.

It was at around this time that the phone started ringing.

We still had landlines in those days, and ours was on a table in the front hall, even though only my parents and my mother-in-law ever called it. Like most other Icelanders, though, our number was listed in the phone book, and anyone who wanted to reach us could do so with ease. One of the first calls was from a man who introduced himself as a pensioner in an assisted living facility in remote Patreksfjörður. I couldn't think of any reason why he would want to talk to either me or Guðni, but when I asked to take a message for my husband, he told me he had seen Guðni on television and thought he should run for president. You know, as one does. Without knowing what else to say, I thanked him and said I would pass on the message.

I thought it was sweet, albeit bizarre, that a stranger had taken the time to look up Guðni's number and call his home. Over the years, people had occasionally joked that he would make an excellent president because he had such knowledge of the field and was not involved with a specific party. I joked right back that he should, because I'd make an excellent first lady. But we took such comments, only ever from people we knew, about as seriously as if they had advised my husband to become a lion tamer. Now, an elderly man who had never met Guðni in person wanted to go to his circus.

The phone rang again. This person said he represented a group of ex-police officers in a nearby village. Would I please pass on the message that they would like to encourage Guðni to consider running?

Over the course of hours, that trickle of encouragement became a flood. When Guðni got home that first night and I shared the news of the phone calls, he didn't seem at all surprised, telling me that he had received dozens of private Facebook messages. An admired member of a national sports team and several famous media personalities swore Guðni to secrecy about their support. Eventually, six-year-old Donnie began to answer the house phone. "Hello, this is Guðni's home."

Meanwhile, as the prime minister caved to pressure and resigned (as PM but not as a member of Parliament), with elections promised for the autumn, Guðni continued to comment on the crisis.

By Friday, someone started a Facebook page encouraging him to run, and the media began calling for an official statement on his intentions.

Suddenly, a ridiculous prospect we had only ever laughed about became a serious matter, drawing enough attention that it required a thoughtful and formal response. Guðni began to think about putting his name forward. As we lay in bed at night, pretty much the only time the two of us had uninterrupted moments to talk, issues flooded our minds, first and foremost being whether this was something he and then I wanted? It was always a joint discussion. Guðni never approached me with a final decision. Only one person serves as president, but the role affects the entire family.

I was one hundred percent on board from the start. The prospect felt scary yet exciting, but I also knew that Guðni would be an outstanding president if he decided it was something he wanted to do and if he won the election. If anything, I needed to stifle my inner Lady Macbeth.

We discussed all sorts of hypotheticals. The number one question was how it would affect our children. We agreed that if we prioritized them, it would be far more likely to provide them with unique opportunities than transform them into entitled nepo babies. Second, would Guðni have a good chance of winning if he ran? (Yes. Some supporters had commissioned a poll.) How would I feel about any negative press coverage? (Less troubled than I expected.) Would we need to remortgage our house to finance a campaign? (No. There are strict laws in Iceland limiting campaign finance.) Would being nationally known become a burden? (Who knew?) What did being president entail exactly? And for me, what would the spouse of a president do?

"I don't even know how to hold my knife and fork properly!" bemoaned Guðni when he thought about the prospect of gala dinners and state visits. We shook our heads in bemusement at the surreality of even contemplating such a prospect.

But one week after the Panama Papers show ended, Guðni was seriously considering running and had begun to realize that he'd need to find a campaign manager and election experts to guide him. But how do you find your own personal Toby Ziegler if you're new to politics and don't yet want anyone to know you're taking the talk seriously? How do you choose who to invite into the inner circle when people from the whole span of your life have generously offered to help in any way they can?

I didn't have the same lifelong connections my husband had, but as it turned out, my network provided the first link in a chain that would, at least initially, be cobbled together more from personal friendships than battle-weary politicos. One of my closest friends in Iceland was an American woman called Liz, who had been living in the country longer than I had. As luck would have it, her Icelandic husband, Friðjón, was one of relatively few political operatives in the country. His reputation was firmly linked with a specific party, but we knew that ideology would not affect their working together; Guðni's appeal was nonpartisan. (In fact, for the nonpolitical position of president, family ties and old friendships often play a bigger role than political ideology.)

Guðni's two younger brothers, Patrekur and Jóhannes, were committed to helping too. As was a historian colleague who had worked on the election campaign for the dean of the university. An elementary school principal with municipal political experience joined as co-campaign manager. Guðni's cousin would look after finances. One of our neighbors offered to watch the kids when needed. The father of one of Duncan's preschool friends would help to rally the troops near his home community up north.

So through the bonds of friendship and a lifetime of being kind and neighborly, we had the beginnings of a team, if indeed one would be necessary.

In the midst of it all, Guðni was invited to Copenhagen overnight to deliver a lecture on the crisis. The Iceland Writers Retreat was about to take place for the third time, and I was almost literally knee-deep in lanyards and goodie bags for 120 people, feeling a bit sorry for myself that I was solo parenting during my busiest time of the year professionally. (The day before, our headlining author that year had written that she was ill and wouldn't make it, and my cofounder Erica and I were scrambling to reschedule workshops and soothe disappointed and occasionally irate participants who thought we'd deliberately avoided announcing the cancellation until it was too late for our clients to change their minds about attending.) As Erica and I discussed whether to put soap or salt in the faculty goodie bags, my phone pinged. It was Guðni.

> I think we should go for it... We can easily have this adventure. No problems, just fun.

I must have stared at my device for a moment too long, because Erica asked me what was going on. For a couple of hours, my mind had shifted away from secret polling and hypothetical dinners with royalty to the reality of a busy household and the biggest crisis facing the Iceland Writers Retreat. Now, with the persistent chime of an iPhone, I realized I needed to carve room in my personal reality for a seismic change. Having a husband as a head of state, or even one running to hold that position, would be a big deal.

I showed Erica the message and then sent a joking reply to Guðni: Have you been drinking?;)

Once Guðni had grown comfortable with the idea of running, I was ecstatic, and we prepared ourselves for the upcoming campaign. We sussed out HQ locations and set aside a date to make an official announcement. I don't remember a specific moment when we broke the news to the kids; they were still so young. The older two knew something was afoot because people were calling their father constantly. Otherwise, as long as they got their episodes of *Ninjago* and not too many unfamiliar vegetables with supper, they were happy.

Then, the day after the first meeting of our campaign team, before any public announcements had been made, we got another shock: Outgoing president Ólafur Ragnar Grímsson had called a press conference to announce that given the turmoil of recent days, an experienced leader was clearly needed to helm the nation through the uncertainty ahead. He had therefore decided that he would run for president after all, for a record sixth term.

We were immediately deflated. No one could unseat a sitting president; Guðni had made public statements to this effect in the past. Against a head of state who had served for two decades, my political neophyte of a husband thought he stood no chance. It felt like it was over before it even began, that we had come crashing down to earth without even reaching cruising altitude.

Meanwhile, the calls for Guðni to run only increased. Although the current president had a great many supporters, the general consensus was that for those who wanted change, Guðni was the only person who had a chance of defeating him. After supporting the initial idea wholeheartedly, I wasn't sure how I felt now. I was so drained from the indecision of a mere two weeks that I couldn't imagine how I would cope with a proper campaign. Twenty-four hours before, internal polling and the word on the street seemed to show that the election would be Guðni's to lose if he announced a run. Now, that was far from the reality we faced. I didn't know how we could do it. Yet a smoldering resentment was also bubbling from within: If we had already made the decision that Guðni wanted to be president, that we thought he was the best person to be president, how could we let someone else decide for us whether he tried or not? The voters elect the president. A president does not indirectly intimidate others into folding when the ante is raised.

The days crept by. I wrapped up work on that year's Iceland Writers Retreat and planned the next issue of Icelandair's in-flight magazine; Guðni and I took the kids to football tournaments and playdates. Friðjón commissioned some secret polling with the sitting president in the mix. In spare moments, I wrote lists (of course!) on how I could be an asset to the campaign: I could speak pretty good Icelandic and could help showcase diversity in society (yes, I realize the irony of that statement!). I had already traveled widely in the country as part of my work as a journalist.

Meanwhile, there were more polls, all of which showed Ólafur Ragnar Grímsson with a significant but not insurmountable lead. (Our still-unofficial team had defined "insurmountable" as twelve percentage points or more. A private poll from April 28 showed a lead for the sitting president of 11.6 percentage points.)

I don't remember a specific moment when we officially decided to take the plunge. The closest thing was probably that text message sent from Copenhagen. In retrospect, I think that from that first phone call from the pensioner, an announcement was inevitable. When the stars align in such an unlikely constellation, you simply can't ignore it. So we picked the day. We called a stylist. We issued a press release for a public meeting on May 5, that year a holiday in Iceland. As my excitement and pride increased, so too did my nerves: Not only did I not have a "personal style," but I had never had any media training. I could only do my best, always tell the truth, and apologize when I made a mistake. But would that be enough?

We had decided early on that we did not want to showcase our children prominently in the campaign. Aside from Rut, who was in her twenties and at university, they were young and had not had a chance to decide for themselves what they wanted to do. But on the day of Guðni's announcement, they would be paraded out in front of hopefully hundreds of people. What if one had a meltdown? Farted at an inopportune moment? Came down with chicken pox?

The announcement was carefully choreographed, the venue selected to highlight a large crowd in a location that was considered neither too upscale nor too mundane. Gerður Kristný, a well-known writer and poet and another friend of ours, would provide opening remarks and introduce Guðni onstage. He would deliver his speech, and the rest of us would emerge from the wings for one nice, happy photo op.

Then the big day arrived—my fortieth birthday. We were most certainly not in Paris, although somehow, in all the madness, Guðni had organized a surprise party for me at the local community center the night before. The evening had also served as an unofficial gathering for the team that would manage the election campaign, including several people I was meeting for the first time or hardly knew at all. It was a touching gesture, especially given everything on his plate at the time. It was also a brief break from the preparation of the announcement, which reminded me of my wedding day but with more children and higher stakes.

Those stakes were encapsulated in Guðni's announcement speech. It would introduce him to the public and lay out his values and vision for the presidency. And with the last-minute addition of the sitting head of state once again throwing his hat in the ring, it would need to provide a counterpoint to what the current president offered. Ólafur Ragnar Grímsson had said he had decided to run again because the nation was facing a crisis and tremendous uncertainty. Guðni took a more positive approach.

I stood to the side of the stage, one eye on my husband and one eye on four remarkably calm kids, as Guðni spoke about his vision of the president serving as a symbol of unity, of a head of state who listened more than spoke. He reviewed his childhood and his love of history. He talked about Iceland's family-friendly society, where people's professional obligations did not need to take over their personal and familial ones. Perhaps the most quoted line from the speech was his promise that as a father of five, if he were to be elected, he would continue to walk or cycle with his children to school (a promise he kept).

He showed confident optimism: "There is nothing to fear," he said. "Of course we do not know what the future will bring. But therein lies the beauty in life's uncertainty." He may not have worked with a team of speechwriters or commissioned numerous focus groups, but Guðni knew how to write evocatively and to deliver his lines in a genuine and intelligent way.

That was our cue. As he finished his remarks to tumultuous applause, the kids, Rut, and I all marched on stage. Two-year-old Edda reached up her arms for Guðni to hold her, while four-year-old Sæþór wrapped his arms around one of his father's legs and looked out shyly at the crowd. A seasoned journalist later remarked to Guðni that the image of this young family man was what guaranteed his victory. I felt elated, proud, and nervous about what was to come.

No matter the final destination, we were now together on the road to the beautiful uncertainty that lay ahead.

8

A Beautiful Uncertainty

Speaking to an audience at the Hóf Cultural Centre in Akureyri, North Iceland, during the election campaign, June 2016.

"I think this is an excellent opportunity to shine a light on important issues… I will not be a housewife who stays at home cleaning."

—INTERVIEW WITH ME IN *FRÉTTABLAÐIÐ* NEWSPAPER, PUBLISHED MAY 7, 2016

51 DAYS UNTIL THE ELECTION

We were swarmed by media and well-wishers—known and unknown—immediately after Guðni's announcement. The youngest kids clung even tighter to us; the older ones shyly stood to the side. I hoped the packed venue was an indication of Guðni's popularity, but there was no time to linger. Now that the kids had been in the spotlight, they wanted supper and to get back to the peace of their own home.

Back at the house, with the kids fed and entertained by cartoons, we turned to our devices to get things going. There was a website to launch, volunteers to recruit, contributions to solicit. Somewhere I am sure someone was strategizing on how to beat a five-term incumbent president, but either I wasn't in that room, or I didn't yet know the Icelandic words for *referendum*, *polling*, and *candidate* (I would be declining them perfectly soon enough).

Turning off Slack (an app I hadn't heard of a few days earlier) and checking Facebook instead, I was bombarded with messages from friends near and far, all positive but ranging from "I'm so relieved! He's going to be a great president" to "What? Guðni from grad school? Running for president?" I also saw numerous requests from new "friends," all of which I accepted in the belief that an election is not the time to be picky.

48 DAYS UNTIL THE ELECTION

During a popular current affairs radio program, Davíð Oddsson, former mayor of Reykjavík, prime minister, and head of Iceland's central bank and now editor of the country's oldest newspaper, announced he was also going to run for president. Davíð's views could be polarizing, and *Time* magazine had named him one of the top twenty-five people responsible for the 2008 global financial crisis, but his supporters were vociferous in their admiration for him, and he was a household name in Iceland. Guðni reminded me that in his more than four-decade political career, Davíð had never lost an election.

"Well," I answered, "neither have you."

47 DAYS UNTIL THE ELECTION

With talking heads musing whether the history professor had enough momentum to overtake both the sitting president and one of the country's most influential former politicians, Ólafur Ragnar Grímsson called a press conference on a Monday afternoon to announce that, now that "two good candidates" had put themselves forward, he had reconsidered his reconsideration. His name would not be on the ballot on June 25.

Two days later, a poll was published that showed Guðni with 69 percent support, followed by Davíð Oddsson at 13.7 percent. The list was now final. There would be nine candidates running for president of Iceland.

Guðni was sanguine. "It's better to be ten goals up than ten goals down, but it's a long race."

That evening, as I prepared dinner for four kids eight and under and a presidential candidate, I got a call from one of a handful of twentysomething hired by the fledgling campaign to manage volunteer recruitment for the cross-country touring that was to come.

"There are a bunch of us together calling potential volunteers," he told me with little preamble. "Can you come in now and work the phones?"

I looked around at the chaos of my kitchen—stray spaghetti noodles fossilizing under the high chair, Bolognese sauce spattered on the wall—and my mind flashed forward to the other duties I had later on that evening: reading *My Big Book of Grimm's Fairy Tales* to the kids for the millionth time, getting them all settled in bed, finishing the next issue of the in-flight magazine and my other freelance projects, and finally numerous discussions with my husband and other strategizers.

"No, I can't," I replied, thinking this guy had no idea what early evenings with young children were like.

"You know, just because we're ahead in the polls doesn't mean we can be complacent. You're going to have to get a babysitter pretty much every day from here on out."

The message was clear: This guy knew campaigns, not me, and either I was committed to the cause or I was a hindrance. I did my best to explain that I agreed there would be plenty of times when I would need a babysitter, but now was not one of them. It didn't even occur to me to retort that the candidate's wife should be campaigning with her partner, not in a dark room at a phone bank. But of course I didn't speak up; I didn't know up from down in political campaigning, and when I thought I did, I was easily dissuaded otherwise.

44 DAYS UNTIL THE ELECTION

I texted my parents to see if they would be willing to fly to Iceland to help with some childcare and housework when Guðni and I hit the road. My mother had been thrilled to hear about the unexpected adventure of Guðni running, so I assumed she would also relish the chance to see her grandkids. After all, even though she and my dad couldn't speak any Icelandic, didn't like to drive when abroad, and had been empty nesters for almost two decades, that couldn't possibly make it more tiring to look after two preschoolers and two early elementary school kids enrolled in soccer lessons and regular playdates. What a relief their presence would be!

Assistance seemed to be a general theme of the campaign. Everyone wanted to help with something, whether giving the kids free haircuts, mowing our lawn, or baking giant whipped cream–covered pavlovas and *kleinur* doughnuts to serve at the campaign headquarters. I was touched at the generosity of strangers and people we did not (yet) know well, working to further the cause of democracy.

43 DAYS UNTIL THE ELECTION

An English-language interview with me on the travel website Hit Iceland was published and shared widely, at least among people I knew abroad. The introduction claimed that the "vivacious" Eliza Reid was "quite an asset to her husband."

Was I an asset, though? I wanted to be and believed I could be. But so far, all I had managed to do was pose for the campaign brochure and reject an invitation to volunteer. I felt rather as if I were a marionette performing under the hands of people who were much more seasoned political campaigners than we were. I was letting them take the lead.

There wasn't much opposition research done. Guðni and I both knew that we didn't have dark secrets we hoped no one would uncover. Guðni had his weaknesses, as all candidates do, but I felt those had an impact on him more than on voters; he wasn't in it for the glory, fame, or perks of power. He simply thought he could do a good job; the downside of that beautiful simplicity was that he had nothing to fall back on when times got tough.

Meanwhile, other candidates had their own cadres of keen supporters: the writer Andri Snær Magnason for his strong stance on environmental protection, Davíð Oddsson for his long career in the public eye, and Halla Tómasdóttir for her private sector experience and because she was the only woman among the top polling candidates.

By coincidence, our good friend Andrew was in town from

the States to update a guidebook. He took the opportunity to chat with locals in swimming pools and cafés throughout the country. His results unofficially confirmed what we thought: Not everyone knew much about Guðni, but he was assumed to be the front-runner and was generally well liked, not least for his knowledge of national history and for being an active family man with young children. There was a strong desire for a president who was apolitical and could rise above the fray, for someone who was down-to-earth and "normal." Even if he wasn't very well known, Guðni was seen as the person who had those qualities.

41 DAYS UNTIL THE ELECTION

Guðni's campaign headquarters opened on a spring Sunday. Housed in an old car showroom, the office met the qualifications needed: centrally located, available to rent for only a few weeks, a couple of rooms for calls and meetings but plenty of open space for welcoming members of the public and hosting events, plus a great corner that could be equipped with kids' toys and a TV. The launch event was jam-packed and featured a stand-up comedian and a beloved, if aging, Icelandic crooner. Volunteers had baked and displayed enough food to feed a small village. ("Icelanders feel about eating cake the way New Yorkers feel about not eating cake: it is a sign of their relentless commitment to self-improvement," wrote Adam Gopnik in *The New Yorker* as part of a feature on Guðni's campaign.)

After enthusiastic applause to Guðni's remarks, we began shaking hands. A stranger approached me to say that she recently lost someone close to her and that just seeing Guðni and me together made her feel better and happier. I was very touched but didn't understand how I could have an impact on anyone. My smile and my buoyant mood were genuine that day, though the word *surreal* was already creeping into my mind on an almost hourly basis.

35 DAYS UNTIL THE ELECTION

Our first campaign stop together outside the capital region was in Akranes, a town almost an hour away. Most of my energy went into coordinating the kids. I arranged for the two oldest to play at a friend's house, and Liz came over to watch the youngest two. Following the playdate, Sæþór went to one sister-in-law's and Edda to the other sister-in-law's. After the campaign stop, I drove a small circuit to collect all four of them. Each out-of-town meeting would involve a similar level of logistics.

After sorting childcare, my remaining brain cells had been diverted from finishing my paid work to fretting about what I would wear, which in turn led to existential worry I was embodying a cliché already. Yet what else would I think about before each event? I wasn't going to be doing anything other than smiling and shaking hands. My husband was the star of the show, the one people had turned up to see. I was but the Garfunkel to his Simon.

In tiny Iceland, when meeting people for the first time, it's vital to explain *hverra manna ertu,* or from whose people you are. The introductions of Guðni's events were all brief, saga-style recitations of his ancestors: he was the son of Margrét, an elementary school teacher, and the late Jóhannes, an athletics teacher, and they were the children of Margrét (housewife) and Guðni (ship captain) and Sigurveig (teacher) and Sæmundur (first mate). If we were campaigning near a community where one of his ancestors had a connection, he made sure to mention it.

Guðni followed his family tree with a brief description of his own professional experience and his vision for the sort of president he wanted to be. Because president is not a political role, there was no discussion of new investments in certain areas or policy changes in others. It was more a matter of introducing his character to people, of explaining his vision of the fairly vague role and its potential as a symbol of unity.

When we were mingling after that first event, someone from the audience approached me and said they thought Guðni was very interesting, but that it was a shame they didn't hear me speak at all. Well, that would be an easy fix for the future. I'd reassign some of my brain cells from fabrics to full sentences. Maybe my harmonies could help Guðni compose an even more powerful melody.

30 DAYS UNTIL THE ELECTION

Several campaign meetings later, I was becoming a pro at describing my own family tree. I told people about my upbringing on a hobby farm (my rural background was a good counterpoint to Guðni's suburban childhood) and my parents' work as English teacher and homemaker (both straightforward, middle-class professions that people could relate to). People loved hearing how

I landed my first date with Guðni at Oxford, and we honed our routine with eye rolling, jokes, and glances of affection.

My experience at *Iceland Review* meant I had already traveled widely around the country and could often highlight something that I enjoyed about a certain community. This was almost always well received, with the exception of one location: There, I mentioned that I'd visited several years earlier to interview a local celebrity who had launched a popular radio station. That trip had been very enjoyable, I added to polite smiles but more awkward silence than appreciative applause. Only later did Guðni tell me that the local celebrity I name-dropped had been convicted of pedophilia a couple of years earlier. Moreover and arguably more seriously, I had confused the convict's small district with the one we were currently visiting. And the neighboring counties had a long rivalry.

26 DAYS UNTIL THE ELECTION

At the end of May, we made a dozen stops in and around the town of Selfoss, almost all of them providing cream cakes, doughnuts, and other baked goods. Face pale and tummy bloated on the long ride home, I made a mental note that five slices of cream cake in one day was too many.

25 DAYS UNTIL THE ELECTION

My parents arrived to save the day. Dad wrote an email to my family back in Canada in which he marveled at how the walk home from preschool took almost an hour instead of the ten minutes he expected because of park stops, pee breaks, tantrums, and other vagaries of toddlerdom. Perhaps the babysitting would not be as smooth sailing as I had thought.

Meanwhile, I tried to keep an eye on Guðni, knowing that I would be his first line of support when he got tired or stressed or unsure of himself. I needn't have worried. He was doing well, especially considering he was naturally an introvert and had never before embarked on an adventure quite like this one.

I, however, was thinking a lot about negative attention. Would I be able to control my reactions when I saw someone criticize my husband in the comments section or on television? Would I comment right back? Burst into tears? It turned out to be much simpler than I thought. First of all, there was relatively little criticism. Some was so fantastical that I couldn't even worry about it, knowing that anyone rational could not possibly believe such ridiculous accusations. Most important was the buffer that campaigning in a language not my mother tongue gave me. I had to consciously choose to read a social media comment, and if I came across a word I didn't recognize, I wasn't going to put it in Google Translate if the context looked insulting. In any case, even the negative words I understood were filtered through a different language, and that helped to soften the sting.

24 DAYS UNTIL THE ELECTION

A poll showed Guðni with a twenty-point lead. I did not feel relaxed. I knew the story of the tortoise and the hare.

12 DAYS UNTIL THE ELECTION

As Election Day approached, we held the biggest rally of the campaign at the Harpa Concert Hall and Conference Centre in Reykjavík. Even though Guðni still had a strong lead in the polls, it was a risk. If not enough people showed up in the vast space, it might indicate that he was losing momentum. Anything could happen.

It was decided that I would introduce him, although the structure in general was to be more of a thank-you rally than a get-to-know-the-candidate event. I didn't want to read from written remarks because it would sound too stilted and contrived. Without notes, though, I risked making mistakes in my Icelandic delivery. I strode onto the grand steps of the hall, a sea of people complementing the view of sunny downtown Reykjavík through the expansive windows in front of me. Next to me was a woman doing sign language interpretation. I looked out at smiling faces in the audience and knew we were among friends here. The atmosphere was buoyant.

I took a breath and began. I would keep it short and simple. People wanted to see me, to know I could speak, but they were there for the candidate, so all I really wanted to do was thank people for everything they had done over the past several weeks. It would be easy to deliver that message from the heart.

"I want to express how thankful I am for the support," I said to the audience of hundreds who stood before me. Then I paused, realizing my mistake. I had just used the Icelandic word for *thankful* in its masculine form. It wasn't an egregious error, and perhaps some self-deprecation would endear me to the crowd. I made my pause look more intentional, then smiled serenely at all the faces and said, "Wait, I'm not a man. I can't be *thankful*." I repeated the masculine ending. "I meant to say that I'm *thankful*," using the feminine form of the word. I was greeted with warm laughter. I was happy I had admitted my mistake and corrected myself. In doing so, I had been more of a hit with the audience than if it had never happened in the first place.

I walked off the stage after introducing Guðni, thinking I had really nailed it.

It was only several minutes later, as Guðni was well into his speech and as I was mentally reviewing mine, that I realized that I had not used the feminine word for *thankful* at all. I had confused Icelandic grammar rules in my mind and instead used a nonsensical word that was closest to calling myself lazy. *I am very lazy*, I had more or less said. I hadn't made the audience laugh *with* me; they were laughing *at* me and my imperfect Icelandic grammar.

10 DAYS BEFORE THE ELECTION

We traveled north to the town of Akureyri for more visits and campaign events, shuttled around in a minibus decorated with Icelandic flags and campaign posters by a car mechanic named Haukur. He had never helped with a political campaign before, he said, but he liked Guðni and had even been one of the people who had called him to encourage him to run. (Being one of the people who reached out to him before he announced his run became a badge of honor, like seeing *Star Wars* in the theater the summer it came out.)

The main campaign event was standing room only. Guðni and I were improving our routines with every performance, making people laugh and, I hoped, showing our genuine natures. After that event, a few people approached me to say that they were voting for Guðni because they had read good interviews with me. I was tickled.

As we rode in the minibus Haukur had rented and decorated, sipping soft drinks another volunteer had procured, to stay overnight at an apartment provided by a supporter, I felt like we could not possibly deserve all this kindness from strangers. We were good people, of course, but weren't others in greater need than us? Didn't others deserve the attention more? It was a bizarre feeling to find myself playing a lead role in a performance I had never expected. But here we were, doing our best, being ourselves. And our hard work, honesty, and dedication were paying off.

6 DAYS UNTIL THE ELECTION

We completed the last of our public meetings on June 19 in Patreksfjörður in the Westfjords, our third event on that day alone. As usual, we had higher turnouts than expected. It was a lovely end to the tours, but as Guðni and I, his brother Jóhannes, and photographer Håkon—our entire entourage—drove on washboard dirt roads around the Westfjords' famous hairpin turns, I almost burst into tears. A particularly sentimental song from our specially curated campaign playlist came on, and I was overwhelmed and just completely physically and emotionally exhausted. After our long days on the road, I was staying up after the others had gone to sleep to finish my own projects such as the in-flight magazine, which was going to print the next week. I felt guilty that my elderly parents were watching the kids all the time and worried that I was being a bad parent because I wasn't spending enough time with my children. (Mothers: Sound familiar?) I was also worried about what effect the likely upcoming change would have on them, even though we had discussed it all endlessly in advance. I was isolating too. I didn't want to talk to Guðni about my exhaustion; if *I* felt this way, I couldn't begin to imagine how *he* felt. I couldn't talk to my friends either. They were working on the campaign and laser-focused on the last-minute details of the final few days; I didn't think they would want to hear me complain.

Everyone was telling us that this election was a done deal, that Guðni would have a clear victory, but it didn't feel that way at all. Although all leading candidates had largely avoided negative tactics, with the occasional exception of debate outbursts from former PM Davíð Oddsson, I wondered if that would change in the last week, when there was nothing left to lose. I worried that I would lose my cool at an inappropriate moment with an angry or emotional outburst.

Having a plan had always given me security, but in that moment, the whole endeavor felt like a seven-week improvisation. For a few moments, in a cramped rented Skoda in the middle of nowhere, it all felt very, very lonely.

That night, I wrote in my (infrequently recorded) diary: "I feel like I would start crying if someone hugged me now."

ELECTION DAY

Turnouts for elections in Iceland are comparatively high compared to other nations. People take their civic responsibility seriously, and many dress in nicer clothes to go to the polling station, making a trip out of it, bringing children with them and perhaps stopping at a café on the way home. Elections are always held on a Saturday.

Election Day in 2016 started with drizzly weather, though it wasn't cold—by Icelandic standards anyway. We dressed up in prechosen Election-Day outfits (the kids mostly styled by my mother, who eschewed recommendations from professionals to coordinate their clothing) and walked to the local school to cast our ballots, our oldest two on their bikes, the youngest two in a large stroller. Journalists had been notified in advance when we would appear, and a bank of cameras and many smiling faces were waiting to greet us. Well-wishers waved at us from cars and honked their horns. The odds all seemed to show that Guðni would win, but two days earlier, we had awoken to a surprise "leave" vote in the Brexit referendum, and I thought it was wiser to take nothing for granted.

After casting our ballots, we stopped at the campaign office, where many supporters would be gathering throughout the day. We shook more hands, and I broke my earlier rule about daily cream cake intake. Somehow the hours passed in the normal business of young families: a trip to the swimming pool, a football [soccer] game, playing with the grandparents.

Polls were set to close at 10 p.m., and the first results were expected soon afterwards. I had arranged a babysitter so my exhausted parents could go to the venue we'd booked for what we hoped would be a victory party. (We decided not to have the kids with us; the event would go well into the middle of the night, and while it might have been a special moment for the oldest two, the youngest two would never have made it.) At 9:30 p.m., a member of the campaign team collected us from our home to take us to the headquarters of the state television network, RÚV. Most spouses and some advisers, including our own Friðjón, assembled in the green room, while all the candidates lined up so cameras could capture their reactions as the first results came in. Small talk with other candidate spouses and advisers was always going to be a bit strange under those circumstances, but the campaign had generally been friendly, and I assumed we all wanted to end it that way too.

The first numbers came in from the southern region just after 10 p.m. Guðni was in the lead, only marginally ahead of Halla Tómasdóttir, a businesswoman who had entered the race polling at about 2 percent but had performed well in debates and seen a surge in support near the end. I pasted a smile on my face for the cameras (which weren't on me anyway) but inside got very, very nervous and started reconciling with the "upsides" of a loss: The kids wouldn't have to switch schools! At least I had finally been to Neskaupstaður! Yet as I looked around, it appeared that all the candidates and Friðjón still expected Guðni to win.

It felt like hours before the next results came in, though it was likely less than thirty minutes, and they reinforced Guðni's lead. Same for the third round of results. After that, the candidates were led into the studios for their thoughts, and soon after, it was crystal clear that Guðni would win (ultimately with 39.1 percent of the vote) and become the nation's sixth president. Halla Tómasdóttir ended up in second place with 27.9 percent. The other candidates congratulated him, and then we left for the party.

It started to feel real, whatever *real* meant. It started to feel big, whatever *big* meant. Or whatever *it* meant, come to think of it. I knew I couldn't dwell on the significance of the moment or I would start crying. Somehow that didn't feel befitting of whatever unofficial role I was about to step into.

We were driven the short distance to the Grand Hotel Reykjavík, where flashbulbs popped and cameras clicked as we emerged from the car and walked slowly, hand in hand, into the main room, stopping to hug and kiss people on the way. Gradually we got to the stage. I couldn't make eye contact with people I knew well, or I would have started to cry. (It became a theme; was anything *not* going to make me want to cry?)

There were cameras, so many cameras. And people, so many people. Clapping, hugging, smiling, laughing, crying. I said something into the microphone, I have no idea what. It was probably short so I wouldn't cry or accidentally say a slang term for penis (I have done this before). Guðni delivered a speech. I have no idea what he said either. It was a blur of flashbulbs, kisses, and thank-yous, and I was riding a wave of adrenaline with no time to think about anything.

We left the party going strong at about 2:30 a.m., though it took an hour to wade through the room to the door. As we stepped out to the car in the endless light of the summer midnight sun, I turned to look behind me and caught a glimpse of my parents, childcare woes forgotten, dancing up a storm to "Uptown Funk."

9

Limbo

Guðni and I wave to friends and supporters outside our home the morning after the election, June 26, 2016.

"Do we have to pay for this?"

—Eight-year-old Duncan upon seeing his first motorcade

The morning after the election, the doorbell startled us awake after only four hours of sleep. My foundation, professionally applied at the television studios the evening before, still mostly hid the circles under my eyes. Added to that the waterproof mascara I did not usually wear, and I was startled to see Tammy Faye Bakker staring back from the mirror. I pulled on some leggings and slipped into a sweater, running my fingers through my short hair as I raced downstairs to open the door. There stood a young delivery boy with a large chocolate sheet cake; it was Guðni's forty-eighth birthday.

The cake was followed by numerous flower arrangements and cards of congratulations—from the former prime minister (of Panama Papers infamy) and his wife, the rector of the University of Iceland, and the Japanese Embassy in Iceland. (Actually, maybe that was a bottle of sake. It's all a blur.) I couldn't keep track of the texts and DMs that were flooding my inbox, and a woman called our landline asking whether she should raise the Icelandic flag outside her home. (Many people have flagpoles, but flags are generally only flown during certain holidays.)

By 8 a.m., television crews arrived, ready to set up for a tradition known as the *hylling*: After a new president has been elected, that person appears on the balcony of his or her house the next morning to greet supporters and deliver short remarks broadcast live to the nation. (Fortunately for democracy, Icelanders have never elected a president who resided somewhere without a balcony.) It would take several hours to get the camera, lighting, and some sort of reporting marquee set up.

Meanwhile, Guðni and I began doing interviews (in my case, after applying a fresh coat of makeup). I did six of them that day, often for Canadian news outlets, which gleefully reported the story of the small-town girl who was about to become a first lady. The most common question, surprisingly, was whether, growing up in the Ottawa Valley, I'd had that specific dream all along? I told one interviewer the event reminded me of having a baby: You're very excited but very tired, and it was the beginning of "the great unknown."

Just before 4 p.m., we pulled the curtains aside and glimpsed the crowds that had gathered. During a blessed break in the rain, I stepped out onto our small balcony to the microphone the television crew had set up. I had already decided that people needed to hear my voice too, even briefly, at these big public gatherings. But I didn't want to read a speech, nor did I want to make a grammatical error in Icelandic that would distract from what I was trying to say. Most importantly, I was worried that my voice would crack from emotion. So I merely stood and said, "Ladies and gentlemen, may I introduce the next president of Iceland, Guðni Th. Jóhannesson!" All five kids joined us, most of them looking out tentatively at the vast crowd, and Guðni said a few words.

Afterwards, we went outside to the yard, my heels sinking into the moist dirt, and shook what felt like hundreds of hands. I noticed someone had evened out the gravel in our unpaved driveway and another had weeded the garden. All I tried to do was accept congratulations without bursting into tears, but that was especially challenging when old mates—including two of the first friends I made in Iceland who had traveled from Europe to surprise me—appeared and gave me hugs.

Then we went back inside to the smell of fresh flowers, to cries from Edda, who was angry there were so many strangers around her house, to complaints from the older boys who wanted some supper *right now*.

Out on the lawn, in my new Icelandic designer dress and borrowed necklace and earrings, I was one-half of the soon-to-be First Couple, the new breath of fresh air so many Icelanders had been asking for. Married to a person who would soon bear the weight of high expectations and consequential responsibilities. A representative of the most senior office in my adopted country, someone who would constantly be seen and critiqued and judged in the court of public opinion, perhaps the most Sisyphean of burdens.

But once I closed the door inside Tjarnarstígur 11, I was Mom. Mom of *I'm hungry* and *my diaper needs changing* and *he's looking at me funny* and *I'm hungry* and *can you reach that toy for me* and *didn't you hear me, I'm hungry*. The heels came off as I thought about preparing our young family for seismic change: new preschools, new schools, new house, busier and occasionally absent parents. But the glow remained.

It was a day that foreshadowed a strange purgatory between our old lives and what was to come. We would be asked to take part in interviews, plan an inauguration, and meet Important People. But we would be walking the tightrope more or less on our own for the next five weeks. The campaign was over, the office closed; our volunteers mostly returned to their own lives. The office of the president offered help and support to the president, and that was not yet Guðni. So the period of transition would be like those seemingly endless seconds after you jump from the airplane and before you activate your parachute.

Blessedly, there was no time to contemplate the levels of support or lack thereof. For at 3:30 the next morning, we awoke again, this time for an international trip. The FIFA European men's soccer championships had been taking place since early that month in various cities throughout France. Tiny Iceland had qualified for the tournament for the first time and, against all odds, had advanced through to the elimination round, garnering international attention. The playoff match would take place in Nice on June 27 against England. Guðni and I would be there.

We would not attend in any official capacity. Icelandair had chartered several direct flights for fans, and along with eight-year-old Duncan and Liz and Friðjón, who had played such vital roles in Guðni's run for president, we had made plans to stay for one night and attend the match.

I realized that life might be changing as soon as we boarded the flight. Instead of being greeted with a curt nod to the right for us to find our seats, we were ushered to the front row of business class. On the other side of the same row sat Iceland's outgoing president and his wife, who were of course going to be attending in an official capacity. It was the first time I was meeting my predecessor, and Dorrit enveloped me in a huge hug accompanied by effusive congratulations. Meanwhile, Duncan was busy testing all the buttons that would control how to turn his seat into a flat bed.

Almost five hours later, we landed in sunny Nice. As the aircraft taxied to a stop, a motorcade of a few vehicles and two motorcycles pulled up. French security takes the visit of a head of state seriously, I thought. Ólafur Ragnar and Dorrit would have a traffic-free journey all the way to the Nice Intercontinental. Then I peered for a moment longer: there were *two* motorcades next to the plane. It turns out that in France, presidents-*elect* are also required to have security.

Duncan gazed wide-eyed at the uniformed officers and tinted-windowed vehicles that would take us to the three-star hotel Friðjón had booked on Hotwire. My son looked at me in awe and asked, "Do we have to pay for all this?"

I wondered how I should explain this new promotion in our modes of transportation. Duncan could tell his friends about it, I said, but he shouldn't brag. It's possible that we might travel with this level of pomp again, I explained, but he shouldn't expect it or feel entitled to it.

We alighted the aircraft, greeted the Icelandic ambassador to France, and smiled at various saluting officers. Someone else collected our bags, and off we drove, sirens flashing, motorcycles blocking any traffic that might impede our progress.

It's unlikely that the manager of the B4 Park Nice was used to the arrival of guests via armed guard. When we pulled up, he rushed out of the hotel to inquire what was happening. Liz and Friðjón, who had driven in the second vehicle of our troupe, explained that Guðni had just been elected the next president of Iceland.

"*Félicitations!*" the manager congratulated us. We were promptly upgraded to a bright, two-room suite with balcony. A few minutes later, a man arrived with a bottle of chilled champagne, a plate of sliced fruits, and gift bags with luxury toiletries.

I could get used to this.

After the security deposited us at our accommodation, we were left alone to explore the town in advance of the match. Nice's crowded streets were teeming with red-and-white-clad England supporters and blue-garbed Iceland fans, all seemingly surprised at the team's success to date. Duncan was in awe of his first palm tree sighting, the heat, and the fact that everyone seemed to want a selfie with his father.

A few hours later, our convoy arrived again to escort us to the match, where we had permission to watch in the regular stands rather than the enclosed VIP area, albeit with a security guard who stood next to us in a suit. When our faces appeared on the jumbotron during "Ó Guðs vors lands," I was glad I had learned all the words to the national anthem.

And that first playoff match against mighty England, the team that hadn't lost a game since exiting the men's World Cup in Brazil in 2014? Iceland won, 2–1. Guðni lost his voice from singing and chanting and cheering. The game has gone down in history as one of the worst England defeats of all time.

Almost as soon as it was done, we were quickly shuttled around the building, burly officers pushing well-wishers out of the way, all the way to the VIP area to sip champagne with men in expensive suits. Then it was back to our hotel, once again the vehicle in front gesturing people out of the way as we passed, sirens on, where four armed guards stood outside as we arrived.

A victory in the quarterfinals meant that Iceland advanced to the semis, and now that the team was on a roll, Friðjón convinced us that we should return to France for that match, which would be against the host nation—in Paris.

A few days later, we found ourselves in the Stade de France for what would turn out to be a semifinal defeat against the mighty Bleus. The day was memorable for something else too: It was July 3, our wedding anniversary. I hadn't been to the French capital for my fortieth, but we managed it for the "silk" anniversary and for the romantic aim of watching a sporting match with our mate Friðjón tagging along. If Iceland's men's team was on a roll, well, so was Guðni, both maritally and politically, even if the execution was quite different than I had fantasized in what seemed like another era, back in my thirties.

Those two brief international trips, taken so close together, set the tone for what felt like the busiest month of the entire presidential adventure. There were, of course, all the normal logistics of a young family moving houses: registering at a new school, filling in change of address details, signing up for new local sports teams. Some indicated the level of privilege into which we were moving: I had never had an interior designer ask me what sort of sink I wanted in the bathroom or countertop in the kitchen, nor had I ever lived somewhere with an en suite bathroom, a walk-in closet, and a garage.

Then there were the details unique to a presidential transition: Guðni was awake late into the nights to write his inaugural address. He was also involved in practical choices such as which songs would be sung during the event. What messages would he send with both the choice of singer and the choice of music?

The interviews also continued. The day after returning from Paris, I had three interviews with various Canadian stations and, the following day, with media from Iceland, Germany, the U.S., and Canada again. Erla María Tölgyes, a generous volunteer from our campaign, sent us a schedule for each day the evening before, including how to coordinate ride-sharing and ensure the kids were picked up from preschool on time. I did a five-hour photo shoot to accompany the cover story of a major local lifestyle magazine to be published right before the inauguration. A stylist brought a rack of outfits—most from the same store and that skewed to the small side. As I tried to wedge myself into yet another pencil skirt, I wondered whether I would have to spend the next several years googling "cheap tummy flattening shapewear." The team at the magazine—makeup artists, photographer, and stylist—kept telling me how relaxed and nice I was. I worried that "relaxed" was code for "this country bumpkin has no place in this world."

Yet when the magazine was published, I noted that the editor had kindly written, "Eliza is a calm and composed woman, a feminist with backbone and a great sense of humor." The feature interview turned out well too, given that inside, I still felt unsure about what I was going to do with my surprise role as first lady or even how to pose for photo shoots.

"I haven't appeared often in the media, but when I have it's been due to my own projects," I told the reporter. "This is the first time that I'm getting attention because of who I am married to. Of course I am very proud of my husband and support him, but it's a rather strange feeling to be in the limelight because of someone else. But that's also an opportunity to use the platform to make my actions count."

I spoke about my interpretation of feminism as a philosophy that should not intimidate people. About how I didn't want to change my style so much that my children would think I couldn't leave the house without applying an hour's worth of makeup first. That as parents, all of us needed to continue to nurture our daughters' independence but also our sons' emotional sides.

"I feel like I am the same person I was in March, which of course I am, but the circumstances are now different," I concluded. "[Guðni and I] continue to be ourselves and we will serve in these roles to the best of our abilities. We are ready."

Yet as a mother of four young ones, exhausted was pretty much my baseline. Now new roles and moving house were added to that, all in the glare of national attention. Questions swirled. Would the kids resent me if I were away more? Would I be lonely? Would my friends still want to hang out with me? Was I even allowed to hang out? What if I made a ghastly mistake and it cost my husband his presidency? Privately, I was indulging in some self-pity.

But then one morning, immediately after being startled from

a deep sleep by my toddler son staring two inches from my face, asking me how big snakes can get, I realized: My husband was going to be *running a country*. The buck was going to stop with him. No, he wasn't prime minister and in charge of budgets and policy, but he would be the highest-ranking person in the nation. If I was losing sleep about not getting to head to the disco as often, how must he feel?

On July 14, Bastille Day in France, a terrorist in Nice drove a cargo truck into crowds of people on the very promenade we had been strolling just a few weeks earlier. Eighty-six people were killed and several hundred more were injured. Guðni posted condolences on his Facebook account and wrote to some of the security officials we had met there. Once again, another epiphany: He had a duty to respond to world events, to represent the people of Iceland on the global stage. This was but the first—and in this case unofficial, done only because we had been in the town so recently—of many moments when Guðni would be called upon to issue statements of sympathy or of solidarity.

On the morning of August 1, Inauguration Day, I posted a photo of Guðni hoisting the Icelandic flag outside our home. The post appeared on the news within minutes. The children's moods seemed to alternate between bemusement, pride, and frustration at the attention. The house filled early in the day with a hairdresser, a makeup artist, a former neighbor to look after the kids, a few more to get them dressed in traditional costume, and several members of my Canadian extended family who had traveled over for the big day. I needed help to put the traditional costume on too. The top and bottom halves of the *skautbúningur* had been generously loaned to me by the families of two former first ladies, and I had gone to numerous fittings in July to make sure that on the day, everything would go smoothly.

We were collected at the appointed hour by Einar, presidential chauffeur, who would drive us to the Alþing in the presidential Lexus marked with license plate 1. Because of the traditional headdress I wore, I needed to ride the 1.5-mile journey hunched over like a glamorous jack-in-the-box. I still managed to wave to the crowds who lined the streets and tried to soak in the atmosphere, to remind myself never to take any of this for granted, to know that if it ever felt commonplace, I was doing something wrong.

When we arrived, Einar opened the door for me, and I emerged as gracefully as I could, giving the crowds another cheerful wave. Then we were whisked inside, first to a church service and then to the inauguration ceremony itself. After signing the documents that would officially usher Guðni into office, we stepped onto the balcony of the Althing in front of the crowds gathered on Austurvöllur Square, waved, listened to a marching band, and raised four cheers for the motherland, as per tradition.

After that and a couple of hours of handshakes and photo shoots later, it was back home to get changed for a new party at Bessastaðir, the presidential residence, where we would move a couple of months later after renovations were completed. As we drove through the Gálgahraun lava field towards the residence, the flag of the president flapped in the wind, an indication that the head of state was traveling in the vehicle. I couldn't stop staring at it. Was this really our life now? It felt surreal yet like it was always meant to be.

For the first time, we entered the residence from the back entrance by the kitchen, walking through the halls to stand in the front room and prepare to greet our guests. Television cameras monitored the progress to report live on who had received a coveted invitation and perhaps whose faces were missing. At the end, weary and happy, we were driven back to Tjarnarstígur 11 as a deep orange globe set over Snæfellsjökull glacier in the distance. The adventure had really begun.

10

Who Am I?

Getting ready for an official photo shoot at the outset of Guðni's second term, fall 2020. I am wearing a traditional "skautbúning" costume.

"Yours is an office which, according to our constitution, doesn't exist."

—Norbert Lammert, president of the German Parliament, to Elke Büdenbender, first lady of Germany, at her husband's inauguration

I took part in my first "spouse program" just over two months after Guðni took office, noting in my diary that I was "a bit unsure about all the babies" in the itinerary but was going along with everything that had been suggested to me as a first lady taking her initial tentative steps in the role would do.

The steps were cautious, but they also needed to be quick. An adviser at the president's office wisely told us early on that our journey was a marathon, not a sprint, but we were nevertheless keen to give it our all from the outset.

In the first months, I zeroed in on the small lessons of what I should or could be doing. I learned to identify the different trees of protocol, attire, and comportment so that later on, I could see how they formed the forest. There was plenty to learn, so many species to discover, that it would be a long time before I saw what they all meant to the bigger picture of how I ultimately wanted to carve out my role as first lady.

Our first official overseas visitors were United Nations Secretary General Ban Ki-moon and his wife, Ban Soon-taek. The visit of this jet-setting couple was perhaps the highest-profile example of learning on the job as soon as Guðni took office. As part of the visit, we would host a formal dinner at the presidential residence.

Before the dinner and the conference he was in the country to address, there was a morning program, during which I was to entertain Mrs. Ban. I had never heard of a spouse program before I was a "principal" in one. I don't recall how much input I had in the creation of that morning's agenda, but the night before, I was sent a to-the-minute schedule of the four stops we would be making.

The first was no surprise, as it had been a somewhat unorthodox suggestion by Guðni upon discovery that Mrs. Ban was interested in children with disabilities. We went to the home of Arnar Björnsson, a six-year-old boy with a nonverbal form of autism. We knew Arnar because he was the son of good friends of ours, and they were willing to open their home for an exactly thirty-five-minute visit.

After we sipped coffee and hugged cheerful Arnar, the minibus that was transporting our small group would then take us to the neonatal intensive care unit at the National Hospital. Again, the stop aligned with our guest's interests and had a personal connection: Guðni's first cousin Margrét was nursing unit manager at the NICU. Plus, there were many babies, and it seemed that babies and first ladies (or other spouses of world leaders) go together like peanut butter and jelly (or dried fish and salted butter if you are in Iceland). But who was I to question whether that was perpetuating stereotypes I didn't necessarily want to propagate? Experienced, diligent people had arranged these visits; meanwhile, I was still learning how to access my new email. Anyway, I enjoyed everything about my new role as spouse program host: meeting people, introducing an important guest to some interesting facets of Iceland, and, I'll admit it, being trailed by a couple of reporters to publicize it all.

The program would finish with a stop at the studio of a local sculptor whose works were displayed at Dag Hammarskjöld Plaza outside UN headquarters in New York and, finally, to lunch at a local restaurant with academics from the University of Iceland who specialized in gender studies.

Mrs. Ban was lovely, if quiet, rather the embodiment of what I had thought the female spouse of a world leader might be: dignified, interested in a detached way, a warm smile at the ready for all she met.

What I thought was most fun, however, was the dinner we held that evening. We had invited about two dozen people to attend the three-course meal. With no formal guidelines on how these evenings proceed, I was as insecure as the time I dared to use my new Cuisinart before reading the manual. Our guests included Ólafur Ragnar Grímsson, the former president who was in charge of the Arctic Circle forum that Ban was in the country to speak at, as well as the minister of foreign affairs and the president of the United Nations Association of Iceland. Both Guðni and the UN secretary general delivered some brief but formal remarks before a toast. Guðni also ensured that everyone around the table had a moment to say a few words and contribute to the conversation rather than having these talented and experienced people satisfy themselves merely with small talk with the person next to them and no real interaction with the guest of honor.

Before that inaugural supper as the nation's dinner-party hosts, I found myself marveling at the minute details of life in a presidential couple, silently clocking simple rules but rarely taking the time to consider what it all meant for the big picture.

Our first official visit came a mere two days after the inauguration and was to Sólheimar, a sustainable eco-community of about one hundred people that was a two-hour drive from the capital. It felt luxurious not to hold my own handbag and to have someone tell me when I needed to reapply my lipstick. I shook so many hands that, years before COVID-19's emergence, I politely requested hand sanitizer for the car. I tried to absorb as much information about the community as possible, knowing that I would be unlikely to retain the nitty-gritty. I smiled for photographs, nodded as we heard details about whichever building we were visiting, shook hands, smiled for more photographs, and repeated the process at the next stop. The next day, I was in an interview about the visit and was grilled on the tie Guðni had chosen, which was red with small primates on it. *Does he like monkeys? What's his favorite animal?* I didn't say he had likely chosen this tie because it was hanging closest to him in the closet, but I noted privately that we would need to consider the unspoken messages of our sartorial choices.

A few days later, we flew north to the community of Dalvík to attend their annual Great Fish Day celebration, during which locals prepare a plethora of variations on fish soup to distribute free to visitors. I learned that day that no matter how much I enjoy a dish, the bloom will be off the rose by the twelfth variation.

Even flying became a new experience. For that domestic flight to Akureyri, the closest airport to Dalvík, our car pulled up right next to the aircraft five minutes before departure, and the captain came out to greet us. Before the safety demonstration, the flight attendant began the announcements, "Mr. President and Madam."

It was exhilarating, fresh, and new. Even though we had been around the country during the election campaign, gripping and grinning, the tone was different now. Guðni wasn't in charge of budgets or policies. He couldn't allocate funds, couldn't change rules on what could be built somewhere or who could live there. But people paid attention to what we did, and we could send signals about priorities by our choices of the events in which we participated. When we visited a particular festival or location or facility, we shone a light on what it was doing, how it was contributing to our society. I loved the diversity of it all, how every day brought something new. I felt the unofficial responsibility bequeathed to us merely by our appearance somewhere. Hardworking people had prepared for our visit, prioritizing what to tell us in a short amount of time, and we owed it to them to listen with interest, to learn about the opportunities and challenges they faced, to help connect them to others to further their objectives, to share our experiences with a wider audience. I wanted to receive what they had to say with the same respect and care they had given us in preparing every single visit.

Even as I recognized my role in these visits, what I had yet to determine was whether I was doing it right. Though with no guidelines or rule book, I suppose technically it was impossible to do it wrong. If Facebook comments were anything to go by, it seemed like the general public was favorable to me. But I wanted something more formalized than "top fan" social media commentators and mentions in a local community's newsletter. I wanted to find out who I was in this new role, to make sure that First Lady Eliza was fundamentally the same human as Ontario's Fastest Typist Eliza and Immigrant Eliza.

Sometimes I looked to previous first ladies for inspiration. Within Iceland, I was only the sixth. The first three served before 1980, in an era when the most scandalous story was of a first lady who was seen in public wearing—gasp!—a house dress. The fourth first lady was very popular and active but died of cancer after her husband had served less than two years in office. My immediate predecessor, an immigrant like me, was also very popular and was welcoming to me when Guðni was about to take office. Dorrit and I both enjoyed meeting people and didn't seem to mind the spotlight. Beyond that, we have different personalities and interests, so I knew I would likely follow a different path than she had chosen in this role.

I also read books about former first ladies. My impression was mostly based on American first ladies, probably because I'm a native English speaker and because they attract so much global attention but also because the other two countries where I have lived—Canada and the United Kingdom—are not republics with presidents (and first spouses). Eleanor Roosevelt made a name for herself beyond her husband's time as president, most notably in her involvement with the creation of the Universal Declaration of Human Rights. Hillary Rodham Clinton famously served as a U.S. senator, secretary of state, and presidential candidate herself (and was also an active policymaker within her husband's administration). A few years after I became a first lady, Jill Biden, the first among U.S. first ladies to hold a doctorate degree, became the first person in the role to work outside the White House during her husband's tenure. I devoured the books I could find on these and other first ladies. I was relieved that I was serving in a much smaller country when I read about press intrusions, massive security bubbles, and strict protocol guidelines, none of which I would have to deal with (although I would later learn that first ladies of even tiny nations also sometimes have to fight to be included in background briefings and have their voices heard).

In fact, many countries have wildly divergent definitions and perspectives on first ladies. Some have no formal job description but a dedicated staff. Others have fairly clear obligations. In Pakistan as of 2024, First Lady Aseefa Bhutto Zardari is actually the daughter of the president and a member of a political dynasty. Her mother, former Prime Minister Benazir Bhutto, was assassinated in 2007.

I was looking forward to having the opportunity to meet many of my counterparts in other countries, to compare notes about our unique experiences. I was touched to receive a kind letter from my compatriot Sophie Grégoire Trudeau soon after Guðni's election. As the then-spouse of a head of government rather than a head of state, there was no protocol precedent for her to get in touch, and I appreciated the gesture.

From others who had gone before me, both in Iceland and abroad, I tried to design the scaffolding for my comfort zone as a first lady. I saw Dorrit earn the Icelandic public's affection with her friendly nature. I watched Michelle Obama deliver impassioned speeches. I tried to carve out room for my own interests and strengths while taking note of hard lessons learned from others—usually following a barrage of local criticism for speaking up "too vocally" about lack of support or recognition, code for straying too much out of their lane, for taking up space. Each new experience added a new brick in the structure I was building of how to be a first lady.

There were lessons in everything. During my first solo speech, at an event for a local Rotary club, I was met outside by a small delegation of senior Rotary members. Lesson #47: A first lady is always greeted by a welcoming committee (and, in fact, I discovered the president's office always called ahead to confirm who the greeter would be).

My first trip abroad as first lady was to London, where I would join Guðni, who had gone a couple of days earlier for meetings. We would meet members of the House of Lords who had connections to Iceland and eventually travel north to Leeds, where Guðni was scheduled to deliver a lecture at the University of Leeds. It was only later that I mastered Lesson #59: Guðni did not require a traveling applauder. This trip was one of only a very few, state visits excepted, where I accompanied him without a specific role.

On this occasion, I was even looking forward to the journey itself. In almost twenty years of a connection to Iceland and including editing the in-flight magazine, it would be the first time I was to travel Saga Class, Icelandair's equivalent of business class. (My trip to Nice for the soccer game was on a rented aircraft with different seat configurations.) I couldn't wait to sip sparkling wine and lean back in my soft, spacious seat.

At Keflavík airport, I was greeted by an on-site police officer and ushered through the staff entrance. I was whisked to the lounge to await my flight while Rikki, another driver for the president's office, stayed with me the whole time. I was asked whether I wanted to board the aircraft first or last. Why, last, thank you very much! As the lounge began to empty, I waited excitedly until the police officer returned to escort me and Rikki to the aircraft. I wondered when Rikki was going to go back to the car, but as we approached the gangway, he stayed silently by my side. I moved to enter the aircraft, smiling at the flight attendants. Rikki followed and put my suitcase in the storage bin above my seat. Was he going to do up my seat belt too? I was beginning to wonder whether this was protocol or whether some higher-ups thought I was not capable of traveling on my own. (The former, it turns out. That was Lesson #60.)

(Speaking of air travel, did you wonder whether the president of Iceland and his or her family have a government jet? No. It's a small country. At the time of writing, I have never stepped aboard a private jet, although perhaps an adventurous soul reading this will feel I haven't been spoiled enough in this life and invite me on a trip.)

I quickly discovered that I was treated to the same luxury boarding procedures even when I wasn't traveling to meet my husband. My first solo trip as first lady happened around the same time when I went to Toronto to take part in a conference organized by the Institute for Canadian Citizenship. That institute's mission is "to unlock Canada for newcomers," and in addition to sharing experiences about Iceland, I was also hoping that my attendance might give me some inspiration for how I could help to celebrate immigrants in my adopted country, a group of which I was a proud member. Since I was visiting my old stomping grounds, this was the first trip where I was asked to take part in numerous television interviews, and I also met old friends who were happy to tease me about my newfound fame.

On the second morning of the conference, a young man at the coffee break complimented me on my necklace. I thanked him and pointed out that it was Icelandic.

"Iceland!" he exclaimed, then paused and puffed his chest out slightly. He leaned in as if about to share a treasured secret. "Well, *I* know the *brother* of the *wife* of the *president* of Iceland."

I felt the hamster on the wheel inside my brain start to run a little faster. This was convoluted, but I must surely know that person too. I connected the dots. Ah, it was *my* brother that he knew! Canada is also a small country.

I was elated to have the opportunity to serve Iceland by traveling and meeting new people, but I always had a nagging worry that I was inadvertently bringing shame to my entire adopted nation. Like almost all women, I had been socialized to respond to positive feedback, and if that was not in abundance, I assumed it meant that I was breaking the rules in some way, and that is not a Good Thing.

As I slowly built a structure of behaviors in which I could feel safe and secure, I sometimes ignored my own instincts. Guðni and I hosted regular receptions at Bessastaðir. I attended most of the larger ones, especially in the early years; it was all so new and exciting. Whether greeting five people or 150, the format was generally the same: Guests would wait in line in the "flower room," with its dramatic views of the surrounding sea and mountains, to shake our hands: his and then mine. From there, guests would proceed to the main reception hall, where they would wait until everyone had been greeted.

People have different reactions to meeting a head of state in person. Some are visibly nervous, avoiding eye contact, giggling sheepishly, or wiping sweaty palms on their clothes. Some are deferential, making a small bow as if in the presence of royalty. Others have gifts to present or photos they wish to take. Some want to stop and talk as if we are the only people in the world, even as a queue mushrooms behind them.

After shaking hands with the president, guests usually moved to shake hands with me. Except not all of them did. Whether they were overwhelmed by their head of state encounter, eager to see the large reception hall, thirsty for a glass of bubbly, or simply didn't see the other five-foot-six human being right next to the president, some shook Guðni's hand and marched straight by me, an invisible prop next to my husband. As I stood, smile at the ready, hand outstretched, these unintentional snubs momentarily disarmed me, no matter how often they happened. To avoid any awkward moments, I would instinctively withdraw my hand and look down briefly as if to nonverbally apologize for expecting to shake that person's hand in the first place. *Don't worry. I can't see you either*, my indirect gaze seemed to say. Then I would blink and greet the next person.

Each ghosting was a minuscule paper cut on my identity, a new grain of sand added to the growing mound of self-doubt that lay within my stomach to remind me that maybe I didn't really belong there. If there were too many of these moments in a single gathering, I found that I was grumpier at the end of the event, a combination of frustration at these guests and anger at myself. Was I arrogant to think that people should also greet me when they had already gripped the hand of the head honcho? What about my silence in failing to point it out?

I didn't tell anyone this. It didn't seem to matter. It was the most wafer-thin of gripes after all, and I was certain no one was doing it on purpose.

There were other occasions I stayed silent too: Guðni and I went on several official visits within Iceland every year. They almost always involved about a dozen stops over a day, including at schools, elderly care homes, health care centers, and various workplaces, with a final gathering that was open to the general public. Guðni is incredibly knowledgeable about Icelandic history, but I am less so, for obvious reasons. On one of the first trips, we were sent another detailed schedule, which included names and times of places we would be visiting as well as the name of the person who would escort us around the elderly home or school or fish factory. There was information on how we would get from place to place (e.g., by car or on foot) and a list of phone numbers for the relevant people taking part in the visit.

That was it.

No biographies of the people we would be meeting or the

local mayor who would be our host for the day. No history of the community, the challenges they were facing, or the special dates they were celebrating. No details of salacious rumors or advice on sensitive subjects that it would be best to avoid. No details of the type of place we would see. Was Sælukot—the event description listed it as "introduction to its activities" and a fifteen-minute visit overall—a youth center? An arts center? A farm? A tourism cluster? I didn't know.

I ought to have asked, of course. How could colleagues who were only just getting to know us be expected to read my thoughts or anticipate my needs? Or maybe I should have done some homework with the help of Google, though I wasn't keen on that, both because I was too lazy to google certain terms in Icelandic and because I didn't think it was my role, given that I was already donating my time, to research and write my own briefs for these visits. Having said that, perhaps I was being unfairly demanding. The president was happy with the level of detail provided; it was his plus-one who was asking for more. My keenness to play an active role as first lady inevitably added to the workload of the office of the president. The team at the office (excluding the residence) was composed of only five individuals after all, and whether that was too few to manage the busy schedule of the head of state *and* the related events of his spouse was a debate for someone above my pay grade.

The first time this happened, I stayed silent. I had assumed such background details would simply be provided. But when I thought about it, I wouldn't really need to know that one of the sagas, written almost a millennium ago, took place in that region or that a famous track-and-field athlete had grown up there. The day didn't end with a locally themed pub quiz after all.

But still, background briefings were something I considered important to my first-lady structural support. With no information beyond what I may have gleaned from years writing for *Iceland Review* and the memory of my campaign flub of mentioning a pedophile still burning in my mind, on these visits, I often erred on the side of silence or generic small talk, which in my case almost always revolved around how much Icelandic I could speak. I don't believe I caused any embarrassment, but I know I missed opportunities, chances where closer bonds could have been formed had I had a more detailed starting point on which to build dialogue.

The second time we went on a visit, I did ask for a backgrounder, but I didn't get a response to the single inquiry emailed to office staff, so I stayed silent again. The third time, I hoped I might get a few Wikipedia links to squint over on the phone in the car, but alas, no. Perhaps it was because the president (Guðni was now rarely referred to by name but more by his role) didn't ask for it; he was steeped in most local history and, in any case, felt secure enough to wing it. Or perhaps there simply wasn't enough time for the tiny team to compile such a briefing.

I wasn't using my voice enough. Or for whatever reason, it wasn't being heard.

But that was only when it came to me personally, how prepared I was for events. What about using my voice to amplify charities and good causes? Isn't that what a proper first lady is supposed to do? (Apparently so, because at an early meeting with presidential staff, I was asked exactly which causes I would choose. "Well, literature and children, of course," began the staffer before I could answer for myself.)

Beyond what was assumed of me, I knew I was interested in gender equality, in literature, in diversity and inclusion. I knew that I wanted to speak up, to use my (accented) voice, even if I chided myself for not always doing it when something affected me personally.

All that time nerding out on primary school speeches came to good use. I accepted many offers to deliver opening remarks and keynote addresses, from higher-profile events like the commencement address at the University of Akureyri, a humanist ceremony for confirmation children, and the International Women's Day event for the Association of Women Business Leaders to more niche gatherings such as a conference on mindful breastfeeding and the annual conference of the International Academy of Sex Research. When I was speaking in Icelandic, I wrote a speech in English, and someone translated it. Then, if it had been returned with enough time, I practiced reading it aloud over and over to avoid mispronouncing terms or putting an emphasis on the wrong word in a sentence. I still stumbled over long compound words on occasion, but the repetition gave me more confidence.

When I delivered speeches, I felt like I was contributing to the reputation of the office of the president. Often, I was the first person in my position to deliver remarks at a venue. I got positive feedback and knew I could do it well. I shared each speech on social media to send the message that I was in this role to do some good. And I enjoyed it a lot more than thinking about what clothes I should be wearing.

Aside from the clothes, I enjoyed almost all of it, even if some things and my own reactions to them frustrated me. In 2017, I delivered thirty speeches, attended thirty-seven events or award presentations on my own without delivering remarks, took part in thirty meetings or interviews on my own, hosted eight receptions alone (plus many others with Guðni), took several solo domestic and foreign work trips, and took part in probably a similar number of events by my husband's side. I know all this because in addition to taking part in such gatherings, I also loved keeping lists of them. And while no one had forced me into any of it, I knew it was all voluntary labor at the expense of my own paid work, which could have an impact in my post–first lady world, both in terms of contracts and in terms of my pension contributions for retirement. To paraphrase Carrie Bradshaw, I couldn't help but wonder: Would a First Husband do this without complaining?

11

Look the Part

Welcoming Germany's President Frank-Walter Steinmeier and his wife, Elke Büdenbender, for a state visit to Iceland, June 2019. I am wearing a secondhand dress and borrowed jacket.

"I was learning how to connect my message to my image, and in this way I could direct the American gaze... If reporters and television cameras wanted to follow me, then I was going to take them places."

—Michelle Obama, *Becoming*

My inner impostor still wasn't comfortable with the fact that my new position might be kind of a big deal. But there was no denying that for a kid whose most elaborate summer vacation was a three-day road trip to Winnipeg, my early months as first lady were not in short supply on the fancy factor: upgrades, motorcades, requests for selfies. So far, so glamorous. But next to glamorous often comes fashion, and there my dreams were different from reality. I had imagined that a couple of weeks before every gala, an immaculate woman would pull up to the residence and unload racks of stylish designer clothing, each item a perfect fit that flattered my larger-than-average figure, obliterating all my stretch marks and saddlebags. Each gown would be loaned to me, accessories included, so I could always present the perfect image of a coiffed first lady of whom the nation would be proud. Best of all, I wouldn't have to spend any time thinking about what to wear and how to accessorize.

In reality, no such woman ever appeared. I spent far too much emotional energy worrying about attire and how I could afford it, and my double chin was as obvious as it ever had been. Though a clearer picture of the kind of first lady I wanted to be was forming, the picture of what I wanted to look like was still amorphous. Partly that was because I resisted acknowledging that appearance was a factor in how I would be perceived. But it was also because I had no confidence in my sartorial skills.

Still, there was no time like the present for a crash course: I was in Toronto for a conference a few months after I became first lady. Knowing that our first state visit would be early in the coming New Year, I needed to select several outfits. I had heard that one of the city's high-end department stores offered free personal shoppers. If preparing for a few days in the company of royalty was not occasion to use their services, what would be?

Shortly before my appointment, a colleague at the president's office forwarded me an email from my new personal shopper, expressing her anticipation at my visit and asking if I had any wishes concerning food, drink, and decor when I arrived. I was particularly intrigued by the third query. Was I supposed to have a preferred wall color? A certain scent of candle? Would the presence of a fawning George Clooney count as decor?

Perhaps this email should have set off warning bells. Perhaps I ought to have reasoned that any establishment that received a message from a presidential office had certain expectations concerning what I might purchase and that anyone who books such services ought to have the checkbook to back it up.

That first—and only—visit to an upscale personal shopper did indeed have some delicate snacks, refreshing drinks, and a calming decor despite not receiving specific guidance from me. I stood on a circular riser in the middle of a large dressing room with mirrors on many sides and dresses, shoes, handbags, and hats strategically set up in a display curated only for me.

I smiled warmly, posed for photos, sipped chilled champagne. I tried on Oscar de la Renta and the newest Dolce & Gabbana. I was introduced to the works of Canadian labels Greta Constantine and Pink Tartan. I learned the stories behind the brands and the messages they were sending with their creations. I discovered that a capsule wardrobe wasn't a tiny closet for pharmaceuticals. The team at the store was professional and welcoming.

I, on the other hand, was a fish out of water, a pair of scuffed sneakers coupled with a tuxedo. I knew from the first ball gown with individually sewn crystals and matching clutch handbag that the prices of most of these designs would be several months' salary at my first job. But I also knew I needed to buy *something*, since part of the unspoken contract of these "free" arrangements is that they're worthwhile for both parties. Anyway, I had a state visit to attend.

I bought some of the lower-ticket items that were still of high quality, many by lesser-known Canadian designers. Almost a decade later, I still wear them regularly. High-quality fashion might just be worth it if you amortize the price over the years in which the clothing is worn.

Having satisfied myself that I didn't come across as too cheap, I concluded that personal shoppers and I weren't a match made in heaven. I was overcompensating for what I thought I *should* be doing as a first lady, not what felt right for me: I had thought that to be a serious first lady, I should be dressing well in a variety of outfits and that I should have a staffer arrange these meetings for me instead of doing it myself. Really, I could dress appropriately without owning dozens of handbags, and it was just as easy to order online as via a personal shopper. I was falling prey to my own prejudices of the job.

I was often asked whether I had a stylist. The short answer is no, although over the years, numerous acquaintances either helped me with some advice or recommended friends who sorted through my messy closet and suggested a few better pairings or new trouser styles. I was grateful for the time they all took, but I didn't feel comfortable taking free fashion advice from professionals I didn't know, and I didn't want to pay for their services, given that "in the real world," I would never have employed them. (I was also often asked whether there was a clothing budget, which there was not. It didn't jibe with my values to spend large sums of my small salary from the Iceland Writers Retreat on my wardrobe. I occasionally received a small discount or free item, but I broke no rules by accepting those and paid going rate for most of the clothing I wore.)

While I was learning how it felt to be first lady from the inside, I was also painfully aware that I was being judged on how I measured up on the outside. When Guðni announced his candidacy for president, I was an unknown quantity. I had no Icelandic family, childhood or university friends, no local roots from which it would be easy to research. I had appeared in the papers and on television a handful of times but was not well known.

What most people knew about the new first lady was that I was from Canada, spoke Icelandic, and had a lot of children. Beyond that, it was frankly how I looked in public that helped form a perception of me. All this coincided with the areas where I felt least secure: my accent and mistakes I made when speaking Icelandic and not my physical looks but my sense of style.

Ever since my first days at a new middle school, when I didn't have the right bicycle shorts or ability to style my hair or apply eye shadow properly, I had resigned myself to the fact that my skills in life lay away from the realm of fashion and beauty. But I also carried with me an almost invaluable tool that had been fostered in me from an early age: I feel comfortable in my own skin. I believe that how we look to others is 90 percent our attitude towards ourselves. If we all had personal trainers, nutritionists, on-call chefs, and a fat checkbook for clothing and accessories, we could all look like supermodels. My choice was to focus on my family, my work, and my love of good food.

I don't dye my hair. I don't have any piercings. I can't touch my toes. I've always thought wax belongs in candles, not on me. I had never owned a piece of shapewear until Guðni's foray into public life. If all those things are priorities for you, great! You do you. However, I oppose societal pressure that implies that people (usually women) are somehow less pretty, less successful, less professional if they don't devote themselves to endless physical maintenance, purely to meet patriarchal standards of beauty rather than a desire for physical fitness and improved mental health.

I have no idea how much I weighed as I entered public life. I didn't feel unhealthy and was grateful I could take pleasure in a nice glass of wine and a good meal; I knew that my old maternity trousers had elastic material so nothing felt uncomfortable. It was more important to think about actual substantive issues than to endlessly worry about my carb intake or how long I could hold a plank.

Once Guðni was elected, I thought it might be a good opportunity to get closer to the shape of before I had children (not that I had ever been able to hold a long plank). I started going to the gym regularly, promising a trainer that I had no intention of cutting out carbs, sugar, or alcohol or fasting for many hours in a day. I had no interest in it, and I felt good about myself as it was. My only goals were to get a bit stronger and have my BMI in the healthy zone rather than "overweight," where it had remained on the very rare occasions I weighed myself after having children.

Just getting regular exercise and lifting weights made me slim down, enough that people began to notice. Within a few months, strangers sent me messages on social media asking me what my "secret" was. Nearly everyone I met in person commented on how great I looked, the implication clear of how they thought I looked before. This fixation with my appearance frustrated me. Didn't people want to ask me about my recent speech instead of whether I ate pasta? Didn't that journalist want to talk to me to promote a new charitable initiative rather than learn what my dress size was? Didn't people realize that I looked great because I was happy and felt good about myself, not because I had marginally more sculpted biceps? I turned down all requests, of which there were irritatingly many, to speak publicly about this issue, fearful of feeding the frenzy that women should exist in a perpetual cycle of self-improvement. One morning in late 2018, I awoke to see the most-read story on a popular local newspaper was a before-and-after feature on me and my "radical transformation." The paper gleefully revealed (inaccurately) that I was no longer "seen in public" wearing glasses and that my fashion style had "completely changed."

Shortly afterwards, I received a long message from a journalist. He began by saying, "I have been told that you have rarely, if ever, been looking so good." (Um, thank you?) Could he perhaps discuss that with me further, answering questions such as what I had done and why and specifically how many pounds I had lost? From the list of queries, it appeared that "never looked so good" equated directly to weight. Needless to say, I declined the interview and also stifled the urge to postpone it until I gained the weight back, which I knew would inevitably happen as the pendulum of my priorities shifted again at some point in the future. (The pendulum was pushed faster a few years later during a book tour in which the only breakfast option was often Cheetos. Don't judge me; that was all to come.)

The only reason I am even mentioning it here and now is to remind readers that self-esteem and attitude have a lot more to do with how you come across than some digital output on a scale. If you feel good, you look good. The world would be a better place if we memorized data on improved cancer survival rates or access to affordable housing rather than calorie intakes and daily weight fluctuations.

Whether it was my more diverse wardrobe, my newfound ability to bench press thirty-five-pound dumbbells, or simply my capacity to adapt to the spotlight, I gradually got more used to being mentioned in fashion pages. On occasion, I even felt pleased rather than resentful. Each time I made a "best dressed" list, an old friend would send me a joking note about how I was the last person they would have expected to see included.

I was also more patient in photo shoots. After a particularly arduous one (for me at least!) for a cover story in a current affairs magazine's Christmas issue, I had little time left as we did the final shoot. I had finally managed to speak up to photographers and say I didn't want images of me arranging flowers or gazing vapidly out the window. But I was struggling to have an interesting look for this most important shot—the cover. Finally, I said to the photographer that the message I wanted to send was *I'm a really nice person, but don't mess with me*. Except I used a different word than "mess."

It was about this time that I was out for coffee with my friend Lisa when she suggested we stop into the Red Cross charity shop. Lisa told me she had purchased all sorts of fashion gems there secondhand, with the funds going to support the Red Cross.

Shopping in charity shops can be hit or miss because there is almost always just one item of everything, and of course, they have been previously loved. But there can be some great finds. On this occasion, I came across a silky black blazer with a large wavy collar. I thought it would be perfect to wear to the Icelandic version of the Academy Awards that I was to attend that evening. The jacket cost about fifteen dollars.

Afterwards, knowing that photos of my husband and I smiling at events always garnered more attention on social media than posts I wrote about speeches I had delivered, I uploaded a photo of the two of us that also congratulated that year's award winners. I had an unofficial rule that I didn't advertise or comment on my clothing choices; I had other issues to focus on. But on this occasion, I did want the fact that my jacket was secondhand to become public, even if I wasn't about to issue a press release about it.

I had my chance when a friend commented about the jacket on the image I posted. "Thanks, I bought it at the @redcross," I replied.

Things took off from there. A story that the first lady had worn secondhand clothing to a gala event made all the major newspapers in Iceland. Then an English translation of one of the articles was noticed by the BBC, which published a piece, and before I could say *circular economy*, I was reaping praise from strangers and fielding calls from the Red Cross offering to set aside some outfits to look at.

I had worn a cheap jacket that supported a good cause and was a sustainable choice. And people paid attention. It reminded me of Michelle Obama's line in her memoir *Becoming* that if the press wanted to follow her, she was going to take them places.

I began to dress in secondhand clothes at other high-profile events. When the German presidential couple arrived for a state visit where we wanted to highlight sustainability, I wore a Red Cross dress and a borrowed white jacket. I wore a used Max Mara jacket to a one-hour interview on a popular television show. I rented a dress to wear at a reception at Buckingham Palace. I even borrowed a friend's Fluevogs (the Dr. Henry, of course) to wear to King Charles III's coronation.

When Guðni was reelected in June 2020, I wanted to wear a secondhand dress. The one I found, in forest-green silk by Marc Jacobs, wasn't a perfect fit. The buttons along the front gaped just a tiny bit at the bust, but beggars can't be choosers when it comes to used clothes. So Helga, a talented woman who worked at Bessastaðir, sewed the dress's bow across the front to prevent any embarrassing photographs. At the end of the evening, I had to be cut out of it. Then I had it cleaned and redonated for someone else to enjoy.

Beyond the environmental components, I learned to send other signals with my choices of attire. I tried to wear as much Icelandic design as I could when I was traveling. It was less of a priority in Iceland because we don't have all that many designers, and the odds increased that I would be wearing the same dress as someone else at any given event. I got many positive comments about my salmon-skin sneakers and fish-leather handbag. I was touched when people I did not know knit a shawl or a traditional *lopapeysa* sweater for me, and I tried to wear those on relevant occasions.

In the autumn of 2019, then U.S. Vice President Mike Pence made a whistle-stop in Reykjavík. It is not inaccurate to say that the American administration was not popular with the Icelandic population. Nevertheless, at the time, the United States was one of the country's staunchest allies and NATO partners, and a head of state (and partner!) should greet people of all sorts, whether or not we agree with their politics. We would give our visitors a warm welcome and help to facilitate a productive discussion.

Yet I could not resist one small dig: I chose to wear a white pantsuit for the occasion. I have always been wary of wearing white because I have a clumsy habit of dribbling food on myself. No one wants to appear before paparazzi with maple syrup from that morning's breakfast on their lapel. This occasion felt worth the risk. I found and purchased a white pantsuit, along with a rainbow bracelet, and wore it to greet the vice president, Second Lady Karen Pence, and their delegation. (If I'm being really honest, my biggest achievement that day was that my next event was a salt cod tasting, and I managed to go through two hours of eating small canapés and sipping red wine without spilling a single drop!)

If the American vice president was offended by my clothing and bracelet choice, he didn't show it, nor would I have expected him to, and nor was that my goal. He was, after all, a consummate politician and a visitor to the country. He and his wife were extremely friendly and polite, and given that neither Guðni nor especially I had any pressing bilateral issues to discuss (that was for the government officials and politicians), we used the twenty minutes or so of private conversation to keep more of a general dialogue, although I did use my overseas origins to highlight some of what I value most about living in Iceland: tolerance, mutual respect, and a growing diversity. I wasn't there to cause a fuss, but given I had a chance to speak to a global leader most people would never meet, I didn't think a reinforcement of my values would go amiss.

Upon returning home, I checked the news to find out what people thought about my wardrobe choice. (I was never going to comment publicly on it. Well, until now, I guess.) There were some great stories about how some offices surrounding Höfði House, where the meetings took place, had been flying rainbow flags. Company representatives assured journalists that they were not criticizing the American administration's reputation for homophobia. It just so happened that they were celebrating a diversity day!

Eventually, the papers also picked up the fact that I was wearing a color that had come to symbolize the suffragist movement in the United States.

I was grudgingly coming to acknowledge that what I wore mattered more than I wanted it to or believed that it should. But if that was still the reality for women especially, then I needed to exploit that for good. I could send some messages with my fashion choices but also indicate that while I had agreed to play the game of looking good, I wanted to use my platform to promote self-confidence and to question the fundamental assumptions of an industry that is built on making women feel like they are not enough. That is not a message I want children of any gender to receive.

It was a balancing act: Fitting into an external image of a first lady while being true to my own identity. Using fashion to send a message—or sometimes simply for pragmatic reasons—while also downplaying the attention given to physical appearances in general.

Yet that feat of tightrope acrobatics was a picnic compared to the other roles I juggled. My life had become a twenty-four-seven mix of the personal and the public, the professional and the political. That was a whole new challenge.

12

The Balancing Act

Posing with one of the presidential vehicles, a 1942 Packard, before our final open house at Bessastaðir, the presidential residence, June 2024.

"You've been going ninety in a locked garage…
We've got to get you out on the open road."

—Amy Hempel, *At the Gates of the Animal Kingdom*

Give my regards to Guðni. I voted for him."

It's always gratifying to receive a compliment, but in April 2017, when a medical practitioner asked me to pass on greetings to my husband, I couldn't help but feel that she was blurring the public and the private. After all, she was conducting a routine cervical exam on me at the time.

Guðni and I were public figures now, even when undergoing intimate medical procedures. We acknowledged that parts of ourselves were public property, like when constituents asked us to pose with them for photos or to lend our voices to their personal challenges or to break through bureaucratic red tape (none of which we could do). I had anticipated that I'd prioritize my life in the presidential limelight over my career, but what I wasn't prepared for was how much I wanted to push back against preconceptions about my role and how much political capital I'd have to spend to do that.

It began with our living arrangements. They were designed to ensure an easier life, to grease the wheels of a demanding schedule, but by merging the public and private identities so seamlessly, they also made it a bit harder to balance both.

Since the country's independence in 1944, all presidents and their families have lived at Bessastaðir, the official residence. Located on the Álftanes peninsula in a rural area of the capital region, which has been inhabited for about a thousand years, the residence is nearly surrounded by the sea. The main structure was built in the mid-eighteenth century, making it one of the oldest houses in the country. Literally meaning "Bessi's Place"—though no one is really sure who Bessi was—Bessastaðir has been a school for boys and the home of writers and regents, farmers and entrepreneurs. Legend has it that the buildings are also haunted by the evocatively named Apollonia Schwarzkopf, who ended up at the pointy end of an eighteenth-century love triangle and died on the premises under mysterious circumstances.

In 1996, the complex was renovated so that the president and their family no longer needed to live on the second floor of the main building but in a separate house next door. That house, by far the largest in which I had ever lived, was clearly designed with a different family structure than ours in mind: It had a huge dining room and entrance but only two bedrooms upstairs—aside from a vast master bedroom. For the first several years, until the oldest could sleep on his own in the basement bedroom, our children shared bedrooms and used our en suite for showers and baths. We furnished the house ourselves, mostly with IKEA items and a scattering of Lego. The only indications that this house was different from any other in Iceland were the hard-to-polish brass fixtures everywhere and the panic button in the bedroom. (Before we moved in, we were asked which side of the bed Guðni slept on, though I always reckoned the button wouldn't be much use to him if he were the one being attacked.) Most of the staff of the president's office had the key code to enter our home, so on occasion, it felt pleasantly reminiscent of my college dorm, where people came and went as they pleased.

The main building was used for all the ceremonial functions of the president. There Guðni received new ambassadors presenting their credentials and hosted receptions from charities celebrating anniversaries to annual awards presentations. Sometimes together and sometimes separately, we hosted lunches and dinners there. Bessastaðir is not surrounded by fencing or other barriers, and aside from a discreet but twenty-four-hour police presence, the relative lack of security never ceases to impress foreign visitors.

There were advantages to living only a few steps away from work (though those steps could be so windy that a couple of times, my glasses blew off my face). The commute was manageable, and my kids grew up with the children and grandchildren of people who lived or worked on the premises.

We moved to the residence in the autumn, which was fitting because I love autumn in Iceland. The light and colors, the sunny skies but chilly breezes, the smell of the sea and of time passing—it all reminds me of the exhilaration I felt when I first moved to the country in early fall and took the bus every day to my job, then to Icelandic class, then to the little one-bedroom apartment we rented. It reminds me of my babies, since most were born in this season: waiting eagerly for them, giving birth to them, feeding, bathing, walking, comforting them under that wind and that light. Autumn in Iceland evokes so many of my happiest memories.

That first autumn, I was excited about the move to a new home, looking forward to hearing the sea just steps from my back door and seeing the sun set with the sparkling lights of the city in the distance, encircled by a view of mountains and water.

In our private home, we worked hard to keep our roles as parents private too. It was important to us that our children felt at home at Bessastaðir but also that they had a chance to grow up anonymously. I was grateful that they would have some interesting experiences as they aged but never wanted them to feel entitled or act too spoiled. (Guðni's daughter, Rut, was already in her twenties and living on her own when her dad became president. Generally, she was left alone to live her life as a private citizen.)

Shortly after Guðni became president, though, we thought we should eat a meal at the official part of the residence to introduce the kids to the people who worked there and to help them feel at home in the complex where they would be living for the next several years (even though we would eat in our own private home in general). Edda's third birthday in mid-August provided the perfect excuse.

Before we sat down to eat, the kids went exploring. Sæþór loved the replica Viking-age sword that was on display on the second floor, while Donnie stroked all the claws on the polar bear pelt that was hanging in the front stairway, a gift from the government of Greenland. (With few exceptions, all formal gifts belong to the presidency, not to the person who holds the office when the gift is given.) They dubbed the dimly lit basement where centuries-old archaeological artifacts were on display the "creepy" room.

In the dining room itself, where presidents past had enjoyed almost all their meals, a French polished mahogany table (that could extend to seat up to twenty-five) was set for six people. I had mentioned in advance that our toddlers were used to plastic dishes and glasses, but the table was set with real silverware and special porcelain dishes marked with an ornate initial *R*. I later learned it likely stood for *ríkisstjóri* ("regent"). It was the set ordered by Iceland's first and only regent, Sveinn Björnsson, who became the nation's first president upon independence three years later. Presumably, no one thought it was economically advisable to buy a fresh set when this perfectly good, albeit no longer accurately branded, china was available.

As a young family of six, we were used to pasta Bolognese or grilled cheese sandwiches. When delicately pan-fried cod with sautéed broccoli and pumpkin was set before us, I looked carefully at each of my children. On the way over, I had reminded the kids that this was a special occasion for a birthday and that the chef had been working hard to prepare dinner and his feelings would be hurt if they looked at something they were wary of and immediately declared, "I don't like it." It would be much better to find something very nice to say or simply to say, "Thank you."

Donnie immediately squinted suspiciously at his dish and stage whispered to me, "What do we say again if we don't like it?" But the atmosphere, made formal with the landscape paintings by Icelandic greats (on loan from the National Gallery), the polished sterling silver candlesticks, and the bouquet of fresh flowers, somehow improved the kids' behavior, so they all set their cloth napkins on their laps and passed around glasses of juice. (It was allowed for the first meal at Bessastaðir.)

I explained that at formal meals here, toasts would be inevitable and that toasts were when people said nice things about other people or important subjects in general. I lifted my glass and toasted Duncan for scoring a goal in his soccer practice, Donnie for looking after his siblings well, Sæþór for ending the year at his old preschool, and Edda for using the toilet like a big girl.

Then set off a cacophony of *cheers!* from all the kids and an eager rush for their own turns as toastmasters. Sæþór to his dad: "For trying his best as president." Donnie to Iceland in general: "For being so beautiful and safe." As soon as the meal was finished and they all ran off to play hide-and-seek, Guðni and I breathed a small sigh of relief. We'd made it through our first presidential dinner with the toughest guests we'd ever have to host.

When Queen Margrethe II of Denmark paid an official visit to Iceland in December 2018, I asked the children if they would like to meet her. I explained that they should bow or curtsy. After the formal dinner, when she was enjoying a digestif with us in another room, the children came in to meet the monarch. The boys were quiet but polite, while five-year-old Edda was unusually shy, running to bury her face in my shoulder and refusing to look at our distinguished guest. I held her as she whispered sadly in my ear, "I thought you said there'd be a queen." I realized then that Edda's image of a queen was a young beauty in a diaphanous ball gown and sparkling crown, not the smiling elderly lady with no fancy headpiece who sat next to us. Thanks, Disney. ("I'm always a disappointment," the queen told me wryly when I explained to her later what had happened.)

A few years later, then thirteen-year-old Donnie had no such qualms when meeting the queen's son, Crown Prince Frederik.

"Your Royal Highness, may I ask you a question?" he inquired of the heir to the throne in the very room where he'd met the queen years earlier. Almost without waiting for an answer, Donnie continued, "Can you please speak to someone here in Iceland so we don't need to learn Danish in school anymore?"

There were moments, of course, when our roles as the presidential couple disrupted our roles as parents, and those times were the most challenging. We missed sports matches and music concerts and had to reschedule some parent-teacher interviews. On our first foreign trip after the COVID-19 pandemic, we traveled briefly to Denmark to attend the World Pride Games, which coincided with Edda's soccer tournament. My parents, visiting from Canada for the first time in two years, promised to get Edda ready to be collected by another parent. A day later, over in Copenhagen, I received a texted photo of an excited Edda in her soccer gear with the caption: Isn't someone picking her up soon?

My heart sank as I realized that after all the time spent writing speeches, planning wardrobes, booking COVID tests, ordering proof of vaccinations, and all the other pre-travel details, we'd dropped the ball on arranging a pickup for our daughter.

Life for our children at Bessastaðir was like life anywhere else, except that a police officer stepped outside his booth to ask the business of any new face that appeared at the door, and they sometimes got delayed for sports matches because people wanted selfies with their dad. (That reminded me of taking drama lessons with the Canadian prime minister's son; I wondered how many people would grow up saying they played sports with the president's kids.) We hosted birthday parties and sleepovers, movie nights and cupcake-making sessions. On Halloween during the COVID pandemic, we hid treats in each room for the kids to find. Once, I launched the "Bessastaðir Olympics" where each child picked an event (from making a puzzle to building a Lego tower to balancing a ball in the air) and had their performance adjudicated by their siblings.

But for me, life at Bessastaðir was unlike anything I'd known. The lines blurred regularly; in a single entry, my diary would give equal weight to the geopolitical events of the day—"the government collapsed"—and the minutiae of parenting young ones—"D. threw up on our bed!"

If balancing being first lady and being the parent of young'uns could be a challenge at times, I found being both first lady and wife an entirely different maneuver when both roles involved my interaction with the same person but in different ways. In a marriage, both parties are equals (or are at least meant to be!). They make decisions together and work out compromises when they disagree. Both parties have different approaches, strengths, weaknesses, and priorities, but they're equally valid. Guðni may have been sole head of the republic of Iceland, but the republic of Bessastaðir had a leadership of two.

In the public eye and the professional world, Guðni and I were not equals. He was more important, the person whose decisions mattered most, the man in whose orbit everyone else revolved. His choices in those fields could override mine. I can't recall any moments when he banned me from doing something; in fact, he seemed to grow uncomfortable when I mentioned the possibility of him exercising this power. I didn't exactly resent this imbalance. After all, we had gone into this adventure with our eyes open. Or at least I didn't resent *him*. But it gnawed at me.

Most often, my discomfort arose when my input would have been relevant had it been sought. When I was sent into quarantine in late 2021 after exposure to a person who had tested positive for COVID, I called my husband (who was out of town) to explain that I would need to ask someone to take the children to school the next day since I had to isolate. Not to worry, answered Guðni, who seemed to know all about my health issue; he had already made the arrangements. Apparently, the police—who conducted all formal processes of quarantining—had first called the president's chief of staff to tell him I was being placed in quarantine. The chief of staff had then called my husband to make arrangements. It never occurred to anyone that I should be in this chain of communication. That I was livid is an understatement.

I decided early on that to be a happy partner to a head of state, you need self-confidence and an independent nature. Like it or not—and he had asked for it!—Guðni's role was at the center of our lives. He had the right and, I would argue, the need to look to those in his orbit, especially me, for support and encouragement. And I did my best to provide that. But when *I* needed support, I tried to look outside the presidential solar system. Guðni is a wonderful partner, but I knew that he would need to focus on being the best president he could, not on whether I was stressed about clothing choices or moody that I hadn't been included in a photo caption somewhere. Being president, even a nonpolitical one such as my husband, is an all-consuming, twenty-four-seven job. And that job must take priority during the time in which one inhabits it. I didn't talk to family in Canada too often, but there was comfort in knowing they were a FaceTime call away, as were all the old Smashers players and other friends who lived in distant lands. In Iceland, I had friends such as Liz with whom I could gripe or unload stresses, and especially as our time in the public roles wore on, I found more trusted colleagues with whom I could express any concerns.

Most of all, I had spent decades corralling my own experiences into an unwritten guide for calming the inner worries in my head. When I was unexpectedly alone in Togo's capital in the middle of the night, I hadn't been able to seek advice from a partner, so I trusted my instincts. When I had failed miserably as a debater at university, friends could remind me that no one judged me for five minutes of less-than-perfect rhetoric. I could acknowledge that the world didn't revolve around me and that I either had the tools to help myself or the contacts and confidence to ask for it. That freed me up to better support my husband and not distract him from his work.

Or that was my plan at least. Did I break my own rules? Of course. When you've had a bad day or an exciting event, you want to share it with your partner. I couldn't help myself! Even if I knew that griping about something about our joint "work" would likely add to his stress, it alleviated mine simply by getting it off my chest, and I did it more than I care to admit. We created some ground rules though, most notably not to talk about work in the evenings. That stricture held sometimes, and sometimes those rules took an about-face and raced down the road paved with good intentions.

A lifelong commitment to a partner is arguably the most important contract one can make, one that is worth investing all one's energy and efforts and then some. I was independent enough to do everything on my own, and I didn't need his praise or validation to feel like I was on the right path. Plus, I was just so proud of him! In his first six months on the job, trust in the office of the president rose 26 percent from the previous year. A poll conducted four months after Guðni took office gave him a gobsmacking 97 percent approval rating. Even after it normalized, that number would remain high throughout his tenure.

I hoped that the work I was doing increased goodwill towards the presidency. I was certainly enjoying it. One reason was that there was no single "regular" day. I could deliver opening remarks at an international conference, visit an elderly care home, and cohost a reception for a new ambassador. Or I could spend the morning visiting a new office complex, speak to a reporter about a pressing issue, and then attend a theater premiere. For different reasons, I especially enjoyed what I had dubbed "no makeup" days, when I had no meetings or events and just worked at my laptop.

But when little things bugged me, I sometimes really let them get to me. And it was hard to know where to express my displeasure, which for me is a more effective way to feel better than simply stuffing all my emotions inside. I wasn't alone, and I generally wasn't lonely, but sometimes I had to prioritize confidentiality over releasing my frustrations. Despite my decade-plus of living in Iceland, where advance planning can hardly be described as a national pastime, I found it difficult to adjust to the last-minute nature of protocol-heavy events. Often I received a schedule only a day before an event, with virtually no background information on people we were about to meet or places we were about to visit.

As first lady, I was pressured to pick causes, especially because I had been vocal about my intention to be active. I had extensive experience promoting Icelandic literature and tourism, but in one meeting, I was told I needed to focus on "problem" areas too. How about something with children? It was all "part of it" I was told. But part of what? My nonexistent job description? My role as wife?

Sometimes I wondered if perhaps the areas I felt most passionate about shining a light on might have simply been considered too controversial or too much hassle to actually put effort into.

I was keen on showcasing diversity and inclusion within Icelandic society. When I moved to Iceland in 2003, 4.3 percent of the population were first- or second-generation immigrants. When Guðni became president in 2016, this figure had grown to 10.3 percent, and by 2024, the figure was 20.1 percent. As an Icelander who had acquired citizenship as an adult, I knew how it might feel to have my formal acceptance into society recognized with more pomp than the form letter I had received in the mail in 2008. In the first months of Guðni's tenure, I suggested that we hold a reception at Bessastaðir for everyone who had acquired Icelandic citizenship in the previous few months. It would be an opportunity to officially welcome those who had chosen to make Iceland their home and to explain our mutual obligations. I envisaged journalists interviewing new citizens at the reception and perhaps inviting a group of schoolchildren to do projects on inclusion. There was so much potential.

My enthusiastic suggestion was met with skepticism. "You are the first lady of all Icelanders, not the first lady of immigrants" was the response as I recall it when I asked for a meeting to discuss the matter. I merely nodded and moved on to a different subject. I did not yet have the confidence in the role to speak back, nor did I even realize that I could. I needed to choose my battles.

But there would be other opportunities to highlight the growing multiculturalism in Icelandic society. In early 2019, I was sent an email invitation to visit the Grand Mosque in Iceland. Housed in a repurposed building and opened in 2012, the mosque offers religious and cultural seminars, Arabic lessons, and other activities. It sounded like an interesting opportunity to highlight diversity within Iceland. But before I accepted any invitations, I liked to learn a bit more, especially about whether the visit could be tied to a specific anniversary or occasion. (There were far more invitations than time to accept them all, so those tied to a special date would generally get priority.) I replied to the president's office that it looked interesting and asked for more details.

Three weeks later, I received a Facebook message from an acquaintance who visited the mosque regularly. She said that officials hadn't yet had a response from the office to their invitation. Surprised, I emailed my colleague again to ask for an update, since I had not heard anything either. Now I got a response quickly: the chief of staff had "concerns" about the organization issuing the invitation and wanted to investigate further. I was told he would be discussing the issue with the president soon. To summarize: No one had responded to the inviting organization, and no one had responded to my request for further information, because no effort had been made to solicit that information. Only when I followed up was I told that a staffer was going to discuss the matter with my husband, who was not at all involved with the invitation.

How would you feel?

Even without the additional information I had asked for, the way the request was handled made the decision for me. I would be visiting the mosque. I did so soon afterwards, becoming, I believe, the first member of a presidential couple to visit a mosque in Iceland.

Were these roadblocks a result of prejudice towards a new group of Icelanders? Sexism towards a female spouse who had been more active than her predecessors on solo engagements in service to the nation? Or were they simply the reality of a busy and overworked office that had to prioritize their projects? I could guess, but I would never know for sure. The result was the same, as was my frustration.

Despite setbacks like these, I reminded myself that I was loving it all, that it was an honor and a privilege to have this position. And when you really love something, when you want to devote your heart and soul to it, all the small things frustrate you. If I had been ambivalent about serving as first lady, I think the microaggressions and tiny details would have washed over me.

But I recognized that this was a once-in-a-lifetime opportunity to have an influence, and when that ambition and drive were stymied, whether intentionally or through lack of resources, it was discouraging and demoralizing. For the missed opportunities, the stunted potential. To paraphrase writer Amy Hempel, it felt as if I were going ninety in a locked garage.

During those first years, I realized that I would need to be my own biggest champion. I needed to trust my own intuition about what to let go and where to push back. To remind myself that I was a good person with good intentions. I needed to work within the parameters of the support I was receiving if I wanted to achieve my objectives and have the confidence to stick to my guns when I thought the circumstances warranted it. I needed to find the right balance of serving as first lady and keeping my children grounded and secure, while also supporting my spouse during his challenging moments and maintaining my own identity as his equal. Easy-peasy.

But I didn't have any regrets and was doing my best. I had had opportunities I had never anticipated and believed I was really making a difference. Sometimes, it felt just like a fairy tale.

13

Fairy Tale

With heads of state of Norway, Denmark, Finland, and Sweden as well as other Nordic royals at King Carl XVI Gustaf of Sweden's Golden Jubilee celebrations, September 2023 in Stockholm.

"Guðni and Eliza are a hit. They are the Barack and Michelle Obama of Iceland."

—Seasoned reporter Heimir Már Pétursson on our state visit to Denmark, January 2017

A horse-drawn carriage is a surprisingly smooth ride. Had I spent any time imagining what it would be like to travel in one, I would have thought that the four wheels provided little cushioning, that the seating would be uncomfortable, and that the sheer unpredictability of having four animals pulling the vehicle would result in a less-than-luxurious mode of transport.

Not so. (Perhaps twenty-first-century horses are better trained.)

These are the thoughts I had as my dreamlike fairy-tale existence as first lady continued with state visits outside Iceland. Just like in fiction, these involved tiaras (not mine), ball gowns (bought on sale), princesses (my traveling companions), and yes, on occasion, a horse-drawn carriage.

My surprise at the smoothness of carriage rides arose during a brief jaunt from stable to palace accompanied by Queen Silvia of Sweden on a state visit that Guðni and I made to the country in January 2018. I didn't share my equine insight with Her Majesty, mostly letting her steer the direction of the small talk. (Later, as we walked inside, she complimented me on the maroon faux fur scarf I was wearing. I thanked her politely, but it took superhuman effort not to add that I had bought it on sale at the local supermarket. I cannot rid myself of the Canadian instinct to play down luxury looks and play up canny spending.)

At that time, I had gained some experience at participating in state visits, though I doubt that any nonroyal ever really becomes blasé about being one of the "principals" on such an occasion. In fact, the real fairy-tale aspect of these journeys had nothing to do with clothing.

The first visit was, understandably, by far the most nerve-racking. As per tradition, due to Iceland's history as a former Danish colony, it was to Denmark. There was no horse-drawn carriage on that occasion, but we were collected from our hotel in the famous Store Krone, the name given to the 1958 silver Rolls-Royce used by the Royal House for foreign guests. As we proceeded the short distance to Amalienborg Palace in central Copenhagen, hopeful faces craned for a glimpse of a famous mug inside the car. (Often, we caught their disappointment that this was not so.) Danish and Icelandic flags lined the streets, and crowds of school-children waved miniature versions. From construction workers to shopkeepers to businesspeople on their way to a meeting, locals stopped, waved, and took photos.

For the last half mile of the journey, our procession was flanked by dozens of the Royal Hussars on horseback, dressed in their finest. We exited the vehicle to greet Her Majesty Queen Margrethe II and her husband, Prince Henrik, to the live soundtrack of a brass military fanfare.

Each state visit has its own unique takes on the traditional format, which stretches back centuries. They involve some ceremonial element, for example the president inspecting troops, and some social element, such as a formal dinner. I'm unsure which came first: state visit template or fairy-tale formula; either way, they bore a strong resemblance, with the exception of ogres and wolves in the latter.

Even in modern times, the beauty of a state visit is how it provides an opportunity for two nations to nurture their bonds of friendship, to showcase areas where they can learn from each other, and to forge personal, cultural, and professional connections. Guðni and I went on nine state visits and three official visits (to Greenland, the Faroe Islands, and Scotland) during his tenure as president. (A state visit takes place when one head of state visits another country at the invitation of the host nation's head of state. The three official visits were not at the invitation of heads of state.) We also hosted visits from the heads of state of Finland, India, Germany, Denmark, and the three Baltic countries (Estonia, Latvia, and Lithuania). From the outset, I was surprised at both the degree to which these visits were choreographed (down to the minute) and the paucity of background briefings before visits.

While almost all such visits contained the same greatest hits—official receiving ceremony, exchange of gifts, tête-à-tête with counterpart, visits to Parliament, numerous stops relating to the theme of the trip, and a (usually gala) dinner—they were each also unique in their own way. For me, that included military jets meeting our commercial plane as we arrived in local airspace (Sweden), a royal representative escorting us from our hotel to a palace (Norway), and the entire diplomatic corps in a city coming out to shake hands with us (Poland). If I let the pomp seep into my soul while Iceland's national anthem played, I usually found my eyes getting moist and my lips quivering.

I was both excited and apprehensive about that first state visit to Denmark, which took place less than six months after Guðni took office. We would be accompanied by a twelve-person official delegation (and an even larger business delegation), including the minister of foreign affairs. Reporters back home would trail our events to comment on how the new president was faring in his first foray onto the world stage. Would he hold his fork correctly? Bow deeply enough? What would I be wearing? (As it turned out, the feedback was mostly glowing—we were even compared to the Obamas.) Guðni relished the irony that he would be staying in a literal palace; on a visit to Denmark just a year earlier, he had prepared by googling "cheap hotel near train station." Meanwhile, I still felt like I was the hero in my own fairy tale, the country girl who would soon be donning a long dress and (borrowed) jewels and dining in a gilded palace.

Yet lurking at the back of my mind was the insecurity that I might inadvertently bring dishonor to my adopted nation. I couldn't speak any Danish, which people born in Iceland are taught at school (although I could speak French, the mother tongue of Prince Henrik). I just had to be myself and trust that that would be enough. I was not nervous about speaking with royalty and was especially looking forward to spending some time with then Crown Princess Mary, a onetime fellow Commonwealth citizen (she grew up in Australia) who, like me, had met her Nordic spouse abroad and ended up moving to his country, learning the language, and having four children with him. But I worried about dribbling sauce on my gala dress or making an offhand remark about a sensitive subject. I wasn't even sure how much I was expected to speak (or not). I had no guidelines under which to work beyond my own common sense and intelligence. I felt untethered but very excited about what was to come.

As with all state visits, we had a full schedule with virtually every minute allocated to a specific activity. On that first trip, we each had an interesting program focused on business and cultural ties. One stop was at the Copenhagen Hospitality School, accompanied by Crown Prince Frederik and Crown Princess Mary. One of the only tips Guðni and I had been given before the visit was to avoid being photographed with food or drink; the resulting images were never flattering. We arrived at the school, a bank of paparazzi capturing our every move, and were presented with… oysters. What to do? We took our cue from Prince Frederik, who smilingly accepted the mollusk, turned his back to the cameras, and slurped it down.

I also took part in a spouse program, a section of the trip when the head of state would be occupied with bilateral meetings and other visits. It was my first program as the guest rather than the host, after having shown Ban Soon-taek around Reykjavík for a morning soon after Guðni took office. Having seen well-dressed, demure-looking spouses watch traditional dances or visit art galleries, I had blithely noted in my diary that "I hope it's not some wifey domestic program." I was asked to share my personal interests in advance with the organizers. I listed them as women entrepreneurs, political developments, and immigration. This first state visit spouse program included a fascinating visit to the UN City in Copenhagen, a hub for eleven United Nations agencies, as well as a discussion with directors from Princess Mary's eponymous foundation...and a trip to a local preschool to see some of the foundation's work in action. (It was of course only this section and a quick sip of champagne at the culinary school that were covered in the *Daily Mail*, which noted that the crown princess "and mother of four dazzled" in Oscar de la Renta. I am not sure if the similar article on the crown prince and Guðni's stops mentioned how many children each of them has.) It was all very interesting of course, and I went along with the proposals that had been presented to me in advance of the visit. I didn't think I had any other choice.

When the visit was finished and we'd returned home, I took stock. How did it go? It was a pleasure to spend time with the Danish royals. They were kind to a fault and very helpful to this wide-eyed couple from Iceland taking their first tentative steps onto the world stage. I was grateful for the tremendous amount of work so many people had undertaken to make sure the visit went off without a hitch, but I also compared my contribution to those of others: Guðni delivered numerous speeches and other informal remarks, and the staff at the office of the president had been working overtime for days on end. And then there was me: I did my best to ask intelligent questions and remain engaged with the diverse program, but I felt like my main contribution to the trip had been to smile for the cameras and showcase different (mostly) Icelandic outfits each day.

I also thought about the next steps. We had met so many interesting people and learned so many important things, but where could we go with that? The places we saw got a boost of press attention, and some of Guðni's visits were used to announce a new agreement or pay tribute to a certain anniversary. But what about the places I saw on my spouse program? What happened after we left and after I had acquired information about them? Was I meant to share that with a similar group in Iceland? Work harder to promote a specific issue? Introduce a new concept or research trend or approach to people back home? I was determined that these visits would be more than merely efforts to keep me occupied.

My own follow-up from that first visit was to try and undertake activities that would have a "what next," whether that was through connecting groups with their Icelandic counterparts or sharing some of the new knowledge I had acquired. I met with representatives from UN Women Iceland as a follow-up to the UN City stop in Copenhagen, and we discussed opportunities for me to help them in future events or campaigns.

But I decided I also wanted to use these visits to confound outdated expectations about female spouses of male heads of state. The most obvious way to do this was to use my voice and not appear merely as some sort of well-dressed prop who smilingly encouraged her husband and showcased her maternal side with plentiful photo ops of interacting with children while wearing heels and pearls. On our next trip to Norway, I enthusiastically agreed to a suggestion by colleagues and delivered a speech on gender equality during my "spouse program." The following year in Sweden, after my brief stint in the horse-drawn carriage, I spoke on literary traditions and at an event on tourism. My persistence, though it did not feel particularly structured, was beginning to pay off, and the staff at the office took on the extra workload without complaining.

Not that my initiative was always welcomed or heeded by those organizing the events. I delivered remarks on Iceland's literary heritage that were billed as part of a "seminar on reading among children and youth" that featured a panel with six women and one man. On another occasion, my interest in the promotion of Icelandic literature was interpreted as a trip to a children's reading center. Before one visit, Guðni received an advance briefing from the foreign ministry while I got printouts from Wikipedia on the most famous of the people we were to meet.

Eventually, I realized there could be no room for nuance in sharing my thoughts on how I could play a constructive role in a state visit. It's a persistent perception that first ladies' interests often relate to children, so I said that when Guðni and I traveled together, I would not take part in events that featured me with children when my husband wasn't there. Sometimes my colleagues criticized me for this, told me that I was being unhelpful to our generous hosts. It turns out that to be a nice first lady, I sometimes had to be a nasty woman. I pointed out when I thought a delegation wasn't gender balanced enough and took note that even when the entire group was more evenly split, until the gender balance at the office of the president itself shifted, it was often mostly women who traveled with me on a spouse program while the men accompanied my husband.

The joy far outweighed the gripes, however. I only wish I had a photographic memory in which to store the elation of meeting volunteers and leaders and visionaries and activists from around the world. To be able to recall at will the beautiful buildings we visited, music we heard, and food we tasted would be divine. I visited UNICEF and a women's shelter in Greenland. I delivered speeches to entrepreneurs in Warsaw, Ljubljana, Halifax, and Bratislava. I visited start-up incubators or companies in Tokyo, Oslo, and Tallinn. The best events were those that led to some sort of follow-up or deepened connections between our countries, whether that was through formal agreements or simply increased visits. Sometimes I received a group of people back in Iceland who had a connection to someone I met on a state visit; it was in nurturing these links that I found the most reward.

Almost every trip featured magical moments. Despite my previous brush with royalty on my backpacking trip in Benin, I was still that small-town, postcard-collecting, book-categorizing country girl. In Helsinki for the onc hundredth anniversary of Finnish independence, we greeted the other Nordic heads of state. It was the third time in as many months that we had seen the king and queen of Norway, and after I offered the briefest of curtsies, the queen leaned in to kiss me on both cheeks. As I withdrew, I realized that I had left a small lipstick mark on her cheek. Too nervous to point it out myself, I hoped one of the many attentive ladies-in-waiting would notice, but I confess that Queen Sonja stepped out onto the balcony of the presidential palace with rosier cheeks than she had expected.

At dinner that evening, I sat across from a former Finnish president. He mentioned that he had spent some time in Africa, and I immediately launched into some stories about my backpacking trip in the western part of the continent. "I have been once to Africa too!" was my enthusiastic message, and surely that was more interesting than chitchat about the weather. It only became clear after dinner that I had been speaking with Martti Ahtisaari, a Nobel Peace Prize winner for his work on resolving international conflicts in Africa and elsewhere. Whether he had judged me for committing a small-talk faux pas or was refreshed by my innocent enthusiasm for a new topic of conversation, I would never know.

Sometimes my old world and my new ones merged in beautiful ways. In October 2019, I traveled to Tokyo for the first time since my backpacking trip more than fifteen years earlier. This time, I had no need to look to the kindness of a stranger to find a place to stay, but I did manage to look up that same woman, Chizuru, who had been so helpful to me so many years before. She introduced me to her two children, and we went out for a noodle lunch together, just as we had before, this time marveling over life's beautiful unpredictability. Back in 2003, when I was dressed in my Teva sandals and one of only three T-shirts I had, no one could have guessed that our next meeting would be when I visited again to attend the enthronement of the new emperor of Japan.

The most surreal foreign trip moment didn't happen during a state visit but when Guðni and I were in Denmark to attend the crown prince's fiftieth birthday gala celebration (which is surreal in and of itself, I suppose). The schedule was just as rigid as on a state visit, but this occasion featured the heads of state of all the other Nordic countries and representatives of most other European royal houses.

Many of us were invited to stay at Fredensborg Palace, which was about an hour's drive from Copenhagen, where the gala dinner was to take place. The dress code was white tie and orders. This means jackets with tails for the men, long dresses for the women (tiaras for those who own them, i.e., royals), and sashes with any Danish orders we had been awarded. (During that first state visit to Denmark, Guðni had been made a knight of the Order of the Elephant, and I had been granted the Grand Cross of the Order of Dannebrog.) Clothing and orders donned, we boarded the "luxury coach" that was to transport us to the palace. We sat in the front half of the bus with various other guests: the king and queen of Sweden, king and queen of Belgium, king and queen of the Netherlands, crown prince of Norway, and more. Various assistants and ladies-in-waiting were in the back half of the bus.

Conversation was light as we drove along the highway towards the capital, diamonds glittering in the afternoon sun. I practiced my French with the Belgian royals. We talked of summer plans and the best time of year to visit Iceland. Sweden's Queen Silvia was silent about my dress choice, which is just as well, as this one had been purchased online in an 80-percent-off sale. We were only about ten minutes into the ride when a traditionally clad Danish aide-de-camp tapped me on the arm and delicately pointed out that my sash was over the wrong shoulder.

This may sound like a minor detail, and while 99 percent of

the population would never notice, one member of the 1 percent might just be the queen of Denmark, our host for the evening. I did not want her to think that Icelanders didn't know how to dress for white tie galas. I needed to maintain national dignity and move the sash to the other shoulder.

There was just one problem: to keep it from slipping, my sash had been painstakingly sewn to my ball gown.

"I have some double-sided tape," Queen Máxima of the Netherlands said to me when she overheard what was going on. "We'll get this figured out." Queen Máxima was born and raised in Argentina and had married into a European royal family, learning Dutch and winning over the hearts of the Dutch people. Perhaps she understood a thing or two about being a fish out of water. We had about twenty minutes before our arrival in Copenhagen.

Queen Máxima's husband, King Willem-Alexander of the Netherlands, jovially assured me that "no one will mind" but offered to switch seats with me. He moved across the aisle to join Guðni and discuss something other than wardrobe malfunctions.

But the double-sided tape didn't solve the more urgent challenge of removing the sash without destroying my purple faux silk dress.

Just as I was about to resign myself to a lifetime of ridicule in Danish tabloids, I noticed that the aide-de-camp who had pointed out the protocol violation in the first place was wearing a ceremonial dagger as part of his uniform.

I asked if I could borrow it and handed the weapon to the queen of the Netherlands.

As we bumped along the road, Queen Máxima held the knife to my neck and, with surgical precision, clipped away at every strand of thread, efficiently removing the sash and leaving both my dress and my neck intact. We spent much of the rest of the journey sharing stories about learning new languages and visiting interesting places.

When we arrived at Christiansborg Palace for the gala dinner and walked down a long hall in front of flashing cameras, only the most eagle-eyed observer would have noticed that the sash was marginally covering my Danish honors.

A misplaced accessory may have been one of the strangest moments on such a visit, but the overall excursion that stands closest to my heart is our 2023 trip to Canada, possibly the first time a "principal" has been on a state visit to their own hometown.

Knowing that virtually every minute of our time was scheduled, we flew in a day early so we would have a chance to spend a few hours with my family. On our holiday visits to Canada with the kids, our days are spent in casual clothes reading books, playing games, and indulging in my mother's bountiful cooking. Mom and Dad knew something was different this time when two unmarked RCMP vehicles pulled up to the gate of the farmhouse to conduct a quick security preclearance in advance of our visit.

Although officials are always aware when a head of state is visiting a country, security needs are usually determined on a case-by-case basis; in Canada, for an Icelandic head of state on vacation, twenty-four-hour security is not required. But on a state visit, there is no room to maneuver once the plane lands, even if the formal program has not yet begun.

So for an afternoon on the farm, we showed up with casual clothes and enjoyed plenty of good cooking, but not before my mother offered the officers freshly baked cookies and showed them where the bathroom was.

Thus fairy tale and real life merged in a beautiful way. I had always felt a thrill to hear the Icelandic national anthem played, to see flags flying in honor of our visit, to greet another head of state in the climax of a time-honored ceremony. But to do so also with the Maple Leaf flying, with my parents and other family members watching, made it all that much more special.

At the state dinner in Rideau Hall that first evening, Governor General Mary Simon delivered remarks, during which she acknowledged my Ottawa-area origins.

"We are proud of all you have accomplished in your adopted homeland of Iceland," she said in her speech. "You have been a great advocate for gender equality and for the immigrant experience and a brilliant example for Canada overseas."

We departed Ottawa at 6 a.m. for a day in Halifax to promote business ties, and the day after that, we found ourselves in St. John's (for the first time since our honeymoon in 2004) to talk literature (me), cod wars (Guðni), and geothermal energy potential (both of us at separate events). But there was even more unpredictability, even sentimentality, to come on this fairy-tale trip.

The office published photos and press releases for all aspects of the visit, but despite the personal connection I had with Ottawa, there was only one moment that made the Canadian national news. Our commercial flight to Toronto was delayed by seven hours, meaning that we had to cancel a special investment event in Canada's largest city. In the meantime, we were in St. John's with no plans and no place to be.

First, we got a guided tour of Signal Hill, a national historic site. But once that was complete, I could see the protocol team looking nervous about how to entertain an entire national delegation for an undetermined number of hours. There were only so many museums in town, but there was a brewery. Not, I hasten to add, that a team of public servants, esteemed business owners, and one presidential couple wanted to start imbibing in the late morning. But the Quidi Vidi Brewery did offer a pleasant location to relax for a few hours, drinking coffee and later having lunch.

I, too, was trying hard to think of something memorable to keep us occupied for a while. I brainstormed a bit with the Canadian delegation. There was one unique ritual for making honorary Newfoundlanders and Labradorians out of visitors. Maybe it would be possible to rustle up a qualified individual to induct all the Icelanders—and some of the Canadians too—into the club?

Thirty minutes later, a young man clad in bright-yellow waterproof overalls and a big fisherman's hat appeared to show us all what a traditional "screech in" was all about. Banging a long staff on the ground to silence the crowd, he announced, "My name is Skipper Dickie, and I'm from—" His lilt was so thick I didn't catch his hometown, and I regretted I'd never be able to send him a thank-you card when it was all over. "I wanted to introduce myself, because in Newfoundland and Labrador, that's what we does," he added. "Be proud of where you're from because it makes you the person you are."

After asking Guðni and me to share our address in Iceland, he elaborated on some of the traditions around this event. First, the vocabulary: "Are ye screechers?" he asked us all.

After several lessons and repetitions, we were able to chorus the answer: "Indeed I is, me ol' cock, and long may your big jib draw!"

After the lingo, it was on to local delicacies: Skipper Dickie handed out cubes of baloney (which he dubbed Newfoundland steak and said was "chock full of vitamin X and W"), then a shot of the local schnapps (the screech part of the ceremony) to wash it down.

The screech provided liquid courage for the final and most infamous part of the ritual: kissing a cod. That's right. Our state visit to Canada ended with a personal encounter with a frozen fish. After each of us had stepped forward to press our lips against the frozen ones of the (unnamed) cod, Skipper Dickie declared us all honorary Newfoundlanders and Labradorians, with certificates to prove it.

In the end, it was this addition of numerous Icelanders and a head of state to the ranks of honorary Newfoundlanders that was featured on CBC's *The National* news broadcast that evening. "We Icelanders know a thing or two about cod, but we do not introduce foreigners to our island in this manner," Guðni joked with host Adrienne Arsenault during the short interview. "It was a very enjoyable occasion."

And so my fairy-tale state visit came to an end. There was more sentimentality—and frozen fish—than I had anticipated, but I wouldn't have wanted it any other way. In my story, I was neither a fragile princess nor a dragon-slaying warrior, but I was becoming the master of my own plotline.

I was also the foil in my husband's own tale, the extroverted sidekick to his thoughtful and gentle leader. There was—and is—no one to whom I would rather play official second fiddle. But in real life, we were equals, and I also wanted to have plenty of solo adventures.

Life as first lady would afford that too.

14

Solo First Lady

Selfie taken at the Zaatari refugee camp in Jordan during a visit with UN Women, September 2017.

"During my years in New York I learned a lot about diplomacy from Secretary General Boutros-Ghali. I think I could have learned even more from his wife."

—Madeleine Albright, in her memoir *Madam Secretary*

We hear you would like to eat Omani food in the traditional way," said the owner of a small restaurant in the village of Misfat Al Abriyeen, high in the Hajar mountains. Indeed, yes, I would.

I sat cross-legged—well, as cross-legged as my non-yoga-toned body can get—on a straw mat on the floor in a covered outdoor part of the restaurant. It was December, but the afternoon temperature was still 82°F, the sun blazing through a cloudless sky. I had reached this spot by climbing through slim entryways and up slippery, precarious steps. There are no cars in the ancient village, whose stone homes were constructed around narrow walkways long before the advent of the automobile. The area was lush with banana, papaya, and date trees.

It could have been like any number of blissful moments on one of my solo backpacking trips of yore: an excursion to a quiet but built for tourists dining area and breaking bread with strangers who wanted to share the hospitality of their homeland. And while I was solo in the sense that I was the only foreigner there, I had arrived with a guide, an official government minder, a personal security guard who I suspected had a government-issued handgun hidden under her abaya, and a handful of other officials. So not quite like the old days.

Although my entourage was more bureaucratic than backpacker,

I was determined that I would show them curious, independent traveler Eliza and not some glamorous image of a president's wife. Sure, my top was silk and my jacket was created by an Icelandic designer, but I had just traipsed up those slick steps myself. I was certainly going to eat the Omani way—whatever that meant.

Several men paraded out large platters of mutton, rice with onions, fruit, chickpeas, olives, and chopped salad with fragrant fresh herbs on the side. The mutton was already cut into pieces and had been cooked "a long time"; usually this meant for days, but they didn't have that much advance notice that I would be visiting. The mutton's head crowned the top of the dish, its gray tongue sticking out and teeth bared.

Eating Omani style would be eating with my hands, I assumed, sitting on the ground in communal fashion. My hosts tore the choicest pieces of meat from the bone and passed them to me.

As it turned out, the Omani way wasn't just communal eating, it was *what* we were to eat. One of the restaurant owners lifted the sheep's head and passed it to me.

"Break the jawbone off, and use that to dig into the brain. It's the best part," he instructed. Did I notice a daring twinkle in his eye? After over a decade in Iceland, I had become grudgingly accustomed to the annual Thorrablót traditions of consuming fermented sheep's parts back home, but never had I been asked to gouge into a steamed cerebrum, encircled by distinguished men eagerly awaiting my reaction.

Now was not the time to pause. If I was going to do this, I needed to do it with gusto. I accepted the mutton's head, broke off the jawbone, dipped it into the brain stem, and after a bit of scraping around, scooped out a small piece of jellied, pillow-soft mutton brain. I popped it in my mouth, chewed, swallowed, and smiled—more from relief that I would likely never need to taste it again than from pleasure at its flavor. The men proceeded to show me photos of then Prince Charles, who had visited the same spot the previous year, although apparently he only partook of the tea. Hereditary monarch: Zero. Small-town first lady: One.

A tally no one would ever care about was not what made the moment so special. I was buoyed by once again being on my own in a fairly distant country, experiencing another moment between strangers that I adored (the experience, that is, rather than the strangers). That energized me, but even better, now I had the added benefit of unofficially representing Iceland. When I had my rose-tinted glasses on—and they seemed to magically appear whenever I was traveling and having fun with new adventures—the possibilities of my role in promoting cross-cultural communications and lasting friendships seemed vast.

I was in Oman for a very short trip to attend an international conference where I would accept the role of United Nations special ambassador for tourism and the Sustainable Development Goals. It was 2017, the UN's International Year of Sustainable Tourism for Development, and Taleb Rifai, the head of the United Nations World Tourism Organization, had met me a few months earlier at a dinner Guðni and I hosted during his visit to Iceland. I think he had been briefed about my interest in travel and tourism in advance of that evening in Reykjavík, and during dinner, he invited me to be one of twelve special ambassadors that they were naming in honor of the special year. The list included Ellen Johnson Sirleaf, the president of Liberia; Luis Guillermo Solís Rivera, the president of Costa Rica; and Marie-Louise Coleiro Preca, the president of Malta. The job description was vague; I could do what I wanted around the goal of promoting sustainable tourism and its potential to foster peace and social cohesion, but the role included solo international visits, not just delivering short remarks when I was traveling with Guðni.

I was thrilled to have been asked. The role aligned perfectly with my interests and was also an opportunity to promote one of Iceland's strongest brand values—sustainability. Tourism is the country's largest export sector and contributes about 8 percent of Iceland's total GDP. Here was an area where I could really step into my own, a sphere that I could own and do with as I wished, helping to tangibly promote Iceland's positive reputation on the global stage. It wasn't the fairy tale of a highly choreographed and ancient tradition that one experienced on a state visit, but it was fulfilling one dream where I felt I could make a difference.

Despite my immediate enthusiasm, there was some discussion within the president's office as to whether I should accept such an invitation. No Icelandic first lady had taken on a position such as this before. How would it benefit Iceland? And of course, was I allowed to accept these sorts of titles since I wasn't serving in an official role? I knew immediately, though, that this was something important to me, even though I also knew that the very small and overworked team at the presidential office would not be able to provide additional support to really maximize the potential of each trip. I was going to take what I could get, and if that meant fewer official meetings on a trip, little social media or other coverage, and not as many opportunities to eat a sheep's brain, so be it.

The special ambassador role, the first title that I had earned on my own, helped to launch me into a new level of independent actions as first lady in which I took on a variety of solo tasks beyond a few speeches here and there. I was stepping into my own, helping to add value to what the office of the president could offer, raising Iceland's profile abroad, and reminding folks that spouses were more than silent accessories. I was making the most of this opportunity, to the best of my ability. I was empowered to speak up, to focus on areas where I knew I could make a positive impact.

The act of actually speaking up also came with a growing sense of pride in my own adaptability. I felt comfortable in front of a crowd, but there were always moments one couldn't fully prepare for, although I was learning to roll with the punches. One winter's day, I had agreed to stop by a Reykjavík secondary school to attend the final day of its International Week. When I arrived, I was greeted by the school principal and vice principal, who escorted me to their auditorium. A podium and mic were set up on the stage.

"You can sit here," someone explained to me, gesturing to one of three chairs on the stage. "We have you set to deliver your speech first, after the opening remarks." I noticed two sets of note cards on the remaining two chairs.

"Right, thank you," I replied, frantically rushing through my mind to recall if I had misread the initial invite or whether they had quite innocently forgotten to mention I would be expected to deliver a speech (the latter, it turns out). I spent the three minutes of the school principal's welcome desperately plotting a rough speech in my mind, hoping that my Icelandic vocabulary wouldn't fail me. Thank goodness I was older and more confident than my days at the Lit back in Toronto. Now I knew that in off-the-cuff remarks, long pauses to rack your brains for an additional point can actually come across as building dramatic tension.

My solo gigs weren't confined to international events or my newly acquired title of special ambassador. I undertook a fair bit of domestic travel on my own too. Some of the early visits were connected to an award called the Eyrarrósin, which was a grant given to cultural projects outside the capital region. I took over as patron from my predecessor, Dorrit, one of only two such patronages that were passed down to me. But soon, I began to get invitations on my own. I traveled to Akureyri to deliver the commencement address at the university there. I visited the Westfjords to take part in a new camp for bilingual children, opened a knitting festival in Blönduós, and spoke at a travel conference in Höfn in the Southeast. These opportunities to meet people in different corners of the country, to undertake diverse projects and lead unique initiatives, all contributed to a multifaceted patchwork of connection in Icelandic society. I was endlessly honored to witness it and take part in some small way.

Someone from the president's office traveled with me on these domestic trips. If flight schedules were such that I would be in a community for several hours although I was invited for just one short event, I often asked whether it would be possible to add more stops, perhaps a visit to an assisted living facility or some local businesses. At first, I was told that I was not going on an official visit, and no more stops should be added. (The message I heard: Who do you think you are? The president?) But after insisting that I felt I could add more value by making good use of my time, this began to change.

As I began to prove myself more, I sometimes stood in for Guðni when he was unable to attend an event. To be clear, I never replaced him for any of his official duties; rather, I made appearances at events when they conflicted with his previous commitments. I visited the Westman Islands for the annual festival commemorating the end of the infamous 1973 volcanic eruption when Guðni had already committed to be elsewhere, and on that occasion, I managed to add on plenty of extra stops. I also hosted my own receptions at Bessastaðir or stood in if Guðni was delayed at other events.

If I thought I could be of help wearing my first lady hat while on personal business, I did that too. In March 2017, I traveled to Washington, DC, to take part in the Association of Writers and Writing Programs annual conference. (The Iceland Writers Retreat had a booth where we could talk about the work we were doing.) It was my first time traveling to the United States since becoming first lady, and even though it was not a first lady–related trip and the Iceland Writers Retreat was paying for it, protocol dictated that the Icelandic embassy be informed of the visit and that I travel on my Icelandic diplomatic passport rather than my Canadian one.

When I arrived at customs, the officer asked me whether it was my first visit to the United States. I explained that it was not, but it was the first time I was traveling to the country on an Icelandic passport.

He gazed sternly at me, silently flipped through some pages of my passport, and looked back at me again.

"Do you like cookies?" he asked, neutral expression on his face.

Was this a trick question? He wasn't smiling and didn't look like he was waiting for me to laugh. If I answered incorrectly, would I be detained? For what? Violation of the sweet tooth act?

He was waiting for an answer. I had to decide quickly, and honesty is always the best policy. "Um, yes?" I tentatively responded. Surely I couldn't face sanctions for liking cookies?

The officer gave a curt nod. He reached under his desk, took out a full box of Girl Scout cookies (Samoas, if you want specifics), and handed them to me. "Welcome to the United States," he said, a grin flashing across his face for the briefest of moments. (It was a more innocent time.)

I was busy most of the trip at the AWP conference, but the former American ambassador to Iceland had asked if I would be interested in having a courtesy call with a good friend of his—Senator Elizabeth Warren. That would be my first-lady assignment on the trip. I attended the meeting with Iceland's ambassador to the United States, Geir Haarde, who was also a former prime minister. The official request was for a "courtesy call," but Senator Warren had visited Iceland several times in the past, and the embassy wanted to use the occasion to raise some specific topics.

Senator Warren was friendly, laid-back, and unintimidating despite her obvious intellectual brilliance, and I was thrilled to have had this half hour with her. I also gave myself a silent pat on the back. I had taken the initiative back in Iceland to find out whether there were people I should try to meet with in DC, and this was the fruit of that labor. I had possibly earned some cachet with the embassy in DC, who saw the potential in using a visit from me—even though I was in town for something else—to arrange otherwise hard-to-confirm meetings. It was exactly how I felt I could be useful, and that motivated me to aim even higher the next time I was in town.

Later that evening, I was at my friend's house checking the news online when I caught one of the top stories. After our meeting, Senator Warren had attended confirmation hearings for Senator Jeff Sessions as U.S. attorney general. There, in a vote along party lines, she was asked to stop speaking following accusations that she had violated Senate Rule XIX. Later that day, Senate Majority Leader Mitch McConnell explained the sanction, saying, "She was warned. She was given an explanation. Nevertheless, she persisted." Almost instantly, the phrase "nevertheless, she persisted" became a rallying cry among feminists.

Senator Warren had inspired me at our meeting with her candor, good humor, and passion for making a difference. I know there is not an ounce of truth to it, but given the timing of our meeting, now among friends, I like to joke that I inspired *her* to persist.

The state visits so far had been energizing and exciting, but I was also keen to travel abroad more as first lady. I didn't think it was good use of my time to go along with Guðni to the few international conferences or other events he attended, because there were no opportunities for me to make a helpful contribution. But I did think that I could help raise Iceland's profile and support good causes by taking advantage of occasions where I could use my skills and interests.

In November 2018, I was in Luxembourg to follow Iceland's national culinary team as they competed in the Culinary World Cup. I observed them in their detailed preparations and as they competed to prepare perfect three-course meals for hundreds and posted on my social media channels as the team was awarded gold medal after gold medal. It got great publicity back home, and a leading dairy producer bought a full-page congratulatory ad in the paper when they returned, raising the team's profile and encouraging future sponsorships, which are necessary if they're to participate in such competitions. During the visit, I also attended a dinner hosted by our honorary consul in Luxembourg. My visit provided a good excuse to gather different parties who had connections with Iceland, and I was always happy to oblige if my presence could help to strengthen those relationships.

In the spring of 2019, I traveled to Stockholm to attend the Dementia X Forum convened by Queen Silvia, whose mother had had dementia. As patron of the Alzheimer's Society in Iceland, I was there to learn about new developments in dementia research and caregiving. I met representatives from dementia associations around the world and sent back information to the Alzheimer's Society upon my return.

One trip that left a lasting impression came about after I started trying to make the most of state visits. When I first met with UN Women Iceland as a follow-up to a stop I made on the state visit to Denmark, I was pleasantly surprised by how quickly they took me up on my offer to help. I later joined them on a trip to Jordan to visit the Zaatari refugee camp near the border with Syria; they were interviewing women who lived there as part of a fundraising documentary. On the flight to Amman, I wrote in my diary that my goal was to showcase "how strong, proud, and dedicated these women no doubt will be," but I didn't want to burst into tears at their stories, nor did I want to stifle my emotion. In the end, I laughed and hugged and cried with the women and wondered, not for the first time, why I'd even tried to plan my emotional responses.

Once again, because I was already in the region, I thought I should try and make the most of it. I was a special ambassador for SOS Children's Villages Iceland, so I spent a day visiting one of the SOS Children's Villages in Amman, as well as an emergency response program that gave classes in English, Arabic, and mathematics for young people, many of whom were illiterate with limited formal education. There I met a twelve-year-old Syrian refugee who was attending school for the first time. An official I spoke to said one of the main objectives of programs like this is to avoid having "a lost generation." The program also supported Syrian refugees and local Jordanian women through offering life skills classes such as marketing and business planning so they can earn some money from the handicrafts they produced.

While some of my solo trips garnered little press attention, others earned an article or two in the Icelandic papers, annoying a small minority of readers who complained that I did not really represent Iceland and shouldn't take formal trips abroad or that I was an "attention seeker" galivanting around for my personal amusement. But one trip was slightly more controversial.

In March 2018, former Russian military officer Sergei Skripal and his adult daughter, Yulia, were poisoned with a Novichok nerve agent in Salisbury, England. Both were critically injured but survived. The British government blamed Russian agents acting with the approval of the Kremlin for the attempted assassinations. Russia denied the allegations. As part of its response to the attack on its soil, the government announced that cabinet ministers and the British royal family would boycott the upcoming FIFA World Cup, set to take place that summer in Russia.

Nordic countries, most NATO member states, and several EU nations also took measures against Russia as a response to what the Icelandic government described as "a grave violation of international law [that] threatens security and peace in Europe." On March 26, in solidarity, Iceland's foreign ministry announced that it would not send officials to the World Cup either, even though the nation had qualified for the first time.

Guðni was not constitutionally bound by the decisions of the foreign ministry or the prime minister's office. He loved soccer and all sports in general and had spent a lot of his tenure talking about the benefits of staying active. He regularly attended a variety of sporting events by men's and women's teams. It would have been a dream of his growing up to be there in person to watch his nation compete in the World Cup.

But he knew that he couldn't go. This was bigger than a boyhood dream.

At the same time, there was vocal pressure within Iceland for someone to attend, to recognize that qualifying for the most watched sporting event in the world was a momentous achievement for a nation of fewer than four hundred thousand people.

A compromise was reached; I would attend. I was not a government representative; I wasn't even on the government payroll. But I was unofficially recognized enough that my presence could provide some attention and support for the team. I was definitely on board with the idea. Admittedly, I knew little about soccer, but having tried my own hand at curling, touch football, rowing, and basketball, it somehow felt fitting for me to leapfrog to a good seat at a world-class event. Despite my lack of skill and interest, athletics kept cropping up in my life.

There were some nuanced logistics to work out: I was not there officially (though I would be traveling with a staff member from the president's office), so I would not sit in the VIP section, nor would I accept the host country's offers of security or transportation. But I was still the spouse of a head of state and needed some guarantee of safety. It was agreed that I would sit in the section reserved for close family supporters of the team members, along with Iceland's ambassador to Russia, and that the embassy would look after my transport.

When the press release announcing my attendance was issued, there were questions about why the office of the president was paying for what was billed as a private visit, but my track record of taking several solo trips as first lady helped assuage concerns. The entire dialogue also helped awaken debate in the press and online about my role—whether it *was* a role and, if so, what it was—which I only saw as a positive development.

It was the first time I had been to Russia since my solo trip fifteen years earlier. When we arrived late at night on a flight chartered for fans for the match, I was immediately impressed by the changes I saw. A slick new highway led us into the city; the hotel menu actually had everything it advertised available to order; a local convenience store boasted a better selection than my go-to grocery store in Iceland; and the behemoth Hotel Rossiya where I had spent my first night in Moscow back in 2003 had been razed to make room for the fan zone where I would meet Iceland supporters in advance of the match against Argentina. The match itself resulted in a 1-1 draw, with Iceland goalkeeper Hannes Halldórsson dramatically saving a penalty kick by legendary center forward and winger Lionel Messi. The result against top-ranked Argentina was treated more like a victory than a tie.

The next day, we headed straight to the airport to return to Iceland. We needed to clear three security lines and a departure passport check. There was only one X-ray machine for all our hand luggage and just a handful of women's toilet stalls in the entire airport, each with queues snaking out the door. Our flight was delayed almost three hours because of some missing paperwork, and once we finally boarded, we were told there would be no coffee or tea served on the way home because the cleaning crew had stolen it all. Now *that* was the Russia I remembered!

That trip to the World Cup was perhaps the most memorable solo travel I undertook in 2018, but it was just one line item of almost two hundred on my "Solo First Lady" annual list (which also included over fifty speeches and over twenty informal remarks or presentations).

I knew I was making a difference, handshake by handshake. But was it enough to carve out my own space in the bizarre world of head of state couples? Although there were no surveys or approval ratings conducted on the first lady, the feedback I was getting was generally positive. Yet outdated expectations lingered in the form of frequent microaggressions that chipped away at my self-worth and frustrated me. Would I never succeed in proving that I was my own unique individual with a voice to share?

That August, we had held an open house at Bessastaðir. We did this three times a year, during which anyone could walk through the main building's rooms, each manned with a volunteer to explain some of the history and furnishings. The residence was not otherwise open to the public. As usual, Guðni and I stood at the entrance and greeted everyone, often a couple of thousand people, many of them foreign tourists, as they arrived. And as usual, several people, after the thrill of meeting the president, strode straight past my outstretched hand. Others stood directly in front of me to pose with my husband for a selfie.

How could I be a role model of equality and leadership if I still didn't always have the courage to insist on shaking everyone's hand at an event I cohosted? If I couldn't eradicate the second-class status of being "the wife," how could I succeed in encouraging others to speak up on occasions when they were boxed into narrow categories?

So I persisted.

15

Not My Husband's Handbag

Delivering a TEDx Beacon Street talk entitled "Pulling Back the Curtain: Life as a First Lady," November 2019.

"I am not my husband's handbag, to be snatched as he runs out the door and displayed silently by his side during public appearances."

—Op-ed by me in the *New York Times*, October 1, 2019

The devil was in the details. After a few years serving as first lady, especially on days when I hadn't had enough sleep or was feeling sorry for myself, I felt that I was being ignored even at the times when my involvement was expected. (As Michelle Obama once put it, "They were using me like I was a candidate, and supporting me like I was a spouse.") It showed up in small ways, like a line in our schedule that said "president will attend," when we had both been asked to an event and both accepted the invitation. Or notes in a schedule or diary that we would both attend when no one had yet asked me. Or Guðni attending an event alone and being asked where I was, as if the invitation that was sent only to him somehow magically extended also to me. And how many times would outlets post newspaper photos of the two of us arriving at a function where the caption said only "President visits…"?

As the first Icelandic first lady to be extremely active on my own, I recommended new procedures. For example, if Guðni and I had been on a trip somewhere together, I also wanted to sign the follow-up thank-you letters. Such letters were generally drafted by staff, but in the first years, I had to specifically ask for letters from me for the parts of the program I had attended on my own. I had no social media accounts until I created and managed them myself, and I occasionally asked that something relevant I had done be included on the social channels of the office of the president. I asked that my name (or at least the title of first lady) be included on all confirmed engagements that I was going to attend and that it not be added by default to events without my accepting them. Sometimes these changes were implemented immediately, while for other requests, I had to ask multiple times.

I knew these microaggressions weren't deliberate. No one was sitting behind a desk somewhere saying, "Ha, Eliza will be *so* irritated when we accept that invitation and don't ask her first!" No one plotted to stay silent on all the work I was doing so it wouldn't get reported or shared. Guðni sometimes raised his eyebrows if I mentioned some minor irritation on occasion, as if to say, "Again? Does any of this really matter? Do you have to make a big deal out of stuff?"

That struck a nerve too. If these tiny actions irritated me, then I needed to tackle them in some way, or they would fester. But on the other hand, they were minute. No one in the public even saw our schedule entries, and if my name was included in a photo caption, half the time, it was spelled wrong anyway. (For some reason, in Iceland, many people, especially journalists, think my first name is spelled Elisa and my last name Reed.)

And yet. As a woman and a feminist, I knew how much societal constructs, social mores, the patriarchy, or whatever you want to label it have traditionally marginalized, minimized, or silenced women's voices and contributions. As a privileged woman, I knew that my negative experiences were much milder than those of many others and that if I did take the trouble to call them out, I would face less blowback and less risk of serious consequences.

One unconscious tactic to avoid having to tackle these issues was simply to preemptively gaslight myself and say that it was all in my mind. Weren't things good enough as they were? I'm an extrovert; perhaps I was just being an attention seeker, someone who craved likes and clicks and media attention. Anyway, who did I think I was? The president? I most certainly was not that person, so why try to upstage him when my proper place was in his shadow?

The pendulum swung back and forth: Stop whining and enjoy what you have. Speak up for diminished women everywhere. Get a grip and recognize who the biggest person in your world is right now. Hint: it's not you. Use this small platform to call out what is going on. But was I doing this for me, or was I doing it on behalf of people everywhere who dealt with the same issues of inadvertent or intentional marginalization but couldn't speak up?

One day around this confusing time, I was with Guðni on an official visit to the Eastfjords. As usual, we had at least a twelve-hour day with stops at numerous places in the community, including a visit to the local elementary school. These stops usually involved the same routine: We would be greeted by flag-waving or singing children, escorted on a short tour, and led to a cafeteria or classroom to meet some of the kids and answer their eager questions.

Guðni has that X factor when dealing with children, a natural connection and interest in them that you can't fake. He relates effortlessly to young people, speaking to them at their level with intelligence, humor, and compassion. It's a joy to watch. I like kids, of course, and I'm pretty confident that I'm a nice person, but I don't have the same magic with them.

In any case, there we were in front of the classroom, having learned about a new project the kids were working on and answering questions about what English Premier League team Guðni supported and what kind of car he drove (the two most common questions). Then someone raised their hand and asked me: "Are you also the president?" I smiled and replied that, no, I wasn't, although I was the president of the family. (Ha ha.)

Later, I thought about it. The question made sense. Very often—though not always, especially in later years—the children had been told "the president is coming" for a visit to the school. When Guðni had showed up with an entourage of people who milled about at the edges of the gathering but only one who stood next to him, they assumed I was also in that role. When I stood next to Guðni and said, "No, I'm his wife," it gave me pause. Did it make the kids wonder why I didn't have my own job to go to? Was that the message I wanted to be conveying to the next generation?

It wasn't that straightforward, of course. No one had ever said it was compulsory to accompany Guðni on these visits. I did it at first because I thought I ought to, but I continued to do it because I enjoyed it. There were still unwritten expectations about the spouse of a president, and one of the major ones was that official visits were meant for a couple. If I hadn't attended, it would have undoubtedly ruffled some feathers, been seen as a snub of a certain community. It was yet another contradiction of the position.

And yet it was vital that young people didn't think the wife of a president had nothing else going on. I could help to shape that image.

In late 2019, I had been invited to deliver a TEDx Talk in Boston providing a behind-the-scenes glance at life as a first lady. On a trip to Poland with Guðni that involved a short layover in Copenhagen, I worked hard on crafting my remarks, which were about confounding expectations. I opened Facebook and came across a piece in *The Guardian* that was being widely shared in my echo chamber of friends. Titled "The G7 Was the Final Straw—World Leaders' Wives Should Refuse to Travel with Their Husbands," the hook of the piece was an Instagram post by then European Council President Donald Tusk that patronizingly described four of the wives of G7 leaders captured in the accompanying image with their backs to the camera, gazing out to sea, as "the light side of the Force." *The Guardian* piece opined that statements such as this reduced these talented women to mere props and that the solution was that they stop traveling with their husbands.

Things were a little more nuanced than that from where I sat. There I was, reading this piece while traveling with my husband, albeit not to an event where spouses would be shunted off on a "keep busy" cultural program. My position was that I had a right to accompany him if I chose to, and that I was making a contribution. But I agreed with pretty much everything else in the piece, as did my numerous Facebook friends who had shared it.

It's too bad I'm first lady and can't say anything, I thought to myself as I sipped my orange juice. *Otherwise, the themes of this story make me so angry I would probably post about it on Facebook.*

By the time I had finished my juice, I had had an epiphany of sorts. As first lady, I had no rule book. What I *did* have was a blue-checked Facebook page and no one telling me what I could or could not post on it. Besides, there was another hour left in the flight before we landed in Copenhagen, so I might as well make good use of the time. I got to work and crafted a long post, linking to *The Guardian* story. Among other things, I wrote:

> I wholeheartedly agree that a couple of decades into the twenty-first century, we can do better than assume the spouses of our leaders have nothing better to do with their time than traipse after their other halves and look at art galleries / visit children / take in the view, while their (almost exclusively) male counterparts take care of Serious Business.
>
> But, wait, am I not one of those women? Yes and no. I make a concerted effort not to be seen as an accessory to my husband (with whom I am of course most definitely proud to be associated). I have most assuredly traveled with him on several occasions, but I can't recall any such excursions where he was making the trip for a conference, summit or meeting. Rather, when I choose to travel with him it is either for an official or state visit, during which I endeavor to hold at least one speaking engagement and/or not exclusively undertake "traditional" spousal activities should I have some separate time, or when I believe the occasion warrants the inclusion of the two of us (I write this, for example, en route to Poland for a ceremony remembering the eightieth anniversary of the outbreak of the

> Second World War). On many occasions, I travel alone, yet nevertheless to represent Iceland in my unofficial capacity as forsetafrú (first lady). It's a privilege and an honor for which I am very grateful.
>
> But when society assumes the presence of these unelected, unpaid spouses as some sort of vital window dressing to affairs of state, then it is time to reexamine our expectations and preconceptions of these all too usually female companions.

I saved the piece as we landed in Copenhagen to be greeted by Iceland's new ambassador to Denmark, Helga Hauksdóttir. We had a few hours to wait before our next flight, so I asked Helga, whom I was meeting for the first time, if she would mind looking at the piece. Would I be pilloried in the press if I posted it? I was nervous, but I wanted to share these thoughts. Helga and a couple of other friends I hastily sent it to thought it was fine.

I posted the story and boarded the flight to Warsaw, this time with no Wi-Fi. When I landed about ninety minutes later, the story had most definitely garnered attention, almost exclusively positive. I was lauded for "speaking my mind," for being "true to [my]self," for being "a badass," and the post was called "timely." Thórdís Elva Thorvaldsdóttir, a well-known feminist activist in Iceland, commented: "Women everywhere have rebelled against archaic structures in the past century, refusing to be reduced to arm candy or window dressing. It's because of women like you that the revolution might even reach the top tier." Touchingly, a number of people said that it was thanks to vocalizing opinions such as this that they were proud to have me as their first lady. The post had been widely shared by Icelandic media too.

(As if to emphasize my point, I was soon after featured in a Polish story titled "Which Lady Looked Best at the Commemoration of the Eightieth Anniversary of the Outbreak of WWII?")

One of the comments on my post was by Krista Mahr, my old editor at *Iceland Review* magazine. "I don't know if you're allowed, but I'm sure people would love to hear your perspective and experiences at *The Guardian*!" Once again, my first instinct was regret. Like anyone with an interest in writing, it would have been a dream come true to have my work published in a highly reputed publication. What a shame that they would probably never be interested. In any case, I was first lady, and that probably wasn't allowed.

Or was it?

I reminded myself that owning no rule book meant I couldn't break any rules. And if I didn't ask permission from people at the president's office or even tell them about it, no one could dissuade me from the idea. So I aimed high: I wrote to a contact at *The New York Times*, who put me in touch with the op-ed team, who loved my pitch.

I got to work on writing it, adapting my Facebook piece to tighten the language and make a clearer but nuanced argument. I included the line "I'm not my husband's handbag, to be snatched as he runs out the door and displayed silently by his side at public appearances." I thought the metaphor was clumsy, but it captured the feeling I often had about being treated as a mere accessory. I talked to Guðni about how I should structure it and about what he thought of the somewhat unorthodox idea in the first place. As usual, he was gently supportive. If you can't already tell by the relative infrequency in which he appears in these pages, Guðni is a very private person. He would never expose his soul in an op-ed, especially when no one had asked for his opinion. But I have always believed these surface-level differences in our personalities are what help make us such a good couple (that's also a sentence he would never write!). Guðni knew it was important to me to speak up, and he would stand by that.

I also sent the draft to a few friends for feedback before submitting. Interestingly, all the women thought the handbag line was the best one of the piece, while all the men said that if I needed to tighten or shorten it, I should take out that bit, which didn't serve much of a purpose. Might men's inability to connect to the handbag metaphor stem from never having their worth downsized to fit neatly under an arm?

I tossed and turned the night before the op-ed was to be published. I was nervous about the response, concerned that I would be pilloried for complaining about a problem that didn't exist, for being a selfish attention seeker who didn't recognize her own privilege. I thought I might make enemies of my colleagues, that they might resent that I didn't give them a heads-up.

Maybe you already know how this goes. In short, none of that happened. The piece was praised and shared widely (even retweeted by a White House correspondent who thought the first lady of *Finland* was a badass). I didn't notice any difference in my colleagues' behavior towards me. I received messages from many people whose spouses were better known than they were and who could relate to the points I made.

I felt empowered to use this flash of attention to continue to speak up in a constructive way. I was interviewed on the nation's main current affairs program about my article. When I was invited to deliver remarks at events, people began to ask me whether I wanted to be introduced as first lady or perhaps as an entrepreneur or a writer? Come December, I was nominated as "person of the year" by several Icelandic media outlets.

Despite the attention this single story attracted, I still had plenty of opportunity to call things out. In October 2021, after the world slowly began to reemerge from the COVID-19 lockdown, Crown Prince Frederik of Denmark led a business delegation to Iceland that included the nation's foreign minister. Guðni and I hosted a meal for all the visitors as well as relevant Icelanders with whom they would meet. It was the first large dinner we had held since the pandemic.

The next day, the visit graced the front page of the main national newspaper. It featured a photograph of the crown prince shaking my hand as he arrived at the residence, Guðni standing next to me, smiling. The photo caption explained that the president had invited the crown prince for dinner at Bessastaðir the previous evening and that the crown prince was visiting Iceland with a delegation that included the (male) foreign minister. And that's it.

I showed the front page to Guðni and asked him what he thought of it. "What a great photo of you!" he exclaimed, not at all noticing what I thought was an egregious, if unintentional, omission in the photo caption.

I thought about leaving it, saying nothing. I was not alone; it happened all the time. There was even a Facebook group called "Do Women Exist? What Are Their Names?" where people shared experiences of being eliminated from photo captions or defined purely in relation to the men beside them. The image with the crown prince was such an obvious example of unintentional bias that I felt I needed to call it out, albeit in a humorous, if pointed, way.

I resorted to the tried-and-true method of reaching many Icelanders quickly—another Facebook post, in Icelandic and in English, with a link to the news story: "Summary of this photo caption on the cover of the newspaper today: One man with a name came to dinner at another man with a name's house. With the visitor was a third man with a name [not pictured]. That is all. #dowomenexist."

You can probably guess the rest. It was another viral moment, an Icelandic tempest in a teapot. I got media request after media request, all of which I turned down. I had said what I needed to say. Interestingly, the only outlet that didn't write something about my comments was the newspaper that had run the photo in the first place. It chose instead to run a piece about the locally designed clothing and jewelry I wore. For days, if not weeks, strangers approached me to thank me for calling out the practice. For every misspelled online comment snidely reminding me that I was not the president and couldn't have hosted a dinner at my own home, there were fifty or more comments offering full-throated support and praising the lighthearted way in which I pointed out the incident. Even the journalist who had written the caption in the first place sent me a thoughtful apology letter; he explained he'd had to write that text before the final image was chosen. Regardless, I had always known he hadn't deliberately set out to insult me; rather, he was merely working within a system ingrained with unconscious bias.

It had taken years, but something was starting to gel. I felt confidence in my solo engagements and empowered enough to criticize when needed. I was in a delicate position and wanted to serve with respect and dignity, but I did not want to self-censor, allow others to silence me, or pay attention to critics. In many, if not most, other nations, the female spouses of male heads of state or government would have been raked over the coals for publishing unapproved editorials in *The New York Times* or posting statements on social media that hadn't been vetted by a team of PR professionals. I know this, because I have spoken to several of them. But Iceland is a global leader in gender equality. We are a small country, but we still have a voice, and we can still hold great sway in certain fields. If there was any country from which to step up and speak out, Iceland was it.

After I had been learning to navigate the waters of serving in an unpaid "job" with plenty of unofficial aspirations, the opportunity to reshape those expectations and views had become my guiding light. I was riding a crest. Now I would make sure to put my hand out assertively at receptions!

The increased confidence led me to reexamine some ideas I'd been keeping on the back burner. I asked again about the prospect of hosting a reception for new citizens. Although speaking up for women (without first asking permission) had turned out well, asking for feedback on an event to celebrate diversity and new citizens still proved challenging. I was told I'd need to choose a recent cutoff date, say, those getting citizenship in the past three months. Yet in doing so, I was also told I could easily offend all the people who had received their citizenship letter in the mail before that date. This wasn't explicitly said, but the message I heard was that it would just be too difficult to arrange without offending vast swathes of people. *Tant pis.*

It was back to the drawing board with that dream, but I couldn't let one setback derail me now. I absolutely didn't need to be the center of attention, but I would not be silent or invisible. The question was, if I was already considered an "outspoken" first lady, should I break some of my own unwritten rules in service of making the most of my time in the role? How much of a big deal did I want my legacy to be? It was becoming more obvious that the choice was entirely mine.

16

Working Woman

Backstage before a live appearance on *GMA3* to talk about the Taste of Iceland festival, May 2023.

"In America, this was expected, while Number 10 was still coming to grips with the fact that I could walk and talk."

—CHERIE BLAIR, *SPEAKING FOR MYSELF*, ON THE TOPIC OF OFF-THE-CUFF SPEECHES

In May 2018, Guðni and I visited a Reykjavík-area assisted living facility to celebrate the 107th birthday of a local resident. We sampled strong coffee and birthday cake and chatted with the birthday girl's many family members, including her adult great-grandchildren. One couple I guessed to be in their seventies sat next to me, and we made small talk: about the impressive life of their venerable relative, how I like living in Iceland, what they enjoy doing. I mentioned that earlier that day, I had delivered a speech at a Nordic conference that was billed as "creative collaboration across linguistic and cultural boundaries."

"You must be busy all the time with this," the woman commented.

I agreed that yes, I was occupied with unofficial first-lady duties, but of course I enjoyed it very much, and it was a tremendous privilege.

The man next to me, who I took to be her partner, then jumped in and added, "You should get a salary for all that work."

I didn't necessarily disagree but stayed silent. This was too nuanced a discussion to have with strangers.

His wife immediately countered: "That role has never been paid." And that was the end of that.

I thought about those spontaneous remarks for a long time afterwards. I was easily doing a full-time job as first lady, all on an unpaid basis. I didn't begrudge that; I knew what I had signed up for, and there was never any talk of payment. Yet as a feminist, I knew that often women undertake extensive unpaid labor that helps to keep not only families but often entire economies running. If someone had told me that a heterosexual couple would initiate a dialogue with me on the topic of compensation for the first lady, I would have assumed that the woman rather than the man would be for it. Upon closer reflection, though—and I probably spent far too much energy thinking about the brief encounter—I realized why that hadn't happened in the elderly care home. To generalize, perhaps a man with a long career would recognize work when he saw it and believe that work ought to be compensated. His wife, on the other hand, might have spent her life in an unpaid grind and thought I darn well could too.

It was another balancing act between my paid professional work and my voluntary labor as first lady. I never resented or expected to be paid for work as the latter. I had not run for office, and there was no official position for me. At the same time, I had no intention of quitting all my jobs because my husband had been elected to a new one. I had always been open about that, even though everyone, from office staff to the general public, assumed I would take an active role in state visits and events of national significance. Though I had always been pretty clear that I was unlikely to snuggle babies who weren't related to me.

I was in the fortunate position of running my own business, so I could pick and choose the projects that I would keep. No one gave me any advice or guidelines on conflicts of interest. Essentially, I relied on my own instinct and integrity. Because I wanted to have time to serve in the role of first lady well, I chose to give up all the projects I had except one: the Iceland Writers Retreat. It was my (and my friend Erica's) creation, and I loved organizing it. I never for a moment considered stopping my involvement with that charity, but I was very careful with not using the office of the president to promote my private endeavor. I would occasionally get apologetic emails from potential faculty members or participants with whom I had already been corresponding with quite pleasantly. Clearly these people had googled the IWR team. Their new messages sometimes addressed me by surname for the first time and often ran along the lines of "Dear Mme Reid, I just googled you and found out who you are. Please accept my apologies for the informal way in which we have been corresponding. I cannot believe I have been writing you like a Normal Person when all along you are a Somebody. I do hope you will forgive my rudeness." These notes always made me chuckle. And each year, participants arrived at the event and couldn't believe it when they learned the woman with the welcome kits and participant badge was the first lady of the country.

As first lady, I continued to take part happily in hundreds of events per year, including writing and delivering dozens of speeches and preparing for gatherings that required more than just attendance. This took me away from additional work I could have been doing for the Iceland Writers Retreat and often cost me personally. Not only in lost income but also most significantly in having to invest in the clothing that is required of a first lady. (Gala dresses, I'm looking at you!)

But wait, wasn't my husband the country's highest-earning elected official? We had free accommodation, all kinds of help. A senior public servant actually said to me once that if I publicly commented on (code for "complained about") not earning money as first lady, the press would attack me because "your husband earns enough to support his family." But it was no longer 1950, and I wasn't selling my quiet servitude for a pat on the head.

I noted how other spouses of world leaders had been pilloried in the press when discussions about their roles and compensation—or lack thereof—arose. French President Emmanuel Macron had to announce his wife, Brigitte Macron, would not be getting any formal "first lady" status after a petition accrued more than 280,000 signatures. And Sophie Grégoire Trudeau was heavily criticized when she mentioned in an interview that she wanted an additional assistant merely to reply to all the correspondence and requests to take part in events she was receiving. Why do we expect women to undertake mountains of unpaid labor, then complain if they fight back or ask for support to do it well? Even my children noticed. Duncan once asked me why I wasn't getting paid to do all the things I did when I seemed "as busy as Dad is." I didn't know how to answer that.

In the fall of 2019, I was approached by the new director of Business Iceland (then called Promote Iceland). The organization is a public-private partnership that, according to its website, "is responsible for the branding and marketing of Iceland and Icelandic export industries [and] supports Icelandic companies in entering foreign markets and facilitates foreign investment in the

Icelandic economy." (In regular speak, it promotes Iceland abroad and encourages investment to the country.) I had first worked with the organization back in 2015 when I got a grant to promote the Iceland Writers Retreat and took part in its "Taste of Iceland" cultural events in the United States, where I spoke about Icelandic literary traditions. Since becoming first lady, I had taken part in several more Taste of Iceland festivals, padding my role as literature lecturer with many more television, radio, and print appearances as well as meetings with local officials. I had also spoken about sustainable tourism at global travel events in Berlin and London and during other visits to the United States and Finland.

Business Iceland's new director, Pétur Óskarsson, brought me in to tell me that according to its data, their events attracted about 50 percent more publicity when I was there. I was also, he noted, the only person on those delegations who was not paid for their efforts.

He thought it was time to change that.

Extensive discussions ensued, but the gist of it was that I would be paid a monthly retainer for taking part in as many relevant Business Iceland activities as I was able, most often speaking and media engagements and international events but also occasionally speaking within Iceland or taking part in online functions. We thought it would be about seven to nine trips per year, with multiple events on each trip.

It was an intriguing, novel idea. I would be promoted on these trips as the first lady of Iceland, so in a sense, I was indirectly being paid because I was first lady. But I wasn't just any first lady. I had extensive experience in exactly what I was being asked to do, and I was very good at it (and had the data to back that up). I would be promoting general Iceland-related projects and not specific organizations, and most importantly of all, I would not cost the taxpayers additional money.

Pétur and I, with some input from the president's office, discussed whether to announce the arrangement publicly. I would not be a staff member so would not be entitled to pension benefits or sick or vacation pay. Nor was it necessary for Business Iceland to advertise for the position, because it was a contract gig. But we all agreed that it was better to be more transparent than less and decided to issue a press release, explaining that I would be working with Business Iceland on certain projects and paid to do so.

I was fired up for the attention this would garner, and I understood that the situation was nuanced. There were no conflict-of-interest guidelines or rules of any sort governing what work projects I could accept. If I were a nurse who took shifts at the hospital while Guðni was president, no one would have batted an eye. But if I had accepted a lucrative post as a spokesperson for, say, one of the banks, which used my contacts as first lady to pad that company's coffers, I am sure there would have been a public outcry. Yet why should I not use my skills and experience for paid work? Iceland has topped the World Economic Forum's Gender Gap Index for sixteen years. If Iceland really was this amazing country for women, we needed to have a dialogue about why women in my position or similar ones were expected to undertake free labor. I did not want to shy away from a healthy discussion about the topic and was confident that in this specific case, I deserved the compensation I would receive. I would bring tremendous value to the organization and to Iceland overall. We were heading into an election year, and I knew there might be some pushback, some accusations of nepotism or corruption. But I was more than happy to address each and every concern. Bring it on.

With some fortunate timing, the announcement went out when I was on a two-day official visit to the western part of Iceland with Guðni. I was able to step away from the program for five minutes to take part in a live interview on the evening news, during which I pointed out that I would continue to be as active a first lady as ever, as evidenced by what I was doing at that very moment. I did miss one state visit, though, to Georgia, as the dates couldn't be moved, and it was arranged after I had confirmed a trip with Business Iceland. I thought it would not send a professional message to cancel a work trip to be in Georgia as my husband's plus-one, however much I may have wanted to be there.

The announcement made the front pages. The nightly news said I would be the first spouse of a president to take on paid work (ignoring the fact that I had been paid for my work on the Iceland Writers Retreat since Guðni took office).

I braced myself for the public reaction. There were plenty of opinions about it. Some called it "poor judgment" or a "conflict of interest" for me to take on this cooperation. Others trotted out the old chestnut that spouses have always undertaken similar work in the past but never "complained" about not being compensated for it. Others still had no problem with a spouse working...*but* thought it should perhaps be as a nurse or a teacher (or other suitably caregiving and feminine role) than a position that they implied strayed into the president's world.

I confess I allowed myself to be provoked by some of the feedback, especially when factual details were reported incorrectly. When people complained that my monthly earnings were far too high, I couldn't counter with the truth that I would have to pay pension benefits and other contributions from that income, or that the 24 percent value-added tax in the figure would also be paid back to the government. When they argued that my job should have been advertised and included a transparent interview process, I couldn't retort that it was contract work, not a full-time position (and that my experience and credentials would shine in a traditional interview process for a similar job). In short, I knew I was a person of high integrity, that I would do a good job, and that Business Iceland would be getting its money's worth without conflicts of interest.

There were no formal polls conducted, but it seems that a majority of people agreed with me and with the Business Iceland decision-makers. I was well qualified, and it was about a broader question of equality. Once again, I was grateful to be living in Iceland, where I felt confident that the tide of public opinion was pushing me along rather than flowing against me. One woman I didn't know reflected a majority of what I saw by commenting on a news post: "In my opinion this woman deserves a high salary for representing Iceland."

After a few successful trips for Business Iceland, the pandemic changed the landscape. During COVID, I took part in online campaigns to raise awareness about Iceland and longer-term planning for how to be ready for tourists once they returned and helped to launch and chair meetings of a new initiative to help Icelandic companies find grants and investment opportunities in lower-income countries. After the pandemic, I took part in numerous events and activities when I was traveling for Business Iceland, including an appearance on *Good Morning America's GMA3*. One year, according to Business Iceland data, I was second only to the prime minister in terms of foreign press coverage among Icelandic political figures. Pétur, the managing director, said inviting me to join the team was one of the best decisions he'd made in the role.

Working for Business Iceland inspired me to branch out even more professionally. Although I did as much as I could for the group during COVID, I decided I also needed to take on more because my first-lady assignments were fewer and farther between. During the first weeks of the lockdown, I devoted myself almost entirely to creating special schedules for the kids to clean and disinfect part of the house, making soups and homemade bread for us and for others who had no time to do so, and completing jigsaw puzzles I had ordered online. Though those activities helped to reduce my fears about the pandemic ruining my children, they were not intellectually satisfying.

In the middle of April 2020, our former president Vigdís Finnbogadóttir, the world's first democratically elected female head of state, celebrated her ninetieth birthday. The big party had been canceled, but she received plenty of love and admiration from

Icelanders on social media. When I was on a long walk with my kids that day, I thought about how Vigdís had attained legendary status within our small nation but that her accomplishments in breaking one of the hardest glass ceilings was all but forgotten elsewhere, at least in the English-speaking world. That's when the idea to write a book about gender equality in Iceland came to me.

I had wanted to write a book for a while but never had an idea I felt passionate about. Besides, before the pandemic, I had plenty on my plate. This idea lingered over many walks, though. I could speak to numerous women, so it wouldn't be history but rather a modern-day profile of Iceland, told through the eyes of its women. I had written many such stories for *Iceland Review* and knew I could pull out interesting and quirky details, making Icelanders relatable to people elsewhere. I'd managed to sit in on a handful of workshops at the Iceland Writers Retreat over the years and had picked up some great tips on nonfiction writing. I could spice it all up with some of my own insider details about serving as first lady.

But was I allowed to do this? It was one thing to write a short op-ed in a newspaper but another to write a whole book. I decided I would do it because I had an important story to tell, but I also hoped it would sell enough copies to make a bit of money. I didn't want to be obliged to donate that money to charity; continuing my own professional development by publishing a book was a logical next step in that journey.

I didn't share details of the idea with the president's office; an "act first, ask later" approach seemed to work better for me. I decided that I would try to write it on my own, ensuring, as always, that I didn't cross any ethical lines doing it. I asked the first women I contacted not to tell anyone that I was writing a book. Even after interviews with numerous women, the news never became public until I announced it.

And once again I wondered what I had been so worried about. My colleagues at the president's office emailed congratulations. I didn't notice any negative reaction to the news. Icelanders pride themselves on a strong literary tradition, and the urban legend is that one in ten citizens here publishes something, so I think people were merely happy I was making a contribution to that landscape.

Almost two years later, my first book was published during the Omicron wave of COVID. I thought the day began auspiciously because I got the Wordle in two guesses. My plan to precede the online book launch with a nice dinner with friends was scuppered when Duncan got COVID and was put in isolation in our basement while the rest of us quarantined upstairs. Somehow it all seemed fitting for a book that was born in the pandemic. That week, I did numerous Zoom interviews from my dining room table, the kids very patient in the background every time I cried, "Shh, going live now!"

Once the peak of Omicron passed, I was sent on a book tour, which proved a great opportunity to promote Iceland in general. I was still a first lady, but I was a solo first lady, so I could travel without protocol hassle. I had enough adventures to provide fodder for further books, from appearing on *Good Morning Britain* to attending a reception hosted by Camilla, Duchess of Cornwall, to a road trip in the southern states that ended with my first visit to a rodeo.

I was given an envelope full of condoms at an event in LA, had to take shelter from a possible tornado in Minneapolis, and spent my birthday alone in Houston at an all-you-can-eat meat buffet.

I loved it all, not just because talking about Iceland and gender equality was one of my passions and not just because I enjoy eating steak. This was different: I was having these adventures as a touring author. Adventures I was enjoying directly because of an initiative of mine. I was getting a glimpse into what the post–first lady life might look like for me, even if I didn't yet know when that life would begin. In the meantime, it helped me be a better first lady as I got more experience in the media and at large events meeting diverse groups of people. And that was good because there were always national and international crises requiring leadership and compassion to help us unite.

17

Eruptions, Epidemics, and Endings

Visiting residents of an assisted living facility in Reykjanesbær. Residents were without heat and hot water for several days after a volcanic eruption damaged pipes that led hot water to the community, February 2024.

"This small nation is more like a large family that knows whatsoever happens to one of us, happens to all of us."

—Former President Kristján Eldjárn, as quoted by Guðni in his address to the nation following a series of volcanic eruptions in and near the town of Grindavík

At 11 p.m. on Friday, November 10, 2023, the Icelandic Department of Civil Protection and Emergency Management ordered a compulsory evacuation of the town of Grindavík (population about 3,800, or 1 percent of the total nation) in the southwest of Iceland, less than twelve miles from Keflavík International Airport and three miles from the famous Blue Lagoon spa, the country's most visited tourist attraction. After enduring weeks of near daily earthquakes, some over 5.0 on the Richter scale and causing severe structural damage, approximately ninety million cubic yards of lava had accumulated under the community. An eruption was considered potentially imminent anywhere on a nine-mile underground corridor that stretched along the peninsula and through the middle of the town.

It was the first time an evacuation of an entire town in Iceland had been ordered since the unexpected nighttime eruption in Vestmannaeyjar (the Westman Islands) in January 1973. On that occasion, a huge fissure had opened just east of the community, spouting lava high into the sky. Ultimately, one-third of the town was destroyed by lava and another third damaged by ash. Now, with that eruption still a living memory for many, residents of Grindavík heeded orders, and the town was officially declared evacuated and all emergency personnel departed by 4 a.m.

Perhaps the process had been so rapid because it was a Friday night, and many residents had already left for a weekend break from the seemingly endless earthquakes straining their patience, leaving all their belongings and pets in the town they expected to be able to return to. (Days later, some residents could return in brief, supervised visits to rescue pets and collect additional essentials.)

That first weekend was a time of unimaginable stress, sadness, and uncertainty for this tight-knit community. The rest of us were nervous as we watched from farther afield, desperate to be able to lend support in some way. (We weren't nervous about our own safety, though. Iceland sees regular volcanic eruptions, and we all knew that the threat was confined to a specific area.) This tragedy, as tragedies often do, also brought about the best of humanity. The Red Cross opened three emergency reception centers for residents who could not stay with family or friends, but there was such an outpouring of offers that they were never full and closed soon afterwards. Someone started a Facebook group; within hours, people posted notices of empty cottages or second homes where entire families could stay for free. Our neighbors in Álftanes, living abroad for a few months for work, invited a Grindavík family of five Polish immigrants to stay in their furnished home for as long as they wished. Public gyms gave free access to all residents; stores donated clothing and food.

The nation was playing a waiting game with nature, but in the meantime, there was work to be done. Government officials were quick to create contingency plans and offer emergency assistance. Guðni and I visited a Red Cross evacuation center to meet those who used it and the volunteers who staffed it. We attended a church service for residents, and Guðni delivered a speech. He issued statements that hoped for the best but assured the nation that authorities were prepared for all outcomes. Many residents said it was the uncertainty that was so challenging.

If there was no handbook for serving as first lady on a "regular" day, there certainly wasn't one for when the nation was facing a crisis—a time when the institution of the presidency ought to serve as a bastion of unity and succor. The unofficial role of comforter in chief was obviously my husband's, but having worked hard to be a visible presence, I knew the more we could each show compassion and solidarity, the better. Yet although my well of empathy was deep and genuine, I sometimes worried about how I would maintain my composure in the face of tragedy and whether that might end up being more of a detriment, some sort of distraction to whatever else was going on. Whereas I usually tried to be a vocal and distinct personality within the presidential couple, my instinct told me that merely bearing witness to big events was going to be enough. Sometimes, rather than seize the moment, the moment seizes you.

The predicted eruption near Grindavík did not come until December 18, and when it did, the fissure opened about two miles north of the town. It was the first of numerous volcanic eruptions that would devastate the community, all in an area that, until 2021, had not seen volcanic activity for about eight hundred years. Gradually, residents would be allowed to return, and sirens were installed in the town for quick evacuation. Most people eventually found other places to live, although many wanted to stay in their homes. There was extensive earthquake damage to the community, including buckled roads and buildings with giant cracks snaking through them. Slowly but surely, residents began to reassemble their lives in a new normal.

The December eruption fizzled after a few days, but on January 14, another small fissure opened, this time less than half a mile from the town, and with web cameras streaming events in real time, the lava crept over three homes, engulfing or igniting them. The television was on all day at our house then, even if we didn't want to watch the destruction of abandoned houses and all the mementos and dreams contained within them. Guðni had one eye on developments as he was in touch with officials and worked on a new speech. That evening, he delivered a live address to the nation, saying, "we will carry on with our responsibilities and we will continue to stand together. We will act out of empathy, compassion and solidarity." I thought he captured the tone that was needed and was very proud of him.

Both of us tried to show moral support to the community as much as we could. We hosted the town's preschool children for a Christmas party and visited assisted living facility residents who had relocated to Keflavík. We met with the town council and hosted all the people who had, at seemingly superhuman speed, worked on building the town's (and nearby power station's) vital defensive walls to stop any future lava flow. Guðni and I usually undertook these visits together, but on one occasion, I attended a church assembly in one location while he visited a gathering elsewhere.

Sometimes I felt a bit uncomfortable alone at these gatherings.

My face was not as familiar as Guðni's, and I felt a bit arrogant walking around as if everyone ought to instantly recognize me. Yet I knew I was there so people would be aware of my presence as a symbol of solidarity. Showing genuine compassion to people in times of crisis was easy, but trying not to cry too much was hard. I didn't think I was "close" enough to the crisis to have earned the right to weep in front of everyone else, yet when others did so or said something kind to me, I often couldn't help myself.

Iceland has tackled the forces of nature for centuries, and the country is well equipped to handle the volcanic eruptions we see, on average, every few years. But they are not the only natural challenges we face. During Guðni's presidency, avalanches hit the village of Flateyri in January 2020 and the town of Neskaupstaður in March 2023. There were no fatalities thanks to the existence of structural defenses and, in the case of Flateyri, rapid response of search and rescue volunteers.

In December 2020, several landslides tore through the Eastfjords town of Seyðisfjörður, destroying or damaging more than ten buildings but once again sparing all residents. The following February, Guðni and I visited the town to hear residents' stories and to thank first responders and other volunteers for their life-saving work.

We met a man who literally ran for his life as the mud approached, grabbing his son and sprinting to the end of the dock out to the fjord. He was preparing for them to jump into the icy Arctic water, but the mud and debris miraculously stopped right before they had to take the plunge. Everyone we met said they wanted to return to the town, but some didn't yet feel comfortable sleeping in their homes.

An old fish meal factory had been converted into a sorting area for all the property and personal items that had been collected from the debris, especially from the town's technical museum, which was destroyed. Next door, in a converted former fishing net factory, we spoke with a burly, bearded man in a wool *lopapeysa* sweater who, with tears in his eyes, told us about the care they took with every item they found, from muddy binders to carpets to dolls. Each piece was painstakingly cleaned and laid flat to dry for owners to sift through and decide whether it was worth keeping.

After a few hours in the town, we knew we were seeing a community whose members were clearly shaken but remained stoic through tragedy, supporting each other and looking for long-term ways to constructively protect their homes in the future.

There were individual tragedies that touched us all too. I often attended the funerals of nationally known figures, usually but not always with Guðni. Most of the time, these were memorials for people whose contributions to society merited the presence of the head of state (or me if he was away). Sometimes, they were for people whose lives had been cut short all too soon, who came to national prominence in death. These were the most difficult.

Presidential couples the world over attend funerals regularly. In Iceland, the same leaders are also used to make this preparation for the aftermath of natural disasters. In 2020, though, a global event unprecedented in our lifetimes shook us all. The COVID-19 pandemic and its aftermath lasted over a significant portion of Guðni's tenure as president. In that crisis too, I tried to be as helpful as possible. While government officials decided on and enforced rules and created economic recovery packages and other relevant policies, we tried to be upstanding role models. Soon after the outbreak of the pandemic, volunteers were encouraged to come forward for testing to gauge how widespread the virus was within society and what percentage of people were infected but asymptomatic. Guðni and I went for our tests trailed by a gaggle of masked media. It is impossible to look photogenic as one swab is thrust up your nose and another down your throat. A tiny victory I noted in my diary: With one exception, in media coverage, we were described as "the presidential couple" or "Guðni and Eliza" and not merely "the president" or "Guðni."

The pandemic brought about unique challenges. I kept my ambition simple and the bar low: Don't break my children. We were incredibly fortunate with our circumstances and did our best to set a good example during the crisis, following all rules to the letter—or, usually, more so.

I wrote letters or recorded messages for every charity where I was patron. I visited Red Cross workers who were helping coordinate the pandemic response. Guðni and I took part in a tourist board campaign that encouraged Icelanders to support the economy and travel domestically in the summer of 2020 during a respite from pandemic restrictions. (It was really the only vacation option unless someone wanted to spend two weeks in quarantine upon their return to the island.) We also visited many regions of the country to showcase the interesting activities on offer in another effort to boost domestic tourism. Once the vaccines became available, we waited our turn like everyone else. Uptake was so high, there was no need for public leaders to act as guinea pigs to prove their efficacy or encourage others to sign up. Guðni got his shot several weeks before I did because vaccinations were prioritized according to risk factors, including age.

Guðni also stood for reelection in 2020. One other candidate ran against him, and polls consistently had my husband with a virtually insurmountable lead. Even though domestic pandemic regulations in Iceland were completely lifted for several weeks before the election (for public health rather than democratic reasons), we chose not to run a large campaign that might encourage big gatherings. We made a handful of trips to the largest communities outside the capital region and left the grip and grin (well, nod and grin) at that. That June, Guðni handily won reelection with 92.2 percent of the vote. By the time the inauguration took place on August 1, restrictions had tightened again, and only a handful of people were allowed to attend the ceremony in the Althing.

The pandemic was teaching me about when I could and ought to stand on my own two feet as a national role model. I was also beginning to do this in my written presence. I consciously curated my social media voice as an active and vocal first lady, but I also issued statements in which I tried to strike a balance between a "first-lady" formality and a more "Eliza" humor. That included a post I made on New Year's Eve 2020:

> Happy New Year, everyone! I send my very best wishes to everyone who has felt the full brunt of the challenges 2020

has hurled at us. For me personally, I admit I have much to be thankful for, but perhaps what stands out most this year is this immigrant's pride in being Icelandic*, or to word it more inclusively, in being a resident of this island: With determination, solidarity, and a respect for scientific wisdom and impartial expert advice, the people of this society have tackled an invisible foe that we will ultimately defeat. Those on the front lines continue to deserve our deep gratitude. In due course in 2021, I look forward to hugging my family and friends, patronizing businesses most affected by the crisis, enjoying the theater and concerts, and witnessing the innovation that inevitably emerges from the ashes of our greatest ordeals.

*Yes, I also consider myself Canadian and only find these two sentiments conflicting if my two nations ever meet in sporting events.

After newsworthy events, while I often simply shared a more formal statement that Guðni had made, I also thought it appropriate to add my own thoughts, although it took time for me to acknowledge that maybe a statement of mine might carry weight or in a small way help shift public opinion. I often "hooked" these statements to anniversaries and holidays when I might be posting something anyway.

In April 2022, two incidents of racial profiling garnered attention. A mixed-race youth was pulled off a public bus by the Viking Squad (the colloquial name given to the special operations unit of the national police force) after members of the public called to say he resembled a wanted criminal. Then, on a separate occasion, this same youth was detained at a bakery, again in response to calls from the public. The criminal looked nothing like this young man except they were both of mixed race and wore dreadlocks. The incidents were prominent in the news, leading the police to become defensive and the family in the center of it justifiably angry. I used the occasion of the national holiday to make a broader statement via social media:

> This the first day of summer in Iceland, a national holiday. It's a time of growth, of renewal, of change. An optimistic time. A time, perhaps, when it's appropriate to consider what we as individuals can commit to renew, to grow, to improve, both in our own lives and for the benefit of society as a whole.
>
> Personally, I have been thinking a lot about racism (as maybe many of you who follow Icelandic news have been doing in the last few weeks). It's not enjoyable to contemplate. It's indicative of my privilege that I can, and do, sometimes decide to simply not think about it, to turn the other cheek when I hear about it, to try not to let it "get me down," because, I tell myself in lazy and self-indulgent moments, I am a tolerant and open-minded person and therefore am not part of the problem.
>
> But that is indeed the rub: We Icelanders are fortunate people. We live in the world's most peaceful country, its third happiest, the one closest to closing the gender gap. But in our own fortune we may be inadvertently burying our heads in the sand by not acknowledging that deep prejudices and injustices exist here, as they do elsewhere.

The first step in tackling prejudice is acknowledging that it exists, that we all carry biases and need to remain vigilant in combating them. Without accepting that stark reality, then we are indeed part of the problem.

The next step is doing something about it.

So in this season of renewal, this is what I am committed to doing: I want to speak up when I can. I want to support my fellow Icelanders and other members of this society who find themselves victims of racism. I want to listen and learn, to think before I act, to help foster productive dialogue. What about you?

We can do better. We must do better.

This particular incident has a very Icelandic coda. In the Icelandic language, there was no word (or words) for *racial profiling*. How can you have a discussion on tackling challenges if you don't even have the vocabulary? So my friend Claudia cobbled together a group of relevant parties, and a word *kynþáttamörkun* (literally "racial defining") was born. Not a solution to the problem, to be fair, but how true to Iceland that one of the first weapons to combat it was creating a word.

I took my position as a role model seriously when it came to geopolitics too. I was not serving in a position where I could take a partisan political stance, but I was able to show solidarity and highlight issues that illustrated my personal values. I am a strong believer in multilateral institutions, in the concept of collective responsibility, and that no conflict should be considered too distant to ignore. We all have a responsibility to highlight injustices and human rights violations. Though it was difficult to make statements effectively but neutrally about domestic news, I grappled with even more impostor syndrome when it came to global affairs. On the one hand, as a public figure, I thought I should occasionally comment on international issues that were occupying daily discourse. But on the other hand, I despise virtue signaling, clicking "like" or reposting something to make myself feel better but doing nothing else. I could not post in a partisan way, telling elected officials that they had to stop x or support y and that they had to do it now. I believed, like all other rational beings, that peace was good, war was bad, and people should be kind to each other. Wasn't that all too obvious to say?

Guðni took office as the civil war in Syria raged and had displaced millions. Like many other nations, Iceland accepted refugees, and we wanted to give them a warm and visible welcome. When the third group arrived in late January 2017, their bus took them straight from the airport to Bessastaðir, where we met them along with the mayor of Reykjavík, the minister of social affairs and equality, Red Cross workers, and numerous volunteers. Guðni and I stood on the steps to greet them on a windy but relatively warm evening. They all seemed a bit tired and dazed after their long journey, but we hoped the winter's gathering sent a message about the importance of welcoming those who are seeking safety. Near the end of Guðni's term as president, we also met with Palestinians who had fled the war in Gaza and been granted asylum in Iceland.

Likewise, when Russia invaded Ukraine in February 2022,

Guðni and I welcomed the Ukrainian refugees who arrived in the country. We toured facilities where they stayed and attended fundraising concerts for them. I attended several (online) meetings with my Ukrainian counterpart, Olena Zelenska, to see how Iceland could provide assistance and conveyed messages to the relevant government ministries.

I met several times with leader of the democratic forces of Belarus Sviatlana Tsikhanouskaya, whose husband, Siarhei Tsikhanouski, was imprisoned as he ran for president of the country in 2020. Sviatlana took his place on the ballot but needed to flee her homeland after she was declared the loser in an election that observers widely decried as unfree and unfair. From exile in Lithuania, she traveled extensively to keep the plight of Belarusians in people's minds. I was—and am—in awe of her tenacity and bravery in stepping into the public eye under such dangerous circumstances. I also had a personal interest in following her story: When I was a teenager, over the course of ten summers, my family hosted children from Belarus who had been affected by the Chernobyl disaster, and I had visited a family in rural Belarus with Guðni in 2006. Sviatlana was of a similar age and spent her summers in Ireland as part of the same program. Now, when I met her, I knew that I could in no way impact Icelandic policy, nor could I offer any formal kind of assistance. But I could remember the plight of the Belarusians when I met others with more power, and I could share and help shine a light on the ongoing human rights abuses in the country. (On June 21, 2025, as I finished writing this book, Siarhei Tsikhanouski was released from prison, along with thirteen other political prisoners. Their fight for a democratic Belarus is far from over, though; more than 1,150 political prisoners remained imprisoned in the country.)

In September 2022, I was attending a saltfish tasting event for Business Iceland when I saw an alert on my phone that Queen Elizabeth II had died. I knew right away that Guðni and I would be invited to attend the funeral as representatives for Iceland. Yet I confess I was honored to attend because of my Canadian roots. When I was growing up, my father explained to me that the queen signed only her name and *R*, for Regina, without a last name. I was very proud that I was also Elizabeth R, just like the queen (Canadian schools in the 1980s didn't talk much about the stark realities of British colonialism). Her funeral would be a somber event, to be sure, but it would also be a global one that millions around the world would be following. How strange to think that I would be one of thousands of black-clad people bearing witness to the occasion in Westminster Abbey itself.

The British government had had Operation London Bridge (as the queen's funeral was dubbed) planned for decades. We arrived in London the evening before the funeral, in time to attend a reception at Buckingham Palace. To smoothly transport hundreds of guests to the reception, we were all driven to a meeting point at the Royal Chelsea Hospital. From there, we gathered in buses to transport us the short distance to the palace. Picture *The Magic School Bus* meets the United Nations. We sat behind the Panamanian and Ecuadorian ambassadors, next to the president of Italy and his interpreter, and in front of the president of Ethiopia. Naturally, we were all dressed in black, and although we chatted, the atmosphere was muted. At the palace itself, grander and more opulent than even the Nordic palaces I had visited, we were greeted by the queen's son, Prince Edward, and his wife, Sophie, Countess of Wessex. Then we entered the large picture gallery and were left to mingle. There were no formal remarks or speeches, but various members of the royal family walked through and chatted with their guests. It would have been the perfect spot for a round of head of state bingo. The higher profile the royal, the more you could see a knot of world leaders drawn towards them. Said prince or princess would inch their way through the crowd as their official photographers snapped pics along the way, images that would be shared back home to placate domestic audiences about their leader's moment to discuss Important Issues and Convey Sympathy to the British royal family. Guðni and I were briefly swept alongside the stream to have a few moments of conversation with the new king, mostly about fly fishing in Iceland. Aside from that, the only working royal we spoke to was a friendly elderly gentleman wearing a name tag marked HRH Duke of Gloucester. (I googled him when I got home—he was the late queen's first cousin.)

Sipping sparkling drinks and dipping into tiny canapés, Guðni and I talked to counterparts whom we had met before. We also spoke with then Tory cabinet minister Jacob Rees-Mogg (infamous for boasting he had six children but had never changed a diaper). Rees-Mogg had attended Oxford, just as Guðni and I had, so I thought that was a good conversation opener. Upon telling him that we had studied at St. Antony's, one of the newer colleges, I added that I had sung with the Merton College choir (Merton College was founded in 1264). I paused for a moment and joked that "they even let me sing with my accent." Rather than smile at my self-deprecation, Rees-Mogg nodded sagely and replied, "Well, you can't hear that when you're singing."

Our practice on the buses came in handy the next day for the funeral itself. It would be a day of "hurry up and wait." My main goal was to stay hydrated enough not to get a headache but not so much that I would need to pee within the five-hour time span in which no facilities were available. London's streets were eerily empty as we were driven through them and past traffic barriers towards the hospital, where we would once again gather before the bus took us to the abbey. We arrived at Westminster Abbey, entering with other heads of state via the side, just over an hour before the service began. I can't think of many other moments when so many world leaders were gathered in one place, all in solemn silence. The front rows of our section were reserved for leaders of the realms and other Commonwealth countries, and after that, we were in alphabetical order, which put us next to Irish president Michael D. Higgins and his wife, Sabina Higgins. The presidential couples of Poland and Portugal were behind us; I noted during the service that both men were talented singers.

And that singing! Choral works, including two pieces composed specifically for the occasion, resonated off the walls of the ancient abbey. The most powerful moment was a trumpet fanfare, then two minutes of silence, then trumpets again that led to the national anthem, now titled "God Save the King."

That evening, we walked around London's quiet streets into a local pub with the Icelandic ambassador where we toasted Her late Majesty and the new king. I felt emotionally drained but honored to have taken part.

We returned to London eight months later for the coronation of the new king. Now we were in the capital for a celebration like only the British can throw, but for us attendees, much of the gathering and waiting felt the same, this time in color. We didn't need to gather for buses, though there was an equal amount of waiting. Small screens had been installed in discreet corners of the abbey, so unlike at the funeral, where our firsthand experience was a primarily aural one, this time we could look up and see what the behatted heads of our fellow world leaders were blocking from view.

In April 2024, Guðni and I visited Grindavík for the fiftieth anniversary of the establishment of the community. It was a muted occasion. To reach the town, we had to pass a police checkpoint proving we had an invitation to visit and drive over a new section of road marked with signs warning drivers not to stop because the road itself was hot from the still-cooling lava over which it had been hastily built. The fresh lava smelled like smoldering leather. We drove past the gym where we had taken our children to countless soccer and basketball tournaments, its parking lot now buckled with fissures. We passed the fish processing facility we had visited during the 2016 campaign and the outdoor area by the harbor where I had delivered the main speech at the Mariner's Day festival in 2019. We drove past the bakery whose owners had nourished the community, literally and emotionally, by steadfastly keeping the doors open as often as possible. It was near the main street where many houses stood slightly crooked, yellow signs plastered across their front windows warning that they were uninhabitable due to structural damage. We drove by the area of town that had actually sunk by three feet or more, so powerful were the earthquakes that had been pounding the area for months. And then, on the outskirts of one of the newer developments, we saw the place where the January lava gobbled up three houses. A single charred piece of iron was all that remained of the new house belonging to a family of five who watched helplessly as their home was consumed by fire on live television.

We switched to huge all-terrain jeeps and traveled up a large hill on a steep dirt road where we could see from above how the protective barriers erected in record time had blocked a stream of lava from flowing directly into the town. The volcano continued to spew fire as we watched in awe.

But still, Grindavík lived on. At the honorary town council meeting, the president of the town council, Ásrún Helga Kristinsdóttir, presented honorary awards to eight citizens for their years of work in the community, including Gunnar Tómasson, who chaired the local search and rescue crew for a decade, and Stefanía Ólafsdóttir, who was vice principal of the elementary school and chair of the church council. They were lauded for their achievements, which included decades of work and volunteer efforts in local sports teams, museums, fisheries, church life, businesses, and other realms. They were also introduced in Icelandic fashion by listing their progeny. Icelanders know that the legacy of many grandchildren and great-grandchildren is often the most valued investment in the future of the community.

At the time of writing, nine eruptions have taken place in the region since the initial evacuation. Residents are able to work in the town, but most have found permanent homes elsewhere, and the community's future remains in question, though I have no doubt that all will continue to be done to keep the spirit of Grindavík alive.

I hope that in decades to come, I will look back on these years and remember the resilience of those who faced unexpected adversities head-on, with courage and tenacity. I will recall those who stepped forward even when fate dealt them a particularly lousy hand. And I will hope we were able to provide even a sliver of solace and continuity during dark times.

18

The Payoff of Persistence

Visit to the White House to attend a Women's History Month event at the invitation of First Lady Dr. Jill Biden, March 2022. If you look closely, you can see "Mom Cell" on my phone. The president surprised my mother with a call.

"Change doesn't come without challenge.
I choose to challenge."

—First lady of Namibia Monica Geingos,
in a 2021 YouTube video posted to
challenge gendered insults online

In addition to serving the people of Iceland, during my final few years as first lady, I worked to consolidate my reputation as an advocate for gender equality, to build the foundations for new exploits in the next chapter of my life and career, and to cement my reputation as a style icon for the ages. Okay, I'm joking about that last part—both the cementing and the reputation in the first place—but I add it because there were still plenty of opportunities for unexpected adventure and humor.

Like that time I was invited to the White House.

It came about from me taking a chance. I had plans to be in Washington, DC, in March 2022 to take part in the Taste of Iceland cultural festival. *Secrets of the Sprakkar* had recently been published, so I suggested a meeting with my American counterpart, Dr. Jill Biden, since I was going to be in the city, to pay her a "courtesy call" as the diplo-speak goes.

In smaller countries, it would be a near certainty that such a meeting would take place if schedules permitted. Things can be a bit more complicated in the U.S., though, especially given that the first lady was also working and that Iceland is a minuscule nation not high on the priority list of bilateral relationships that needed particular nurturing. Nevertheless, it was worth a shot.

It was several weeks before we got a response, but when it came, it was especially positive. Yes, the first lady would like to meet with me. But she also wanted to invite me as her guest to a Women's History Month event that she and the president would be hosting in the White House. I didn't need to think twice.

When the big day came, a representative of the Office of Protocol arrived at the Icelandic embassy to exchange gifts. I had a signed copy of my book, wrapped in easy-to-pack paper with a small red, white, and blue bow—it wasn't a formal state visit, after all, and I didn't think there was need for an extravagant present. Since I was in the country for my work with Business Iceland, I wasn't with anyone from the president's office anyway, and my luggage space was limited.

The first lady's gift to me in return was a beautiful but large glass serving bowl discreetly engraved on the base with an image of the White House and her signature, all wrapped in shimmering gold paper. It was far too large to fit in my suitcase, but it eventually found its way back to me two years later when a staff member at the embassy was relocating to Iceland and packed it with their things.

After the premeeting formalities, Iceland's ambassador, Bergdís Ellertsdóttir, and I were collected at my hotel by a White House driver and a protocol person. (Two other members of the Icelandic embassy team would be present at the larger event later that day.) It was the first time there had been such a high-level bilateral meeting involving Iceland at the White House since a 2016 state visit with all the Nordics. I was thrilled and, I confess, a little bit chuffed that I was responsible for this accomplishment.

Bergdís and I were deposited at the diplomatic reception room entrance off the South Lawn. As the "principal" guest, I sat on the right-hand back seat of the car; that's the side that is closest to the entrance on any given occasion. As the vehicle pulled up, two marines stood to attention by the doors. Someone announced, "Doors. Open!" and they followed the commands, opening them up and welcoming us to the White House, where I was formally greeted by Rufus Gifford, the chief of protocol. We spoke together in the diplomatic reception room and then walked to the Red Room. We were all quite excited. By now I had been to numerous palaces, to Rideau Hall (home of the governor general in my hometown) and to presidential residences in several countries, yet something about the storied White House made this one extra special. Perhaps it was that I was here without Guðni, invited because of something I had done on my own.

It wasn't long before the first lady arrived. By now, there were many people in the large room, from security guards to advisers and embassy employees—I would guess maybe ten or so. But Jill (as she asked me to call her) greeted me warmly, and we sat on the sofa together to chat, Ambassador Bergdís in a chair next to us. It was an informal catch-up rather than a serious dialogue—although with all the people taking photos and notes standing along the walls behind us, there was a limit to how casual it could really be.

It felt like only a few minutes had passed before the president joined us. If I thought the first lady had arrived with a larger entourage than I was used to, its size suddenly seemed tiny. We posed for photographs, and then the three of us sat down for a chat. The president wanted to discuss his grandkids a lot. He was clearly accustomed to a retail style of politics, having been first elected to the U.S. Senate before I was even born. After a few minutes, someone brought a chair over for Ambassador Bergdís to sit near us. I had had many interactions with Bergdís before, not only at her post in Washington but also when she was based in Brussels and New York. I bear tremendous admiration for her professionalism. And now the two of us were having tea with the Bidens in the Red Room of the White House, and I could almost see her tittering with excitement.

We must have spoken for about thirty minutes, and then it was time for the Women's History Month event, to be held for a large audience in the East Room at the White House. I had a seat in the front row across the aisle from Speaker of the House Nancy Pelosi—who was treated like a rock star—and members of the American women's national soccer team. There was a row of TV cameras along the back.

If receptions at Bessastaðir were like senior prom, then this was the *Vanity Fair* Oscars after-party. The atmosphere was electric, dynamic—or maybe it was just that everyone had a negative rapid COVID test and could once again meet in person. It was the biggest event the Bidens had held since moving in over a year earlier. At the beginning, a chirpy female voice welcomed everyone and then announced over a loudspeaker, "And now! Please welcome! The president and first lady of the United States!" She was nearly drowned out by whoops and cheers as Joe and Jill Biden walked hand in hand to the front of the room.

The president began by introducing himself as "Jill Biden's husband" and then mentioned several of the pioneering women who were in the room, including Avril Haines, the first female director of national intelligence, Energy Secretary Jennifer Granholm, and other female cabinet members. (Vice President Kamala Harris had been scheduled to introduce the president, but her husband tested positive for COVID that morning, so she was unable to attend.) After reviewing his administration's success with matters of the day's theme, the president mentioned that his wife had "a special guest" who was "a real champion of gender equality." Everyone clapped, and he gestured for me to stand. I stood and turned around to wave at the crowd, since I thought that was what I should do. In my mind, I was thinking: *That shows you, grade 6 bullies!*

I was interrupted from my reverie by a small murmur that evolved quickly into laughter. Wow, I was really killing it, and all I was doing was waving! Then I heard a discreet *psst*, and I realized that after I had turned my back to the stage, the president had gestured for me to join him. I sheepishly turned around and walked up to more applause, this time mixed with friendly laughter and finally a standing ovation. I hoped I wasn't blushing too much and thought about my parents back on the farm, who knew I was at the White House and may even have been watching the C-SPAN coverage.

The event ended with an eloquent speech by Jill Biden, who spoke about the importance of role models who you don't find in the history books, including her own mother.

I felt like I was having an out-of-body experience, but the best was yet to come. As the gathering wound to a close, I exited a side room to have some time to bid farewell to the Bidens. I thanked Jill especially for her speech mentioning family role models.

"I have a very strong mother too," I told her.

Then the president jumped in. "How are your parents? Are they still alive?" he asked.

I confirmed that they were indeed alive and that they knew I had been at the White House.

"Well, let's call your mother!" exclaimed the president.

I had heard that President Biden had a reputation for calling people out of the blue but didn't know that it was not merely lore, especially for people without voting rights in the U.S.

I learned that it was also true that the president didn't have his own cell phone, so he took mine after I dialed for him. I hoped my mother would pick up, even though I have an unlisted number.

She did.

"Hi, this is Joe Biden, President Biden," he said when my mom answered.

"Oh, hi, how are you?" she replied in a friendly tone, as if he were the neighbor she hadn't spoken to in a while calling to borrow some brown sugar.

The president said he was well and explained that he and his wife were standing in the White House with her daughter and that we were talking about mothers, and he wanted to call and ask how this particular mother was doing.

"Well, I'm just absolutely fine," replied Mom warmly. "And I'm so proud of all the women that you've put forward in your country and the ones that we're promoting in our country these days. It's about time." It sounded like someone had sent Mom talking points. Mom also spoke to the first lady, and after another minute or so, the call ended.

Bergdís and I returned to the hotel and relived the highlights of the visit over a glass of champagne. It was certainly not a run-of-the-mill day for either of us. I had surprised myself with how much of a "did that really just happen" high it was. It was like the first time I met European royalty, except I recognized their faces, and the tone was less formal.

But my adventure had had a purpose too: I had been invited to meet the spouse of the world's most powerful head of state entirely on my own merits. I also had a chance to meet her husband. It was a unique opportunity to raise Iceland's profile in a pressing human rights arena, even if we are still better known as a photo-ready, subarctic Eden than a gender paradise. For me, it represented the culmination of my work to forge my own network and purpose in this weird role.

My visit to the White House lingers longest in my mind, but there were other moments I was proud to be a part of. Moments when I felt like I'd earned my invitation based on the way I was using my platform as first lady. Within Iceland, I spoke regularly at gatherings of the Association of Women Business Leaders and rang the bell to open the stock exchange in honor of International Women's Day in 2022. I stepped in to speak with activist and actor Ashley Judd at the Reykjavík Global Forum when the prime minister had to cancel. And in the autumn of 2023, I was honored to be asked to be among the group of activists and other stakeholders to announce that there would be a new women's strike held in the model of one almost fifty years earlier that had become a pivotal moment in Iceland's fight for gender equality. (Typical me, I had wavered a bit before accepting the invite, wondering whether I was "allowed" to attend such an announcement on the chance that it was too political. It seems I never learn.)

As I took part in more visible activities on my own, the sisterhood of "first spouses" (who, in truth, weren't all women) provided me with more inspiration and support. In 2024, the first lady of Austria, my friend Doris Schmidauer, invited me to address an audience of several hundred at the Hofburg Palace in Vienna for an annual event the presidential couple held on International Women's Day. I had met Doris in New York only the previous autumn; we were introduced by German first lady Elke Büdenbender, who was convinced we would get along well. She was right. Doris and I connected immediately. She has a warm and engaging personality and is interested in many of the same things I am, including increasing gender equality. Austria is in twenty-first place in the World Economic Forum's Global Gender Gap index. Doris's primary concern is achieving a fairer distribution of unpaid care work while also increasing women's representation across business, political, and social fields.

In fact, after I had accepted the invitation to speak at Doris's event, I discovered that I was going to be in Berlin with Business Iceland at a similar time. So I took a day trip from the German capital, along with Elke. It was a "first-lady road trip"—except on a plane and with staff (hers, not mine). The talk was very well received and resulted in several contacts within German-speaking Europe for me to speak at events and possibly to facilitate connections with activist groups between the two nations.

What sticks in my mind, though, is the day I spent with two other women who were serving in the unique and usually informal role of first lady of their country. Many of these women see each other regularly because they attend the United Nations General Assembly week or annual NATO gatherings. In Iceland, it is usually the prime minister who represents the country at such events. Iceland is not a member of the European Union, so we did not attend the annual EU gatherings of nonpolitical heads of state. Despite the irregular contact, the unique situation in which we found ourselves connected us, and I am grateful to have formed friendships with several other individuals who have served or are serving in this role.

There are even a couple of organizations that work to connect spouses of world leaders and to leverage the indirect influence they command. I have met founders of the Global First Ladies Alliance but also connected to first lady of Ukraine Olena Zelenska through the Summit of First Ladies and Gentlemen, which she founded. That group meets annually in Kyiv, and the gathering became even higher profile after Russia's invasion of Ukraine in February 2022. Although I was never able to attend in person, I participated virtually several times.

I did meet Olena once in person in London, when alongside First Gentleman Aleš Musar of Slovenia, we participated in a panel on soft power at the Brand Finance conference in 2024. There we discussed our unofficial yet influential roles and how we can use them to serve our countries' national interests. One of the Ukrainian advisers mentioned that an initial challenge of their conference had been that many spouses are not able to travel officially alone. All of us had vague or nonexistent descriptions of our roles, which were usually unofficial. I realized that I was one of the lucky ones to be able to use the role independently of my husband as much as I did.

And I continued to do so. I was at the opening of the Special Olympics in Berlin in 2023; it was held on Iceland's national day, so Guðni was not able to go. I was in New York to speak at several sideline events during the time of the annual UN Commission on the Status of Women week, its second largest event after the General Assembly each September. I had been invited by UN Women Iceland and the Reykjavík Global Forum and met with several groups to discuss Iceland's role in the fight for gender equality. Even though I didn't represent Iceland in any official capacity, it felt like people knew my presence in my unofficial role could help make a difference and would attract attention for the issues they wanted raised. I had earned the right to be at the table.

I had also learned that if I really wanted to do something, I shouldn't expect it would just happen of its own accord. I shouldn't expect people to read my mind; things went smoother when I was proactive. I got more background briefings and fewer assumptions about what kind of first lady I *should* be. I was given the support to be the kind of first lady I *wanted* to be. There was still the occasional bump in the road, though they were fewer.

After the pandemic, I tried a third time to work on a reception for new citizens. This time, I was met with more willingness to make the idea a reality, but we were stymied once again, now by strict privacy laws that meant that other ministries could not share names or contact information of new citizens with us.

Fortunately, there were other goals to focus on. In my early years as first lady, I was often invited to various "spouse" events on the sidelines of UNGA (the UN General Assembly week). They almost all sounded interesting and exciting, but Iceland's prime minister or foreign minister usually represented the country at UNGA, and I knew Guðni was unlikely to attend. Finally, near the end of his second term, I realized that if I wanted to experience New York that week, I would just need to figure out events and opportunities where I could help talk about Iceland.

In 2023, I went to New York during UNGA on my own, with no staff and no partner. But I headlined an event at the New York Public Library with another good first-lady friend, Finland's Jenni Haukio, during which we talked about Nordic literary traditions. (In addition to holding a PhD in political science, Jenni is also a writer and poet.) While in New York, I also participated in a panel at the annual Clinton Global Initiative conference. It was a fun and productive few days, although I noted that in the year that I was finally in town for these events, I was not invited to many of the gatherings held for spouses of global leaders, gatherings that are important not just for maintaining friendships and contacts but also for input into the issues of the day, simply because my husband was not in the city with me at the same time. (It's likely that international protocol officials did not know about my presence for the same reason. I think a rogue solo spouse was a bit of an anomaly.)

My last foreign trip as first lady was, appropriately, a solo one.

In June 2024, I went to Slovenia at the invitation of the spouse of the president, Aleš Musar, whom I had met in person for the first time at the soft power event in London earlier that year. Aleš had only been serving in the role for about a year, but I knew that he was a kindred soul as far as using the position of presidential spouse to promote important issues.

Aleš asked me if I would speak at the annual Bled Water Forum, which became the *raison d'être* of a visit that also included an outing to the national library of Slovenia, a meeting with members of the literary community, and a trip about the beautiful town of Bled. In preparing the visit, much of which was done with the two of us communicating directly, Aleš also acknowledged that there were really no guidelines on how a spouse was formally meant to host another spouse. In fact, he had had to invoke a never before used article from his nation's protocol rules concerning guests, since a visit of this sort was a first. We were breaking new ground! That commonality between us seemed fitting near the end of my time as first lady, during which I had focused so much on carving out a place for myself where I could be of use.

It was my last year serving as first lady, and as my husband's second term drew to a close, I was starting to think about my legacy. A president's legacy is supported through public record and actions. By default, a spouse will almost always disappear into the ether or be known solely for tasks undertaken in relation to the principal—or for controversies—unless they work hard to define themselves. I was happy that I was well known within Iceland for the promotion of gender equality (and, I hoped, for being an active and effective first lady), but gender equality was a topic with which Iceland was already often associated and one where I didn't see much wiggle room for nuance in the dialogue. Was I ready to speak up under circumstances where the dialogue required even more delicacy? Could I reveal more of my personal opinions without breaching the barrier of the overtly political? I wanted to be brave enough to do that too.

Then, an opportunity presented itself. December 10, 2023, was the seventy-fifth anniversary of the Universal Declaration on Human Rights, a document that had been crafted in no small part due to the help of former U.S. First Lady Eleanor Roosevelt. The Icelandic branch of Amnesty International asked me to deliver some remarks in honor of the occasion.

It was a fraught time. The terrorist attack on Israel on October 7 had been the most significant attack on Jews since the Holocaust. Meanwhile, the Israeli government response had garnered international condemnation for the vast number of Palestinian casualties.

Like most others, I was following developments with shock and concern—or whatever other diplomatic words one uses in these situations. I felt that as a spouse of a world leader, I should *do* something, but what? Tweet? I didn't influence policy, and I was not in a role where I could criticize or encourage government action. But was that just an excuse not to speak up? Was I worried about backlash to my statements? I didn't know.

As I prevaricated, Guðni and I met with Palestinians in Iceland, both citizens who had lived for a long time in the country and those freshly arrived from the conflict. I met with the wife of the sole resident rabbi. I shared information on how to support causes such as the International Red Cross, UNICEF, and UN Women. I had also been personally criticized—probably more than at any other time when I served as first lady—for interviewing former Secretary of State Hillary Rodham Clinton and Canadian writer Louise Penny at a literary festival in Reykjavík that November. Although we were there to discuss the thriller they wrote together, there were protests that Clinton would be attending; some felt she had not condemned the war in Gaza vociferously enough. Others sent messages that if I spoke to Clinton and Penny about their novel, I would be responsible for killing babies in Gaza. (Iceland recognized the independence of Palestine in 2011, becoming the first Western European state to do so, and notwithstanding sympathy to Israel for the attack committed against its people on October 7, from the outset of the conflict, Icelandic public opinion was firmly sympathetic to the Palestinian people.) Over the years, my skin had grown thicker for criticism and personal attacks. It's an unfortunate aspect of serving in a public role, even an unofficial one with no direct influence on policy or expenditure.

I had my personal views on the war, of course, but I was waiting for an opportunity where I could discuss them with care and nuance without overtly straying into political territory. I wanted to be able to address the tremendous polarization, the sentiment that expressing sympathy for what happened to Israel on October 7 was anti-Palestinian or that calling for a ceasefire and, later, using the word *genocide* in relation to Israel's actions in Palestine was denying Israel a right to exist or was anti-Semitic. I wanted to express sympathy with those on both sides whose lives had been affected, who had lost loved ones and relatives. The speech for the Universal Declaration on Human Rights anniversary was the perfect opportunity, and I worked hard to write something that captured the nuance but I hope also left room for what regular people could do. I reproduce my remarks almost in their entirety here. (Bear in mind that a year later, in December 2024, Amnesty International issued a report calling Israel's actions in Gaza a genocide. This would have likely been reflected in my remarks had it been the case at the time.)

> It was three-quarters of a century ago today, soon after the end of a massive global conflict, that the UN General Assembly gathered to adopt a declaration on universal human rights. Not a treaty or a legal document, but a declaration, a statement of inalienable human rights that has inspired numerous legal binding treaties and agreements in the intervening decades. And a declaration that has become the most translated document in the world, available in more than five hundred languages.
>
> The declaration is not perfect, but it does lay out common goals for nations and states, a guiding light, one hopes, for states to bear in mind when creating the policies for a just society.
>
> Three-quarters of a century later, we are, of course, living in a world where human rights are violated on a daily basis, on a scale both large and small.

The UDHR was created to be a nonpartisan document, but it is often hard to extricate its contents from politics, whether those of a group or of a nation.

Yet it should not be. Does any rational person really disagree with the statements that "all human beings are born free and equal in dignity and in rights?" That "everyone has the right to life, liberty and security of person?" Or with so many of the declaration's 28 other articles?

We live with incredible privilege here in Iceland. The privilege that most of us live in relative safety and security, in what is called the world's safest country, with one of the world's highest standards of living. We live in a healthy democracy, where we have good access to our elected officials, where we have a right to protest peacefully, to engage in activism, to rally for change...and where our voices can sometimes be heard more, even if it doesn't always feel like it. I am personally grateful for this.

I am also grateful for the work of our elected officials and public servants, who I generally believe are serving we citizens and residents with integrity and hard work, while with many complex circumstances to consider. I trust that they also use this declaration as one of their guiding lights.

And what of our place in the world? What of our obligations, not to tell other nations what to do, but to speak up for injustice when others are unable?

Today's event is organized by Amnesty International, and, as usual, they are doing incredibly important and vital work in raising awareness about global human rights violations. Their websites—both Icelandic and international—highlight the work of specific individuals whose human rights are now being violated, whose stories illustrate larger problems.

What larger problems? Well, where do I start? I am thinking of the thousands of civilians, of children, who have been killed in Gaza and of those who have lost loved ones and been displaced. I am thinking of those affected by the attacks on people in Israel on October 7. Of Afghan women who have systematically had their rights to education, to expression, to freedom, eradicated. Of queer activists in Russia and many other countries whose vital work has been declared illegal. There are simply too many ongoing human rights violations to mention them all now.

But let us not allow "too many to mention" to immobilize us into inaction. We cannot do all things for all people. But we can use our voices, use our influence, to continue to speak up for what we believe is right, live according to our consciences.

At the same time that we demand improvements, changes, the return of liberties, ceasefires, peace, let us also remember basic human kindnesses and dignities to each other. Let us recognize and be thankful for this declaration on human rights, and the strides we have made towards further legal parameters to protect human rights.

We must be rightly horrified at the travesties that are taking place even as I speak. But we can also celebrate the fact that other horrific outrages have undoubtedly been prevented thanks to this declaration and other more legally binding frameworks and agreements that have built on it.

I want to end by thanking those of you working often behind the scenes to implement change, thanking the Amnesty team and supporters for everything you are doing and the causes and people you are keeping in our hearts and in our minds. And I want to encourage all of you to remain passionate about the need to continue championing for just societies, not only here in Iceland, but around the world.

The audience reacted to my speech very positively. I was happy that I had used the chance to say something that I hope contained some real substance. And therein lay another objective of the speech: to remind people that when given the opportunity, it was good to speak up, to use any platforms we have to the fullest. (I was not to know whether I had been successful at a secondary goal of testing the waters of speaking more explicitly to political issues. When you don't have a whole PR team behind you who can make off-the-record calls to sympathetic journalists or produce slickly designed reels of key clips ready for viral sharing, then hitting the right moment with a statement, no matter how nuanced, is largely a matter of luck and timing.)

I had always been trying to live by that mantra of using our platforms, especially for the past nearly eight years. I felt as if I had a lot more ahead of me, but as it turned out, more change was afoot.

19

Curtain Call

We were presented with special sports jerseys during an official visit to the town of Seltjarnarnes, April 2024.

"We are interconnected as never before, and, if I may add especially in the current climate, we bear a responsibility as never before to be role models: To use our voices, to fight for what is right, to speak up about injustice, to elevate the voices of those who cannot. To be vigilant in fighting for a more equitable world."

—From a speech I delivered at the Canadian High Commission in London, March 2022

Ever since I was four years old and burst into tears on Christmas morning when I discovered that some *stranger* had filled my pristine and empty stocking with gifts, I had found change intimidating. Leaving my role as first lady was no exception.

Unlike the spouse of someone who was running for reelection and was then defeated, I had had some time to get used to what was to come and, of course, formulate a plan. Guðni's second four-year term would come to an end on July 31, 2024, and it was tradition for presidents to make an announcement during their annual New Year's Day address about whether they planned to stand for reelection or not. Except for the nation's first president, who died after eight years in office, all the nation's heads of state had served at least three terms (there are no limits); Guðni's immediate predecessor had served five terms, or twenty years. Given that and my husband's broad popularity, it's fair to say that people expected him to announce on January 1 that he would seek reelection. The only question would be if anyone would be foolish enough (or vain enough) to run against him.

But Guðni has never needed to do something just because everyone else was doing it. He had given his all in the role, and now it was time to move on to something else. At the end of the day, he had to make that choice for himself and himself alone. During the days and weeks that he was making the decision, I kept my eye on the kids and how they would handle things, and of course, I reassured Guðni that I would be by his side no matter what. Regardless of my personal feelings, the last thing I wanted to do was put unfair pressure on him to make a decision based on what others thought he should do. I would always support him.

I knew that I would look back on these years with fondness. I was immensely proud of what Guðni had done during his two terms in office. Perhaps I was most proud of the way in which he was able to combine his deep knowledge of the Icelandic presidency and its purpose with honesty, compassion, and an ability to bring out the best in both people and organizations. When he ran in 2016, Guðni said that he hoped he would be able to remind people that we all matter, and I was convinced he had achieved that goal.

On the late morning of December 28, I went with Guðni to the hall of the main residence building for him to record the New Year's address, a couple of the kids in tow after I reminded them that this particular speech was going to be memorable. The team of the president's office knew the speech's contents by now, but the camera crew who had arrived to record the message and who would be sworn to secrecy until the broadcast did not. There was the usual jovial post-Christmas banter, *hangikjöt* (traditional smoked lamb) and *laufabrauð* (fried flatbread) ready to be served after the work was finished, but I could sense a somber tone. We knew what was coming. I wonder if the crew picked up on it. In any case, it wasn't long because they began filming and would hear it for themselves.

Of course I had read Guðni's speech and provided some input, but it was still going to be difficult to hear the words spoken out loud. I felt like I was once again diving into unknown waters. But seeing Guðni's obvious peace with his decision gave me comfort that this was the right next step.

At 1 p.m. on January 1, 2024, the broadcast aired, the bombshell dropped, and once again the messages started pouring in, from friends and strangers alike, almost all of which were some variation on thanks for the service and a respect for, if surprise at, the decision. I quickly learned that there are two phrases for "sorely missed" in Icelandic (*sárt saknað* and *eftirsjá að honum*, if you were wondering), but there wasn't time to wallow in the language's vocabulary. As usual on this day, we were busy with a ceremony for new recipients of the Order of the Falcon, followed by a New Year's reception at which several hundred people were invited. I'm someone who is rarely moved to tears (though, as evidenced from the frequency it's mentioned in this book, I often fretted over the prospect), but there were a few times when I couldn't quite manage to get the words "Happy New Year to you too" out because my voice was quaking.

The innumerable kind messages from people, which continued to stream in over the following days and months, both written and in person when I was grocery shopping or at the swimming pool, were both humbling and bittersweet. I felt as if I were preparing to say goodbye to an elderly relative during her final days. She was someone I had loved deeply, had lifelong fond memories of, but I had always known that this time would one day arrive. It would be a loss, and I knew I would need to grieve it.

As usual, I shifted into overdrive. On the family front, we were building a new house. The kids would also have a big change, especially the youngest two who didn't remember life before the presidency, whose informal extended family included kindhearted souls who worked in and around Bessastaðir and for the president's office. I got used to answering the question "I guess you're looking forward to taking some time off?" by nodding politely but not agreeing with the question too wholeheartedly. The truth was I felt like I was now operating at two hundred percent, which was a way of compensating for the fact that I was worried because I didn't yet have a plan, and change was looming. Happily, Guðni knew that he would return to his beloved world of academia. But what work would I continue with? I have never seen a job advertisement asking for the skill set of a spouse to a former head of state.

I was only forty-eight years old. I didn't want my work as first lady, the network I had developed, the experience I had accumulated, to be the high point of my career. I wanted to build on it, to further challenge myself, and, I hoped, to continue having a positive impact on the world around me. After that dip in Lake Baikal with the honeymooning Swiss couple, I was even meant to have another quarter century to my lifespan. But was leaving the position of first lady like reaching some sort of political menopause where society would write me off, even though I still believed I had so much to offer?

Still, in eight years, I had tried not to let others limit my dreams or tell me what I was or wasn't qualified for. I couldn't let the lack of a handbook for post–First Couple life limit me now. If I stopped to consider it, I did have several projects lined up already. After finishing *Secrets of the Sprakkar*, I had written my first novel, a murder mystery set in Iceland, and had sold it in a two-book deal. That manuscript needed to be submitted just before Guðni's term would end, though the nerves at how my debut fiction would be received would last for many more months. (It turned out to be a critically acclaimed instant bestseller that was optioned for television.) Once that mystery was finished, I would need to start on book two in the series and keep my fingers crossed that the television option I had sold would also become a reality.

I booked several speaking engagements too. My penchant for public speaking had never dissipated, and now I had more of a platform to talk about storytelling as an instrument for social change, about how to make the most of unexpected opportunities in life, or about more practical topics such as gender equality and sustainable tourism. Being a former first lady of a tiny country was not an obvious sell for the lecture circuit, but I worked to leverage my network to find the right audiences to share my messages.

Meanwhile, a process for systematically securing the president's legacy was kicking in. Guðni would return from a day at the office talking about the rules on how his correspondence would be archived, what his postpresidential website would look like, and who might act as a part-time assistant for work that related to his life as a former head of state. Despite some brief discussions that I would also have access to this assistant, I was now resigned to the fact that none of this would apply to me. It was a little disheartening to hear that no one really cared whether all my speeches or letters or documents that I wrote as first lady were kept for posterity. (I had only just discovered that all Guðni's work-related handwritten letters had been scanned and stored for the archives. None of mine had been, simply because I didn't know that was done—or maybe it was only done for someone who held an official position. Nor did I know that the presidential website was an unofficial archive of events, or I would have worked harder to ensure that all my first-lady activities were included; most but not all were.) Nothing would happen unless I took the lead myself. Perhaps it was for the best that I would be a one-woman show going forward, even when I made appearances as "former first lady."

That spring, we held a number of farewell events. I hosted a reception for all the organizations I had served as patron. We welcomed thousands of members of the public to a final open house at the residence (everyone shook my hand too, because now I assertively put it out there to be shaken). In a nod to my inner eight-year-old, I was interviewed for a documentary on bridge! We also invited all the people who had been working to build barriers around the town of Grindavík and protect the region's vital infrastructure—hot water and electricity—from the now regular volcanic eruptions. Recognizing the crucial but sometimes overlooked work of the teams who had tirelessly kept the people of this region safe seemed like a fitting final gathering, as did, on a tiny scale related to my personal gripes, the photo caption on the front page of a newspaper the next day, in which Guðni alone was praised for hosting his final reception underneath a photo of the two of us shaking hands.

Those slights persisted among some groups. The lack of structure around how to support my work and how to even define it had carried over into the flow chart of a postpresidential transition. But I had always tried to break my own ground, and some of that had seeped into the public consciousness. (During the campaign to elect the new president, there was even a separate debate for the spouses of leading candidates.) I had moved the needle.

A few days into the New Year, writer Andri Snær Magnason, who had also run for president in 2016 and finished in third place, was interviewed on a local podcast in which he spoke about Guðni's tenure and about how my husband had been a good man in the role.

"But Eliza," he said, "had the skill to build a network… Guðni wasn't as into that…and there was Eliza at coffee with the Bidens. She knew perfectly how to play that game, and you could say that she helped round out what was lacking in Guðni."

A few years before, in fact, when Guðni was running for reelection, the head of the women's shelter in Reykjavík posted a kind story on Facebook about an unofficial visit I had made to the shelter one Christmas Eve, spending time with the women who lived there, "somehow both just one of them and also a dear guest," and noting that "in all her visits to the shelter, Eliza has shown her talent at making people feel comfortable. She blends into a group of women who have emphatically been told that they are not important." That's why, she concluded, she would be voting that day for "Eliza's husband."

I was regularly asked whether I would consider running for office one day. That spring, when Guðni and I were in Scotland on an official visit, I was approached by a local official who had taken part in one of our meetings that day. As we chitchatted at an afternoon reception, he asked me whether I was thinking of going into politics. I smiled politely and thanked him, giving him a nonanswer. "I mention it," he added, "because, with all due respect to your husband, you seemed more interested in that side of it than he did."

It was flattering and curious, coming from someone I had met only briefly. But I didn't have an answer, and I still don't. I love politics, I loved serving in a public role, but if there is anything my life has taught me, it's that you don't know what the future will bring.

Still, it was rewarding to have this unofficial and unbiased acknowledgment that I had been effective. Author and feminist Roxane Gay wrote that "change requires intent and effort." I felt that I had been making change, incrementally. I wasn't going to shift the world in a big way, but I hoped that what I did could have ripples elsewhere. I didn't consider myself an activist. I was merely trying to speak up about the issues I felt passionately about and enjoy the ride. To make the most of the chance I had been given or, as I had said in a speech in London in 2022, to use my voice and to be vigilant.

I knew I wouldn't be going back to wiping snot off sofas and proofreading annual reports. (If anything, our kids were now more likely to be breaking curfews than dishes.) But in all seriousness, there was no going back. I could go up, but only if I worked at it.

From June onward, I knew not only that my time as first lady was finishing that year, but also who would be filling my shoes. For the first time in the nation's history, the spouse of the president would be a man, Björn Skúlason. How he would forge that new path would be up to him, but I was prepared to offer any assistance I could.

Guðni was so contented as everything wound up. He was leaving the presidential office with an approval rating of over 80 percent. But it wasn't external validation that satisfied him; it was knowing he had done the best he could and was leaving while he could still give his all. I was happy for him but sad for what I was giving up and lonely that I didn't have many others with whom I could confide that melancholy because it was cloaked in privilege.

Still, I knew that given time, I could look back on what I had achieved. Had I used the opportunity I had been given? Had I pushed my own comfort zone? Increased my sartorial skills? Improved my Icelandic? Learned to speak up for myself more effectively? Remembered my roots and refused to let the glamour and perks shift my values? Protected my family from letting such privileged circumstances evolve into entitlement? Grown in compassion, tolerance, and understanding of the different challenges people face and how public figures can help to alleviate them?

I felt as if I had. Moreover, after all the lists, diary entries, accumulated stories, and new rules—both broken and kept—I knew, deep down, that I had let the unexpected lead me on a wonderful adventure. I am deeply grateful for that.

20

Pollyanna

After many years of trying, I was thrilled we were able to host a reception for new citizens of Iceland in May 2024.

Serving as first lady of Iceland has made me more of an optimist.

You may think that I have a fairly entrenched Pollyanna attitude if I was convinced my grade 6 bridge club initiative would be a smashing success or I celebrated an intramural touch football championship as if it were the Grey Cup victory. And it's true that once Guðni was elected president, I was already confident that the new role would offer adventure, fulfillment, and possibly even intrigue.

It's also true that there were downsides, many of which have been outlined in this book. Aside from my own tiny quibbles, I also met people who were experiencing acute, sudden grief, who had lost homes or loved ones or endured violence or other unspeakable tragedies.

But just think: I also got to glimpse, in the most ordinary ways possible, the best of humanity. Yes, again there was big-picture stuff like awards for bravery or sporting records, artistic accolades or grand openings. What really sticks with me, though, are the everyday acts of people of all ages, genders, backgrounds, and abilities who were slowly but surely, possibly without even trying to do so, making their communities, our society, and our world a better place.

They are people like the members of the Suðri Lions Club who fundraised for a new vital signs patient monitor in the health care center in Vík, the conductor of the Karlakórinn Heimir choir in Skagafjörður who led the rural community in song for almost four decades, the ninety-nine-year-old Winnipeg resident of Icelandic descent who proudly prepared traditional *vínarterta* cake for the arrival of special guests, the capital area elementary school children who won the contest for entering the most words into a new Icelandic language training dataset for speech recognition (meaning that in the future, we'll be able to speak to our devices in Icelandic), and the American immigrant who founded an award-winning puppetry festival in the town of Hvammstangi, population six hundred. I could go on and on.

My optimism was also increased through my own pride in my achievements and my persistence to make a difference.

After I was told early on that as first lady, I was representing all Icelanders, not just immigrants, the dream to host a reception for new citizens took a back seat to "quick win" events and projects I thought I had a better chance of accomplishing. But it never quite went away, despite privacy regulations and other roadblocks. As I realized my time in the role was coming to an end, I became ever more fixated on the idea. Such an event would underscore to new Icelanders the importance and responsibility of citizenship while reminding those of us "older" Icelanders that we too have obligations to ensure that everyone can contribute fully to society and help to make it a richer nation for all of us. It would be a chance to renew our shared commitments to the continuous improvement of our communities. The more I thought on it, the more I decided that if there were only one more thing I could accomplish as first lady, hosting this single reception with Guðni would be it.

Finally, in May 2024, it happened! We invited everyone who had acquired Icelandic citizenship since the beginning of that year to Bessastaðir (overcoming privacy regulations by having the Directorate of Immigration send the invites on our behalf). We invited media to cover the story; television reporters spoke to both new citizens and to me about the idea. In two batches, we received people from almost thirty countries. They dressed in their finest and seemed so proud and happy to be there. There was the professor at the University of Iceland, originally from Iran. The couple from Morocco and Poland who had fallen in love after meeting here. Even a woman who claimed she moved here for the outdoors and the weather (I'm pretty sure she was originally from Germany). And there was a young doctor and activist from Afghanistan, Noorina Khalikyar, whose citizenship had been fast-tracked after she had to flee from the Taliban's new takeover in August 2021. Unlike many Icelanders of Afghan origin who had recently arrived, she had no previous connection to the country. When I asked her why she escaped to Iceland of all places, she answered simply, "I googled 'safest country in the world for women,' and this is what came up."

Who wouldn't feel more optimistic about change after meeting people such as this, just a tiny fraction of those who are now proud to call Iceland home?

That reception, that celebration of diversity and inclusion, was really personal for me. Far from shoehorning me into a limited sphere of influence, my experience as a first lady who was also an immigrant allowed me to send a message that speaking Icelandic imperfectly and with an accent reminds us that we need to make more room for others who wish to do so too. It highlighted the positive diversity of our country and helped me always remember that many voices in Iceland don't get the same level of attention as others, and that needs to change.

Being an immigrant in Iceland is an important part of my identity, and generally speaking, as first lady, it was always critical to me to maintain my own identity in this adventure. So I chose to be vocal and engaged, to use any spotlight I had to shine on areas that I felt were important: gender equality, diversity and inclusion, the promotion of Icelandic cultural pursuits, tourism and sustainability, and innovation. And I wanted to send a message that as someone who happily undertook probably thousands of activities on a voluntary basis as first lady, I could also simultaneously earn my own living working at jobs I enjoyed.

Meanwhile, serving as first lady in this specific country—the world's most peaceful, third happiest, and closest to closing the gender gap—enhanced my belief that each individual can make a difference, that we are all role models and have voices that deserve to be heard. Because here in Iceland, on our good days, we can celebrate change and realize that progress for all of us is not going to happen without concerted effort, and if we don't stay focused, there can easily be a backlash.

On October 24, 2023, Iceland's women took another day off to mirror the original event from 1975 when 90 percent of the country protested ongoing wage inequalities by not doing their work—both paid and unpaid—for the day. The success of that first strike remains a beacon for activists and others to show the impact of collective action and positive protest. Almost half a century later, despite tremendous achievements, we still hadn't reached the ultimate goal, so an event was held again, this time specifically asking nonbinary folks to take part too and placing an emphasis on the eradication of gender-based violence.

I had already made plans to be abroad that day, so I couldn't gather downtown, but I did take the day off where I was. Meanwhile, I asked several others if they would be heading into town to listen to speeches and sing songs. While the event itself drew record numbers of people, several of those I spoke to beforehand said that they couldn't make it—they had to watch their kids because their husband's work was too important or variations on that theme. Those responses surprised and disappointed me. Complacency is dangerous. We have come a long way in Iceland concerning gender equality, but what if too many people think that that is good enough? Does the privilege that so many of us have blind us to the ongoing inequalities and struggles of others? Is getting near the finish line an excuse to slow the pace and conclude there's no need for extra exertion?

I don't think that "good enough" is good enough. I think that those of us who had the ability to take a day off, to show the value of our work, had an obligation to do so for all those others who supported the cause but really couldn't manage it. I think when we have an opportunity to push for progress, whether that's in gender equality or human rights and democracy more broadly, when we find ourselves on the cusp of change, we need to grasp hold of it with all our might.

At the end of the 2023 gathering, Una Torfadóttir, an up-and-coming local indie singer, performed a cover of the 1975 Women's Day Off anthem, "Áfram stelpur," with its iconic motto that galvanized a nation: Dare I? Will I? Can I? Yes, I dare, I can, I will. I was sent a short video that panned over the crowd of thousands as they sang along in unison, a sea of motivated jubilance belting out the inspirational lyrics under an azure sky. I posted it online with the permission of the videographer, Eva Björk Ægisdóttir. To this day, it is easily the most viewed and shared post on my social media.

Foreign audiences love the story of Iceland's Women's Day Off, and local audiences continue to be inspired by it. I share the motto "I dare, I can, I will" and repeat it again at the end of talks. It's my call to action to audiences: What do they dare to do to build change?

It's also a motto I had tried to hold with me as I navigated my role without a handbook. Did I dare to break some of the unwritten rules? Did I not break enough or perhaps break too many? Could I figure out what I wanted to achieve and implement it without losing my own identity? Throughout my life, I've reveled in planning the details, working out all the small stuff. I compose to-do lists, ticking off task by task. I've tried to anticipate next steps, predict outcomes, to know how I might react when faced with certain challenges, some bends in the road. I've used past mistakes to inform future decisions. Taking the time to do that left me free to embrace the giant, amorphous opportunities, the ones you might miss if preoccupied by routine, the ones that are the markers of a life well lived.

I believe that we are all the authors of our own destinies, even if we don't know where the story may lead. We need to have flexible ambitions and hone our adaptability to make the most of those unexpected moments in life. We should strive to be happy and to make others happy, to live with no regrets. You never know the path your life will take, but you should enjoy being on the journey too. The key is to be willing to embark on the voyage in the first place, even if it's to a destination unknown.

Moving on from the most unexpected chapter of my life would take a different leap of faith than the one that led me into it. Now there may be less adrenaline and perhaps more equanimity. Fewer ball gowns and more flip-flops. But eventually, I would realize, just as much adventure and many opportunities to build on the unique story I had spent the last eight years writing. I just needed to keep my eyes and heart open.

The weather on August 1, 2024, began with rain that would clear just in time for the inauguration of Iceland's seventh president and only the second woman to hold the role, Halla Tómasdóttir (yes, the same woman who had finished second to Guðni in 2016). Guðni's term had ended at midnight on July 31, and according to the constitution, the prime minister, the president of the Althing, and the president of the supreme court jointly maintain the office in the approximately fourteen-hour period before the new president signs the oath of office in the Althing.

It was a bittersweet day for me. A time to reflect on the past eight years but also to look forward. From our new home, still with plywood stairs and no bathroom door, I dressed in my ball gown, sash, and Order of the Falcon. For the final time, we were collected by Rikki, now steering the 1942 Packard, and escorted by two police officers on motorcycles. The vintage vehicle drew attention along the four-mile route to the Althing. Other drivers on the highway slowed as they passed us to flash their lights and crane their necks. Pedestrians had their phones out. Many waved, and it felt like all were smiling. One car inched by us slowly, and a young woman in the passenger seat held up her hands to form the shape of a heart. My eyes glistened with tears.

That evening, after the church ceremony, after the inauguration in the Althing, after a champagne reception to toast the new presidential couple, Guðni and I invited our two good friends Liz and Friðjón to dinner at our house. They had had a ringside seat from the beginning of the adventure, and it seemed only fitting to be with them as we commemorated the closing chapter. We would order Chinese food and raise a glass. And not just any glass. On our first state visit in 2017, Prince Henrik of Denmark had gifted us with a magnum of 1989 Château de Cayx from his private French vineyard. We'd kept it on its side in its wooden casing for almost eight years, waiting for the right time to open it but never quite landing on an occasion that would live up to the bottle's origins. Now seemed as good a time as any.

As the food arrived, we took out the bottle and four glasses. Friðjón is an enthusiastic oenophile, and he had already scanned the label and pasted it into a wine lover's app to reveal the drink's unique tasting notes. There was mention of delicate plums, a hint of pepper. This was going to be special, a rare Bordeaux wine, one fit for royalty no less!

I knew as soon as I began twisting the corkscrew that something was amiss. The cork virtually dissolved at its touch and crumbled into the bottle. The liquid was a murky brown rather than a deep red, the bouquet more fetid leather than rich tannins. The '89 Château de Cayx was spoiled.

It was an unexpected ending, yet apt. Sometimes you get a dud bottle. Sometimes things don't happen the way you expect them to. Sometimes you need to wing it and in doing so maybe even make something better from the situation than you thought possible.

I unearthed a different bottle of wine, one I had probably bought solely for the appealing label, and doled out the kung pao chicken and egg noodles. A dusty light bulb, a reminder of how much work was left to do on the house, swayed gently over our plates. We shared some stories and laughs around the kitchen table. It was all going to be okay. I smiled at my husband, smiled at my friends, and looked forward to the next chapter of life's beautiful uncertainty.

ACKNOWLEDGMENTS

My husband likes to call me "Analyza" because I have a tendency to overthink actions and decisions, especially those in the past that are now beyond my control. It's really not a good use of time. But perhaps it's why the acknowledgments is often my favorite part of a book; this section provides some space for me to overexplain all of the areas where I overanalyzed in the main text. Lucky you, dear reader.

So, a few caveats: Conversations in this book are reproduced to the best of my memory, but memories are obviously fallible. Facts are mentioned as accurately as possible, and with the assistance of many of those I thank in the paragraphs that follow, although needless to say, any errors remain mine alone.

You will probably not be surprised to discover that even after writing this book, I still worry about my relationship to the rules. I know that first ladies often write memoirs, but are they allowed to write ones that detail cervical exams, wardrobe malfunctions, and plenty of imposter syndrome? Is it bad protocol to talk about royals even though I hope it's done in a kind way? Will my family, friends, and named acquaintances think I mentioned them too much? Or not enough? I don't know the answers, but I have trusted my intentions and I hope readers will too.

A great many people helped me in the writing of this book, by sharing information, providing me with relevant history, reading full drafts, or simply refreshing my memory of Dutch coalition negotiations and the vodoun religion in Benin. I am grateful to all of you (and to anyone whose name I have inadvertently neglected to mention!).

Here goes: Guðrún Ágústsdóttir, Zuhaitz Akizu, Jann Arden, Jóhann Gunnar Arnarsson, Tammy Axelsson, Elke Büdenbender, Amanda Burt, James Cann, Peter Damisch, Helga Kr. Einarsdóttir, Bergdís Ellertsdóttir, Friðjón Friðjónsson, Serena Goebel, Sif Gunnarsdóttir, Björn Helgason, alumni, faculty, and staff of the Iceland Writers Retreat (especially faculty such as Danny Ramadan and Curtis Sittenfeld in 2025 who helped brainstorm titles), Ásrún Helga Kristinsdóttir, Heiðrún Kristjánsdóttir, Katrín Jakobsdóttir, Jóhannes Ólafur Jóhannesson, Elliot Johnson, Dan Kois, Elizabeth Lay, María Erla Marelsdóttir, Magnea J. Matthíasdóttir, Lachlin McKinnon, Martin Mevius, Aleš Musar, Pétur Óskarsson, Elizabeth Renzetti, Ríkarður Már Ríkarðsson, Doris Schmidauer, Ragnar Schram, Una Sighvatsdóttir, the St. Hilda's Smashers of 1996–97, Ildikó Somorjai, Kati Süle, Erla María Jónsdóttir Tölgyes, Marilyn Valgardson, Elizabeth Vlossak, Stewart Wheeler, Hattie Williams, Claudia A Wilson Molloy.

Jonas Moody deserves a special shout-out for being the first reader of every chapter and providing excellent and constructive feedback (such as "this chapter ends like slamming into a brick wall"—that's hopefully been fixed to the degree that you won't know to which chapter this comment refers).

My deep gratitude to current and former staff of the Office of the President of Iceland, both those at the office and those who work at Bessastaðir. It is a small but mighty team who look after Iceland's head of state (and spouse!), and that cannot always (or ever?) be an easy job. I don't think anyone would doubt your commitment to the office and the institution of the presidency, and I thank you for your service. Some of you were specifically helpful in the preparation of this book; your names are also listed earlier.

Once a book is written, it is transported into the great sausage-making factory that is bookmaking. There are many people to thank here too. It starts with my awesome agent, Samantha Haywood at Transatlantic Agency in Toronto. The team there includes Eva Oakes and Megan Phillip. Anna Michels at Sourcebooks and Adrienne Kerr at Simon & Schuster were once again wonderful editors with whom to work (extra shout-out to Anna who helpfully pointed out a sentence in one draft that included a whopping four clichés!). Over on the production and promotional side, I'd like to thank Nicole Winstanley, Shara Alexa, Lisa Wray, Rita Silva, Cali Platek, Kaitlyn Lonnee, Paul Barker, Wendy Blum, Kayley Hoffman, and Janice Weaver for S&S Canada, and Patience Bramlett, Jillian Rahn, Kirsten Clawson, Angela Corpus, Gianna Antolos, and Daisy Rankin at Sourcebooks. Thank you also to the photographers who captured the images in this book.

Kæru landsmenn á Íslandi: Takk. Takk fyrir að taka á móti mér. Takk fyrir að gefa mér tækifæri til að blómstra. Takk fyrir að vinna að því að bæta við okkar fallega samfélag. To my fellow countryfolk of Iceland: Thank you. Thank you for welcoming me. Thank you for giving me the opportunity to blossom. Thank you for doing your part in working to build a better society.

Final words, as always, to my family, both in Iceland and in Canada. Thanks to my mother, Allison Reid, who allowed me to read the entire manuscript to her over the course of a Christmas vacation (that's parenthood for you, even when your children are middle-aged!) and to my stepdaughter, Rut Guðnadóttir, for her encouragement about the parenthood section. Duncan, Donnie, Sæþór, Edda, and of course Guðni are the most important parts of *my* story, but this book is not their story, and I did my best to respect their privacy within its pages. My whole family—immediate, extended, in-law—has my gratitude for the creative, kind, encouraging, and simply happy environments in which I have always lived. I am so fortunate.

READING GROUP GUIDE

1. What identities do you have for yourself (e.g., mother, father, friend, coworker, etc.)? Do you feel comforted or confined by these identities?

2. How well do you react to the unexpected? Is there a situation you can recall where you reacted particularly well or poorly to something unexpected in your life?

3. Were you interested in politics when you were a child? Were you aware of the general political atmosphere? If not, when did you start to become aware?

4. What do you picture when you hear the words "first lady"? What do you think the responsibility of a first lady is/should be? What do you think the responsibility of a first gentleman is/should be? Are they different?

5. What causes or charities would you champion if you had the time and means to do so?

6. Do you find humor helpful in dealing with challenging times? What is it about jokes, satire, and other forms of humor that allow us to better handle difficult subjects?

7. How do our pasts shape who we become as people? What parts of your background and culture influence how you participate in the world around you?

8. Describe a time when you've felt out of place in a group or situation, no matter the reason. What made you feel this way? How did you react to that feeling?

9. Eliza faces many microaggressions because of her position, such as people shaking hands with her husband and ignoring her. Have you faced these kinds of microaggressions in your life? How do you deal with them? How did Eliza?

10. If you are in a position of power, privilege, and influence, is it your responsibility to call out wrongs you see in the world? What if you aren't in that position? Is it everyone's responsibility, no matter the power they hold, to speak up about injustices?

11. How concerned are you with the idea of legacy? What would you like to leave behind for future generations?

PHOTO CREDITS

Chapter 1: Courtesy of Golli

Chapter 2: Courtesy of the author

Chapter 3: Courtesy of the author

Chapter 4: Courtesy of the author

Chapter 5: Courtesy of the author

Chapter 6: Courtesy of the author

Chapter 7: Courtesy of Axel Sigurðsson

Chapter 8: Courtesy of Håkon Broder Lund

Chapter 9: Courtesy of Anton Brink, Reykjavík Museum of Photography

Chapter 10: Courtesy of Helga Einarsdóttir

Chapter 11: Courtesy of Gunnar G. Vigfússon

Chapter 12: Courtesy of Una Sighvatsdóttir, Office of the President of Iceland

Chapter 13: Courtesy of Kungahuset

Chapter 14: Courtesy of the author

Chapter 15: Courtesy of John Werner Photography

Chapter 16: Courtesy of Robin Crawford

Chapter 17: Courtesy of Hilmar Bragi Bárðarson, *Víkurfréttir*

Chapter 18: Courtesy of Davið Logi Sigurðsson

Chapter 19: Courtesy of Silla Páls

Chapter 20: Courtesy of Árni Sigurjónsson, Office of the President of Iceland

NOTES

"Each of us needs": Chris Hadfield, *An Astronaut's Guide to Life on Earth: What Going to Space Taught Me about Ingenuity, Determination, and Being Prepared for Anything* (Random House Canada, 2013), https://books.google.ca/books?id=Cm9Srav-opoC&pg=PT265.

CHAPTER ONE: OVER THE HILL

an "incredibly weird job": Eliza Reid, "I'm a First Lady, and It's an Incredibly Weird Job," *New York Times*, October 1, 2019, https://www.nytimes.com/2019/10/01/opinion/first-ladies.html.

CHAPTER TWO: FOLLOWING THE RULES

"Bert: Ernie, how do I look?": "Sesame Street: Same Old Bert," *Sesame Street*, May 17, 2010, YouTube video, 2:22, https://www.youtube.com/watch?v=pD0CL4KJOa8.

CHAPTER SIX: IN A FAMILY WAY

"We could sit together": Guðni Th. Jóhannesson, Gunnar Thoroddsen. Ævisaga (Reykjavík: JPV, 2010), pp. 159–160.

CHAPTER SEVEN: PANAMA

twenty-seven people: Mariko Oi, "Panama Papers Money-Laundering

Trial Begins," BBC, April 8, 2024, https://www.bbc.com/news/articles/cnek443n8zvo#.

"I'm starting to feel": "Viðtal við Sigmund Davíð um Wintris—Kastljós 3. apríl 2016" [Interview with Sigmund Davíð about Wintris—Spotlight on April 3, 2016], sveinbjornt, April 3, 2016, YouTube video, 8:20, https://www.youtube.com/watch?v=3lHs-iUeAWE.

third largest corporate bankruptcy: Jenny Anderson, "How Iceland Emerged from Its Deep Freeze," *New York Times*, July 3, 2015, https://www.nytimes.com/2015/07/05/business/international/how-iceland-emerged-from-its-deep-freeze.html.

CHAPTER EIGHT: A BEAUTIFUL UNCERTAINTY

"I think this is an excellent opportunity": Snærós Sindradóttir, "Í mesta lagi tólf ár á Bessastöðum" [At most twelve years at Bessastaðir], *Vísir*, May 7, 2016, https://www.visir.is/g/2016160509227/i-mesta-lagi-tolf-ar-a-bessastodum.

2008 global financial crisis: "25 People to Blame for the Financial Crisis," *Time*, October 6, 2011, https://content.time.com/time/specials/packages/article/0,28804,1877351_1877350_1877340,00.html.

a poll was published: "Guðni með tæplega 70% fylgi" [Guðni with almost 70% support], *Morgunblaðið*, May 11, 2016, https://www.mbl.is/frettir/kosning/2016/05/11/gudni_med_taeplega_70_prosent_fylgi/.

"quite an asset to her husband": Súsanna Svavarsdóttir, "Eliza Reid: *The Canadian* Girl Most Icelanders Want as Their First Lady," Hit Iceland, May 2016, updated December 15, 2022, https://www.hiticeland.com/post/eliza-reid-the-canadian-girl-most-icelanders-want-as-their-first-lady.

"Icelanders feel about eating cake": Adam Gopnik, "Guðni Jóhannesson, Iceland's Historic Candidate," *New Yorker*, July 4, 2016, https://www.newyorker.com/magazine/2016/07/11/gudni-johannesson-icelands-historic-candidate.

CHAPTER NINE: LIMBO

"the great unknown": Anna Margrét Björnsson, "Video: Interview with Iceland's New Canadian First Lady," *Iceland Monitor*, July 2, 2016, https://icelandmonitor.mbl.is/news/politics_and_society/2016/07/02/video_interview_with_iceland_s_new_canadian_first_l/.

"Eliza is a calm and composed": Erna Hreinsdóttir, editor's note, *Nýtt Líf*, no. 8 (2016): 8, translated from Icelandic.

Guðni posted condolences: Sunna Kristín Hilmarsdóttir, "Guðni Th. sendir samúðarkveðjur vegna árásarinnar í Nice" [Guðni Th. sends condolences for the attack in Nice], *Vísir*, July 15, 2016, https://www.visir.is/g/20161376960d/gudni-th.-sendir-samudarkvedjur-vegna-arasarinnar-i-nice.

CHAPTER TEN: WHO AM I?

"Yours is an office": Anna Sauerbrey, "Germany's First Lady Problem," *New York Times*, April 6, 2017, https://www.nytimes.com/2017/04/06/opinion/germanys-first-lady-problem.html.

assassinated in 2007: "Aseefa's Nomination as First Lady Sparks Debate," *Tribune* [Pakistan], March 11, 2024, https://tribune.com.pk/story/2459057/president-zardari-decides-to-name-daughter-aseefa-as-first-lady.

"to unlock Canada": Institute for Canadian Citizenship, accessed June 16, 2025, https://forcitizenship.ca/.

CHAPTER ELEVEN: LOOK THE PART

"I was learning how to connect": Michelle Obama, *Becoming* (Crown, 2018), 372.

style had "completely changed": "Eliza Reid þá og nú—Þvílík breyting," *Morgunblaðið Smartland*, November 22, 2018, https://www.mbl.is/smartland/stars/2018/11/22/eliza_reid_tha_og_nu_thvilik_breyting/.

secondhand clothing: Marta María, "Eliza mætti í jakka úr Rauða krossinum" [Eliza arrived wearing a jacket from the Red Cross], *Morgunblaðið*, February 27, 2018, https://www.mbl.is/smartland/tiska/2018/02/27/eliza_maetti_i_jakka_ur_rauda_krossinum/; "First Lady Wears Thrift Store Jacket to the Edda Awards," *Iceland Monitor*, February 27, 2018, https://icelandmonitor.mbl.is/news/culture_and_living/2018/02/27/first_lady_wears_thrift_store_jacket_to_the_edda_aw/.

noticed by the BBC: Alistair Coleman, "Icelandic First Lady's Charity Shop Chic," *BBC*, February 28, 2018, http://www.bbc.com/news/blogs-news-from-elsewhere-43228332.

cut out of the dress: Marta María, "Eliza í kjól úr Rauðakrossbúðinni á kosningavökunni" [Eliza in a dress from the Red Cross on election night], *Morgunblaðið*, June 29, 2020, https://www.mbl.is/smartland/stars/2020/06/29/eliza_i_kjol_ur_raudakrossbudinni_a_kosningavokunni/.

the suffragist movement: Anna Sigríður Einarsdóttir, "Sendi Eliza pólitísk skilaboð með hvítu dragtinni?" [Was Eliza sending a political message with the white pantsuit?], *Morgunblaðið*, September 4, 2019, https://www.mbl.is/frettir/innlent/2019/09/04/sendi_eliza_politisk_skilabod_med_dragtinni/?fbclid=IwAR306Q7HYzhmZ_BRTgId3KtQ5lJg38CBngCIBPLOF3scoq2cj_lrP_V5qiE; "Colors Speak Loudly during Pence's Visit," *Iceland Monitor*, September 5, 2019, https://icelandmonitor.mbl.is/news/politics_and_society/2019/09/05/colors_speak_loudly_during_pence_s_visit/; Lee Moran, "Mike Pence Got Colorfully Taunted on His Way to Meet Iceland's President," *HuffPost*, September 5, 2019, https://www.huffpost.com/entry/mike-pence-iceland-flags_n_5d70d003e4b01108045a1cc7.

CHAPTER TWELVE: THE BALANCING ACT

"You've been going ninety": Amy Hempel, *At the Gates of the Animal Kingdom* (Penguin, 1991), 49.

trust in the office rose: "Traust til forsetans eykst mikið" [Trust in the presidency increases significantly], *Morgunblaðið*, February 27, 2017, https://www.mbl.is/frettir/innlent/2017/02/27/traust_til_forsetans_eykst_mikid/.

97 percent approval rating: Garðar Örn Úlfarsson, "Vinsældir forseta í tölu sem sést eiginlega aldrei segir professor" [President's popularity in numbers never really seen, says professor], *Vísir*, December 20, 2016, https://www.visir.is/g/20161133181d/vinsaeldir-forseta-i-tolu-sem-sest-eiginlega-aldrei-segir-professor.

When Guðni became president: "Immigrants 18.2% of the Population of Iceland," Statistics Iceland, December 12, 2024, https://statice.is/publications/news-archive/inhabitants/population-by-origin-1-january-2024/. Statistics Iceland considers a first-generation immigrant as a person born abroad with both parents foreign born and all grandparents foreign born, whereas a second-generation immigrant is born in Iceland having immigrant parents.

to visit a mosque: Alma Mjöll Ólafsdóttir, "Eliza Reid forsetafrú segir sjálfsagt að sýna íslömskum vinum samstöðu" [First Lady Eliza Reid says it goes without saying to show solidarity with Islamic friends], *Heimildin*, March 27, 2019, https://stundin.is/grein/8717/eliza-reid-forsetafru-segir-sjalfsagt-ad-syna-islomskum-vinum-samstodu/.

CHAPTER THIRTEEN: FAIRY TALE

"Guðni and Eliza are a hit": Eiríkur Jónsson, "Obamahjón Íslands" [Iceland's Obamas], Vefsahn.is, January 26, 2017, https://vefsafn.is/is/20170508112946/http://eirikurjonsson.is/obamahjon-islands/.

Oscar de La Renta: Sinead MacLaughlin, "The Hard-Working Princess! Mary Enjoys a Glass of Champagne after Hosting a Gala Dinner for the President of Iceland in an Elegant Navy Gown," *Daily Mail*, January 25, 2017, https://www.dailymail.co.uk/femail/article-4155938/Princess-Mary-stuns-visit-Iceland-President.html.

"very enjoyable occasion": "#TheMoment Iceland's president and first lady got screeched in," CBC News: The National, June 1, 2023, YouTube video, 1:23, https://www.youtube.com/watch?v=dN54kN7QcDI.

CHAPTER FOURTEEN: SOLO FIRST LADY

"During my years in New York": Madeleine Albright, *Madam Secretary: A Memoir* (Harper Perennial, 2013), 214.

The list included: United Nations World Tourism Organization, *UNWTO Annual Report 2017*, https://doi.org/10.18111/9789284419807.

Tourism is the country's largest: "The Share of Tourism in GDP Estimated at 8.5% in 2023," Statistics Iceland, February 29, 2024, https://www.statice.is/publications/news-archive/national-accounts/the-share-of-tourism-in-gdp-2023-provisional-estimates/.

"She was warned": Daniel Victor, "'Nevertheless, She Persisted': How

Senate's Silencing of Warren Became a Meme," *New York Times*, February 8, 2017, https://www.nytimes.com/2017/02/08/us/politics/elizabeth-warren-republicans-facebook-twitter.html.

would not send officials: "Iceland Takes Diplomatic Measures against Russia," Ministry for Foreign Affairs, Government of Iceland, March 26, 2018, https://www.government.is/news/article/2018/03/26/Iceland-takes-diplomatic-measures-against-Russia-/; Matt Bonesteel, "Iceland and England Won't Send Government Officials to Russia World Cup, and Others May Follow," *Washington Post*, March 27, 2018, https://www.washingtonpost.com/news/early-lead/wp/2018/03/27/iceland-and-england-wont-send-government-officials-to-russia-world-cup-and-others-may-follow/.

CHAPTER FIFTEEN: NOT MY HUSBAND'S HANDBAG

"I am not my husband's handbag": Eliza Reid, "I'm a first lady."

"They were using me": Robin Givhan, "Michelle Obama Wanted to Gain the Public's Trust. So She Started with a Garden," *Washington Post*, March 21, 2018, https://www.washingtonpost.com/news/arts-and-entertainment/wp/2018/03/21/michelle-obama-wanted-to-gain-the-publics-trust-so-she-started-with-a-garden/.

The Guardian piece opined: Zoe Williams, "The G7 Was the Final Straw—World Leaders' Wives Should Refuse to Travel with Their Spouses," *Guardian*, August 28, 2019, https://www.theguardian.com/lifeandstyle/2019/aug/28/the-g7-was-the-final-straw-world-leaders-wives-should-refuse-to-travel-with-their-spouses.

"I wholeheartedly agree": Eliza Reid, Facebook post, accessed November 2018, https://www.facebook.com/elizajeanreid/posts

/pfbid02Bb1u6TB6vj6vUtWQBerT3TAiD6m EpZXyhEyw2Daq vmyZHGt6ZR3WroNQJEPdn7MMl.

"Which Lady Looked Best": "Która z dam wyglądała najlepiej na obchodach 80. rocznicy wybuchu II wojny światowej?" [Which lady looked best at the celebration of the 80th anniversary of the outbreak of World War II?], *Viva*, September 2, 2019, https://viva.pl/moda/ikony-stylu/agata-duda-na-obchodach-80-rocznicy-ii-wojny-siatowej-34056-r3/.

nominated as "person of the year": "Hver er manneskja ársins 2019?" [Who is the person of the year 2019?], RÚV, December 19, 2019, https://www.ruv.is/frett/hver-er-manneskja-arsins-2019; Tinni Sveinsson, "Þau eru tilnefnd sem maður ársins 2019" [They are nominated for person of the year 2019], *Vísir*, December 23, 2019, https://www.visir.is/g/2019191229714/thau-eru-tilnefnd-sem-madur-arsins-2019; Sunna Kristín Hilmarsdóttir, "Ummæli ársins: Villimannseðlið, sómakenndin og þú sem ert nóg" [Comment of the year: The savage instinct, sense of dignity, and you who are enough], *Vísir*, December 24, 2019, https://www.visir.is/g/2019191229737.

"Summary of this photo caption": Eliza Reid, "Summary of this photo caption on the cover of the newspaper today," Facebook, October 13, 2021, https://www.facebook.com/photo.php?fbid=406341104389299&id=100050402383504&set=a.246394553717289.

tempest in a teapot: Hólmfríður Gísladóttir, "Forsetafrúin spyr: #erukonurtil?" [The First Lady asks: #dowomenexist?], *Vísir*, October 13, 2021, https://www.visir.is/g/20212169049d/forsetafruin-spyr-erukonurtil; Jelena Ćirić, "Iceland's First Lady Asks: Do Women Exist?," *Iceland Review*, October 13, 2021, https://www.icelandreview.com/news/politics/icelands-first-lady-asks-do-women-exist/.

clothing and jewelry: Marta María, "Geislaði í eldri skyrtu og nýrri íslenskri hönnun" [Radiant in an older jacket and new Icelandic design], *Morgunblaðið*, October 13, 2021, https://www.mbl.is/smartland/tiska/2021/10/13/geisladi_i_eldri_skyrtu_og_nyrri_islenskri_honnun/.

CHAPTER SIXTEEN: WORKING WOMAN

"In America, this was expected": Cherie Blair, *Speaking for Myself: My Life from Liverpool to Downing Street* (Little, Brown, 2008), 211.

"creative collaboration": Vigdís International Centre, "Roots and Wings—A conference on creative collaboration across linguistic and cultural boundaries is held in Verold 24–25 May," Facebook, May 14, 2018, https://www.facebook.com/watch/?v=1728551193890526.

280,000 signatures: Adam Lusher, "Brigitte Macron Will Not Get Official 'First Lady Job," *Independent*, August 8, 2017, https://www.independent.co.uk/news/world/europe/brigitte-macron-first-lady-controversy-announcement-latest-update-emmanuel-macron-wife-petition-transparency-charter-official-title-job-french-president-france-salary-cost-opposition-thierry-paul-valette-a7883131.html.

Trudeau was heavily criticized: "'I need help': Sophie Grégoire Trudeau's Plea Sparks Anger in Canada," *Guardian*, May 16, 2016, https://www.theguardian.com/world/2016/may/16/i-need-help-first-lady-sophie-trudeaus-anger-canada.

"is responsible for the branding": Business Iceland, accessed June 17, 2025, https://www.islandsstofa.is/en.

Iceland has topped: "Gender Parity: Here's What Leading Countries Are Getting Right," World Economic Forum, June 21, 2023, https://www.weforum.org/stories/2023/06/global-gender-gap-parity/.

take on paid work: Heimir Már Pétursson, "Eliza mun taka þátt í fjölda viðburða með Íslandsstofu á næsta ári" [Eliza will participate in several events with Business Iceland next year], *Vísir*, October 30, 2019, https://www.visir.is/g/2019191039842.

Some called it "poor judgment": "Álfheiður sakar forsetahjónin um dómgreindarleysi: 'Er þetta ekki óeðlilegt? Hagsmunaárekstur?'" [Álfheiður accuses the presidential couple of lack of judgment: "Isn't this unusual? A conflict of interest?"], *DV*, October 30, 2019, https://www.dv.is/eyjan/2019/10/30/alfheidur-sakar-forsetahjonin-um-domgreindarleysi-er-thetta-ekki-oedlilegt-hagsmunaarekstur/.

"deserves a high salary": Unattributed quotation from an unidentified Icelandic news outlet's social media post, copied by the author into a personal diary, c. 2019.

appearance on *Good Morning America*: "How to Improve Gender Equality," *Good Morning America*, May 12, 2023, https://www.goodmorningamerica.com/video/99287964.

CHAPTER SEVENTEEN: ERUPTIONS, EPIDEMICS, AND ENDINGS

"This small nation": Address by President of Iceland Guðni Th. Jóhannesson at the Beginning of a Volcanic Eruption at Grindavík, January 14, 2024, https://gudni.forseti.is/media/12127/20240114-grindavík-eruption-address.pdf.

An eruption: Melissa Scruggs, "Iceland's Ground Swells as Volcanic Eruption Looms near Grindavík,"Temblor, November 16, 2023, https://temblor.net/temblor/nov-2023-iceland-volcanic-eruption-looms-near-grindavik-15694/.

residents could return: Barney Davis, "Every Resident of an Icelandic Town Was Evacuated Due to a Volcano. Daring Rescuers Went Back to Save the Pets," *Independent*, November 25, 2023, https://www.independent.co.uk/news/world/europe/iceland-grindavik-volcano-eruption-b2453338.html.

The predicted eruption: Mitchell McCluskey, Taylor Ward, and Jessie Yeung, "Volcano Erupts on Iceland's Reykjanes Peninsula Weeks after Town Evacuated," CNN, December 19, 2023, https://edition.cnn.com/2023/12/18/europe/reykjanes-volcano-erupts-iceland/index.html.

"we will carry on": Address by President of Iceland Guðni Th. Jóhannesson.

There were no fatalities: Andie Sophia Fontaine, "Three Avalanches Strike in a Single Night; One Rescued, Multiple Boats Damaged," *Reykjavík Grapevine*, January 15, 2020, https://grapevine.is/news/2020/01/15/three-avalanches-strike-in-a-single-night-one-rescued-multiple-boats-damaged/.

several landslides tore through: "The Landslide in Seyðisfjörður Is the Largest Landslide to Have Damaged an Urban Area in Iceland," Icelandic Met Office, January 8, 2021, https://en.vedur.is/about-imo/news/the-landslide-in-seydisfjordur-is-the-largest-landslide-to-have-damaged-an-urban-area-in-iceland.

He was preparing for them: Kristín Sigurðardóttir and Rúnar Snær Reynisson, "11 ára drengur og faðir hans hlupu undan skriðunni" [An 11-year-old boy and his father ran from the landslide], RÚV, December 19, 2020, https://nyr.ruv.is/frettir/innlent/2020-12-19-11-ara-drengur-og-fadir-hans-hlupu-undan-skridunni.

upstanding role models: "Iceland Provides a Picture of the Early Spread of COVID-19 in a Population with a Cohesive Public Health

Response," Decode Genetics, April 15, 2020, https://www.decode.com/iceland-provides-a-picture-of-the-early-spread-of-covid-19-in-a-population-with-a-cohesive-public-health-response/.

It is impossible: Kolbeinn Tumi Daðason, "Guðni og Eliza mættu í skimun" [Guðni and Eliza attended the screening], *Vísir*, March 13, 2020, https://www.visir.is/g/202019400d/gudni-og-eliza-maettu-i-skimun.

visited Red Cross workers: "Hjálparsími Rauða krossins" [Red Cross helpline], President of Iceland, March 18, 2020, https://gudni.forseti.is/fréttir/2020-03-18-hjálparsími-rauða-krossins/.

"Happy New Year, everyone!": Eliza Reid, "Happy New Year, everyone!," Facebook, December 31, 2020, https://www.facebook.com/elizajeanreid/posts/1096986254071544/.

"This is the first day of summer": Eliza Reid, "This the first day of summer in Iceland, a national holiday," Facebook, April 21, 2022, https://www.facebook.com/elizajeanreid/posts/pfbid02fST2vu NnL3SiugsRSGbKX7uGUs6p1FA7Hhxm9anUGQw7FUNPCd7kYohm9Z3jYcs2l.

They all seemed a bit tired: Brynjólfur Þór Guðmundsson, "Andúð á þeim sem loka landamærum" [Hostility towards those who close borders], RÚV, January 30, 2017, http://www.ruv.is/frett/andud-a-theim-sem-loka-landamaerum; "Icelandic President Invites Syrian Refugees to His Official Residence," *Iceland Monitor*, January 30, 2017, http://icelandmonitor.mbl.is/news/politics_and_society/2017/01/30/icelandic_president_invites_syrian_refugees_to_his_/.

Sviatlana took his place: Sviatlana Tsikhanouskaya, "I Am the Belarusian President-Elect, and Together We Will Prevail," *Politico*, November 14, 2022, https://www.politico.eu/article/sviatlana-tsikhanouskaya-belarus

-opposition-leader-democracy-elections-alexander-lukashenko-vladimir-putin-russia-ukraine/.

fight for a democratic Belarus: BBC News, "Eliza Reid: Iceland's First Lady on Equality and Representation," last modified June 20, 2025, https://www.bbc.com/news/articles/c9397rrkwedo.

never changed a diaper: Benjamin Kentish, "Tory MP and Father of Six Jacob Rees-Mogg Says He Has Never Changed a Nappy," *Independent*, July 22, 2017, https://www.independent.co.uk/news/uk/politics/jacob-reesmogg-never-changed-a-nappy-lbc-nigel-farage-nanny-conservatives-a7854791.html.

Along with their achievements: Heiðursviðurkenningar á hátíðarfundi bæjarstjórnar Grindavikurbæjar í tilefni af 50 ára kaupstaðarafmæli bæjarins 10. april 2024 [Honorary awards presented at the meeting of the Grindavík town council on the occasion of the town's 50th anniversary on April 10, 2024], April 10, 2024, https://www.grindavik.is/gogn/2024/Heiðursviðurkenningar%20textar_24.pdf.

CHAPTER EIGHTEEN: THE PAYOFF OF PERSISTENCE

"Change doesn't come": "The First Lady of Namibia Monica Geingos Shares a Powerful Message about Women's Rights," Global Citizen, March 18, 2021, YouTube video, 3:21, https://www.youtube.com/watch?v=UxFCCTKh8dk.

It was the biggest event: "Women's History Month Event," The Biden White House, March 15, 2022, YouTube video, 19:40, https://www.youtube.com/watch?v=0i_U0ls7oNA.

I was really killing it: Bjarni Pétur Jónsson, "Vandræðagangur á Biden og Elizu í Hvíta húsinu" [Biden and Eliza awkward in the White House],

RÚV, March 16, 2022, https://www.ruv.is/oflokka-eldra-efni/2022-03-16-vandraedagangur-a-biden-og-elizu-i-hvita-husinu.

She did: Fanndís Birna Logadóttir, "Ræddu jafnrétti á Íslandi og forsetinn hringdi í móður Elizu" [Discussed equality in Iceland and the president called Eliza's mother], *Vísir*, March 16, 2022, https://www.visir.is/g/20222236088d/raeddu-jafn-retti-a-islandi-og-forsetinn-hringdi-i-modur-elizu.

Iceland recognized: "Iceland Recognises Palestinian State," Al Jazeera, December 15, 2011, https://www.aljazeera.com/news/2011/12/15/iceland-recognises-palestinian-state.

This would have likely: "Amnesty International Investigation Concludes Israel Is Committing Genocide against Palestinians in Gaza," Amnesty International, December 5, 2024, https://www.amnesty.org/en/latest/news/2024/12/amnesty-international-concludes-israel-is-committing-genocide-against-palestinians-in-gaza/.

"It was three-quarters": Speech by First Lady Eliza Reid for Amnesty International on Human Rights Day, December 10, 2023, https://gudni.forseti.is/media/12038/20231210-amnesty-international_eng.pdf.

CHAPTER NINETEEN: CURTAIN CALL

"We are interconnected": Eliza Reid, speech delivered at the Canadian High Commission, London, March 2022, quoted from author's personal diary, unpublished.

She knew perfectly: *Rauða borðið*, "Forsetaframboð, Siggi hakkari og áhrif loftslagsbreytinga á heilsu," aired January 4, 2024, on Samstöðin, https://www.youtube.com/watch?v=sIhxUSqUXdc.

"Eliza's husband": Sigþrúður Guðmundsdóttir Facebook post, accessed June 2020, https://www.facebook.com/1073616254/posts/10219880676462000/.

"change requires intent": Roxane Gay, *Bad Feminist: Essays* (Harper Collins, 2014), 201.

He was leaving: Darren Adam, "Guðni Heads Towards Exit with Huge Approval Ratings," RÚV, July 18, 2024, https://www.ruv.is/english/2024-07-18-gudni-heads-towardss-exit-with-huge-approval-ratings-417952.

ABOUT THE AUTHOR

Eliza Reid is a bestselling writer, public speaker, gender equality advocate, and cofounder of the acclaimed Iceland Writers Retreat. From 2016 to 2024, Eliza served in the unofficial role of first lady while her husband was president of Iceland. She was born and raised in Canada but has lived in Iceland for more than twenty years. Her first book, *Secrets of the Sprakkar: Iceland's Extraordinary Women and How They Are Changing the World*, was an instant bestseller in Canada and Iceland, was a *New York Times Book Review* Editors' Pick, and was translated into numerous languages. Her first novel, an Iceland-set mystery called *Death on the Island* (*Death of a Diplomat* in the UK), was an instant *USA Today* bestseller, was an instant bestseller in Canada and Iceland, and was optioned for television in a preempt deal.

Eliza lives in the outskirts of Reykjavík with her husband and their four children. Despite their dwindling popularity, she still collects postcards.